W9-ASV-298

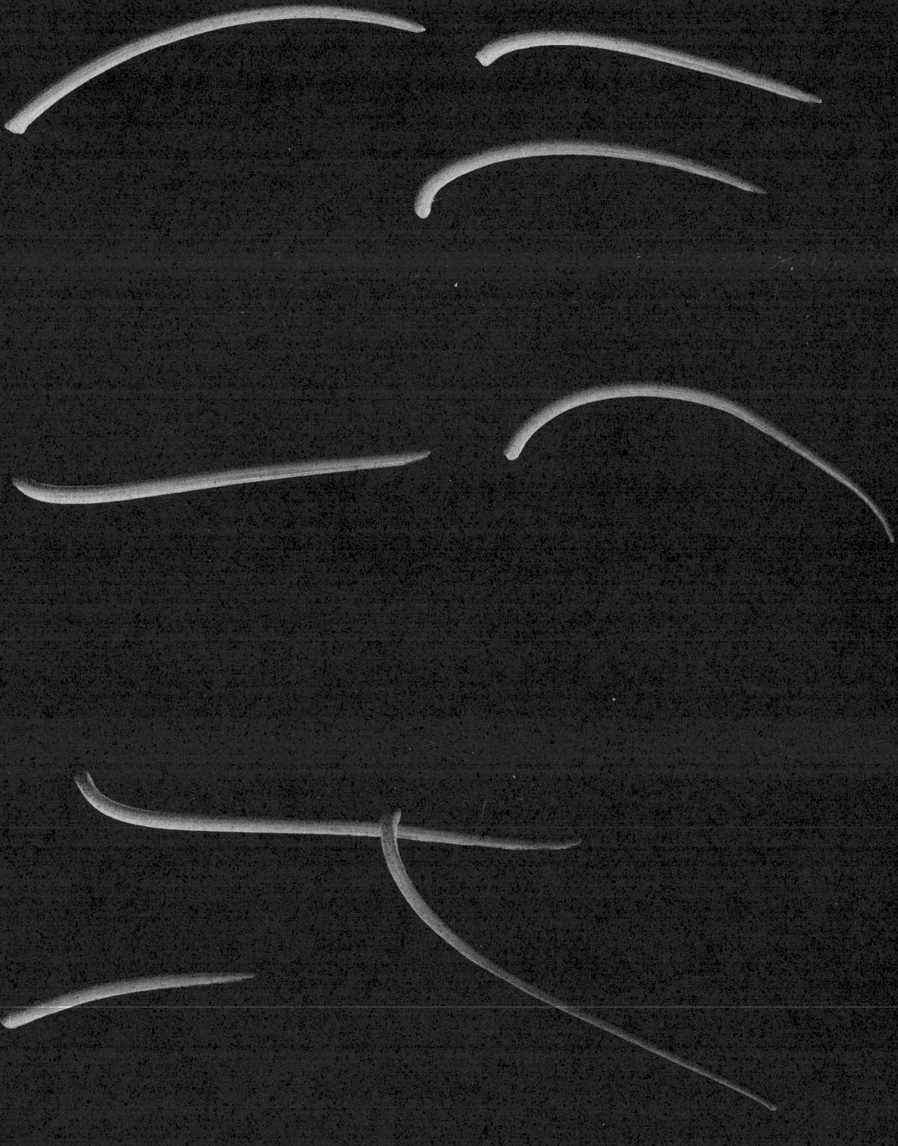

INFOGRAPHIC

GUIDE TO

SPORTS

An Hachette UK Company
www.hachette.co.uk

First published in Great Britain in 2014 by Cassell Illustrated
a division of Octopus Publishing Group Ltd

Endeavour House
189 Shaftesbury Avenue
London
WC2H 8JY

www.octopusbooks.co.uk
www.octopusbooksusa.com

Distributed in the US by
Hachette Book Group USA
237 Park Avenue
New York NY 10017 USA

Distributed in Canada by
Canadian Manda Group
664 Annette Street
Toronto, Ontario, Canada M6S 2C8

ISBN 978-1-844037-85-8

A CIP catalogue record for this book is available from the British Library

Printed and bound in China

1 3 5 7 9 10 8 6 4 2

INFOGRAPHIC GUIDE TO SPORTS

Daniel Tatarsky

CONTENTS

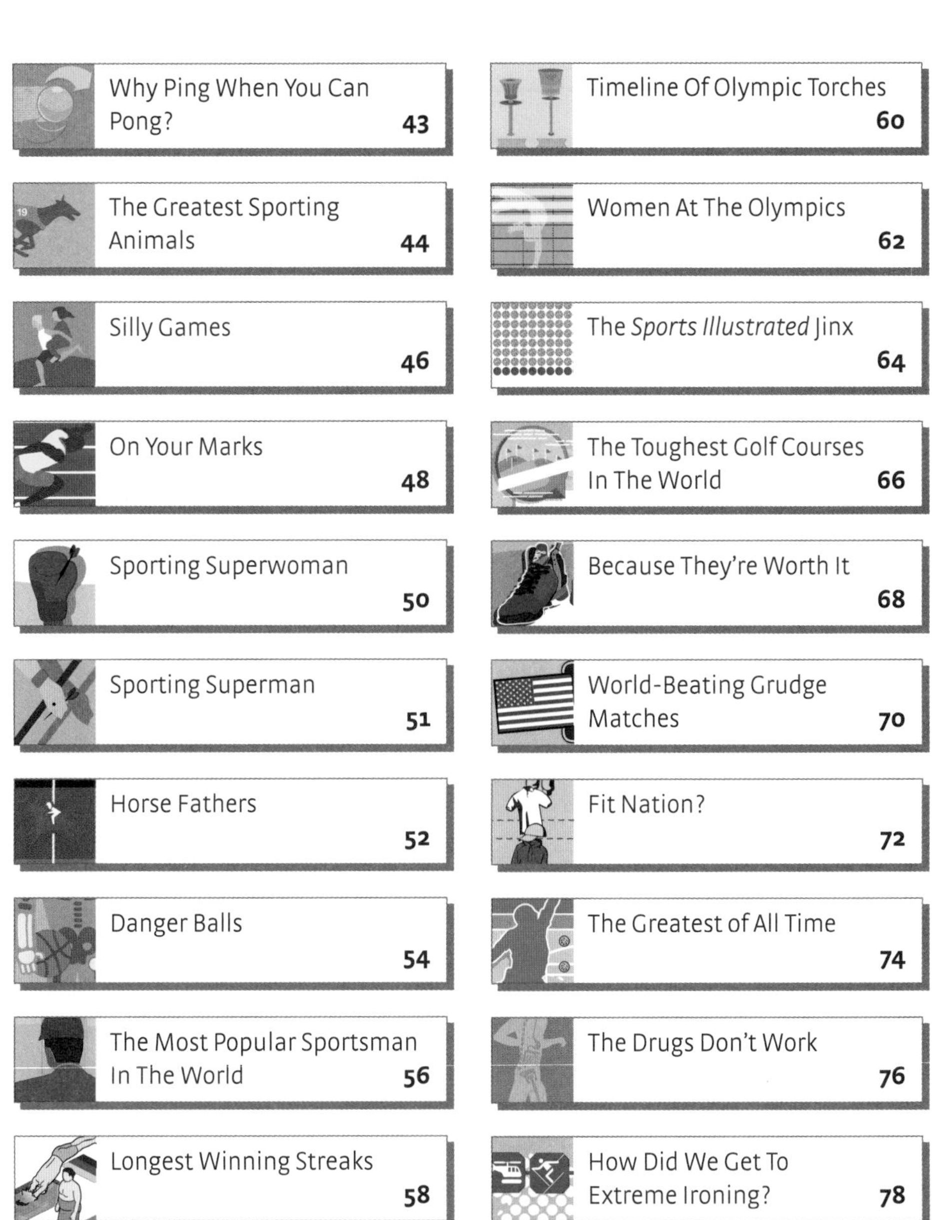

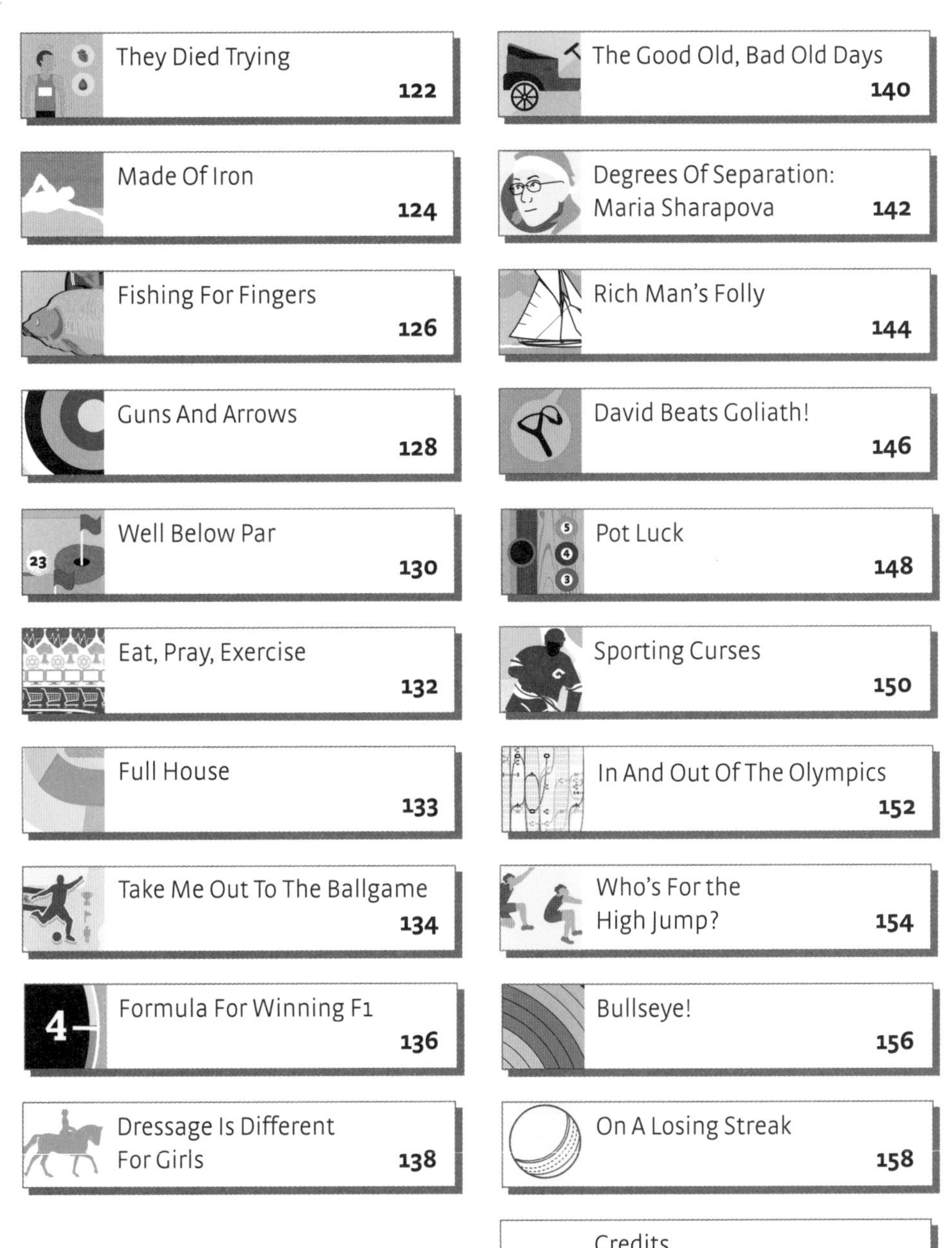

Introduction

by Daniel Tatarsky

Albert Camus, that renowned author, philosopher and soccer player, wrote "After many years during which I saw many things, what I know most surely about morality and the duty of man I owe to sport and learned it in the RUA (Racing Universitaire Algerios)." RUA was the team for whom Camus played in goal during his youth, until contracting TB at 18. It is hard to argue with Camus' assertion that sport teaches us about life, but it is also true to say that it teaches us much about ourselves. I certainly learned that you need to be first in the shower if you want the hot water.

As in life, in sport there are winners and losers, and there are those who say it is not necessarily important into which of these camps you fall. The significant thing should be how you deal with the result, for it is this that indicates and builds your character.

There is a massive industry based around the statistics of sport. In every corner of the world, wherever games are played, there are people making notes on every element of every sport. The speed, the height, the time in possession, in defense, offense, etc., etc.; it goes on and on, but in all sport, without exception, there is only one stat that really counts: who won. I'm not sure who said it, but second place is nowhere, it's just the first loser. It doesn't matter who gained the most yards, shots made are irrelevant, time in the opponent's half won't win you a trophy. So why are so many people spending so much time recording and analyzing data that doesn't necessarily have any direct bearing on the outcome? It's simple. It's because we love stats.

I can spend hours looking at a league table, comparing the figures, and hopefully some of the joy I experience searching stats comes across in these pages, enhanced as they are by beautiful and exciting graphics. There is a statistic relating to art galleries that says the average person spends 40% of their time looking at the labels, 30% at the paintings and the rest in the café or gift shop. This book can't offer coffee or gifts, but there are plenty of the first two elements. It covers almost every sport from Archery to Zumba. Although zumba isn't a sport, and if you doubt me, check the graphic entitled When Is a Sport Not a Sport?

If you're looking for a book that tells you who won the Baseball World Series in 1963, or how many Olympic gold medals Mark Spitz swam to,* then you will need to look elsewhere, but if you want a book that starts as many debates as it ends, then look no further. In these pages you will find everything and anything, from Ali's Shuffle to the decibel level of female tennis stars – described, drawn and dissected. Have fun, and remember: a good loser is still just a loser.

**Oh ok, it was the New York Dodgers, and Spitz won two in 1968, seven in 1972.*

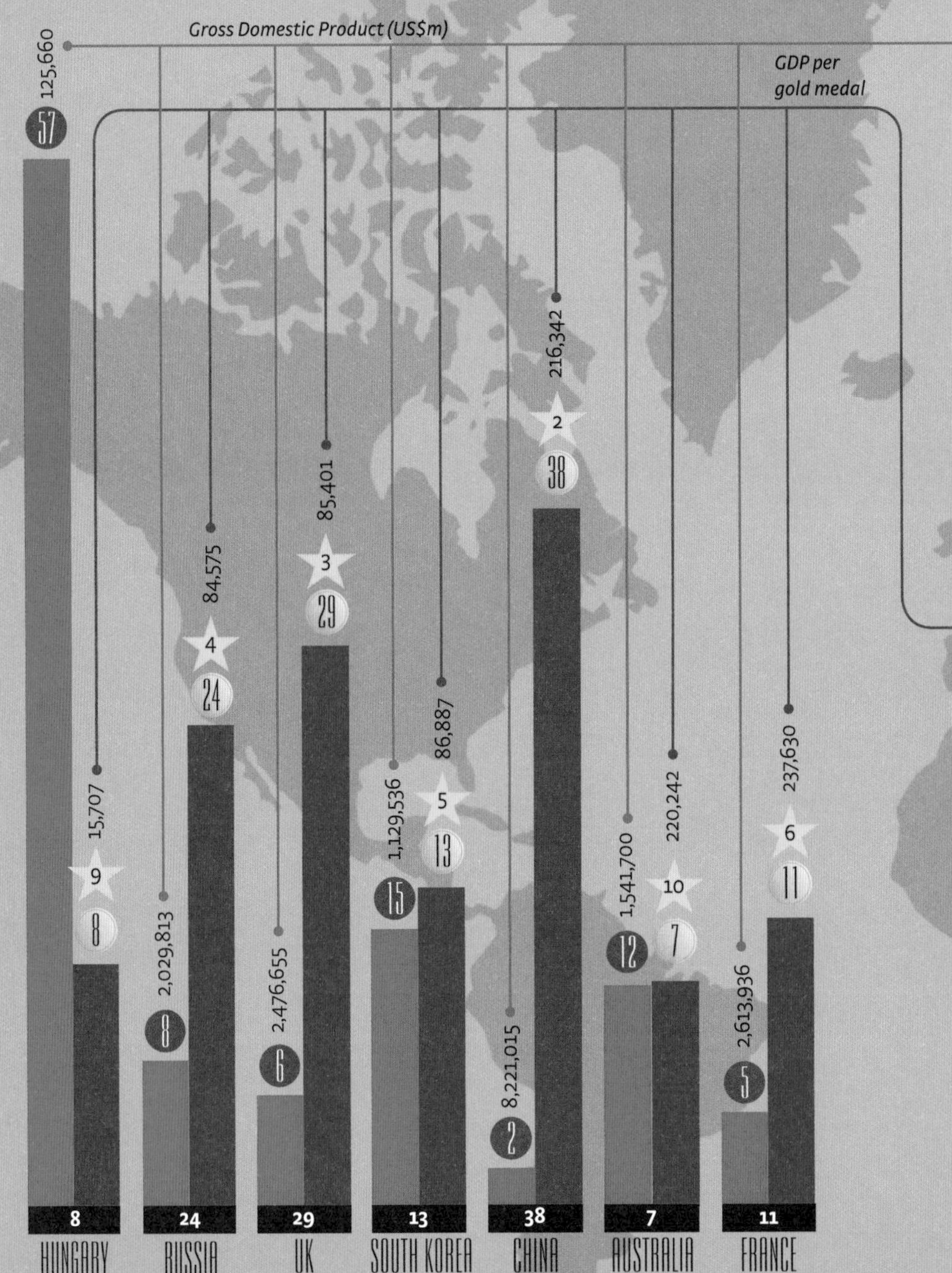

Gross Domestic Product (US$m)
GDP per gold medal
125,660
57
15,707
9
8
2,029,813
8
84,575
4
24
2,476,655
6
85,401
3
29
1,129,536
15
86,887
5
13
8,221,015
2
216,342
2
38
1,541,700
12
220,242
10
7
2,613,936
5
237,630
6
11
8
24
29
13
38
7
11
HUNGARY
RUSSIA
UK
SOUTH KOREA
CHINA
AUSTRALIA
FRANCE

IF THE **GOLD** STANDARD WERE **GOLD** MEDALS

A country's Gross Domestic Product – the value of everything produced by each country in a given year – marks its place in the world market. A country's gold medal haul at an Olympics marks its place in the world sporting arena. Dividing GDP by GMH gives an idea of how efficient (i.e. lowest cost) each country is. [Figures based on London 2012 Olympics and IMF data for the same year.]

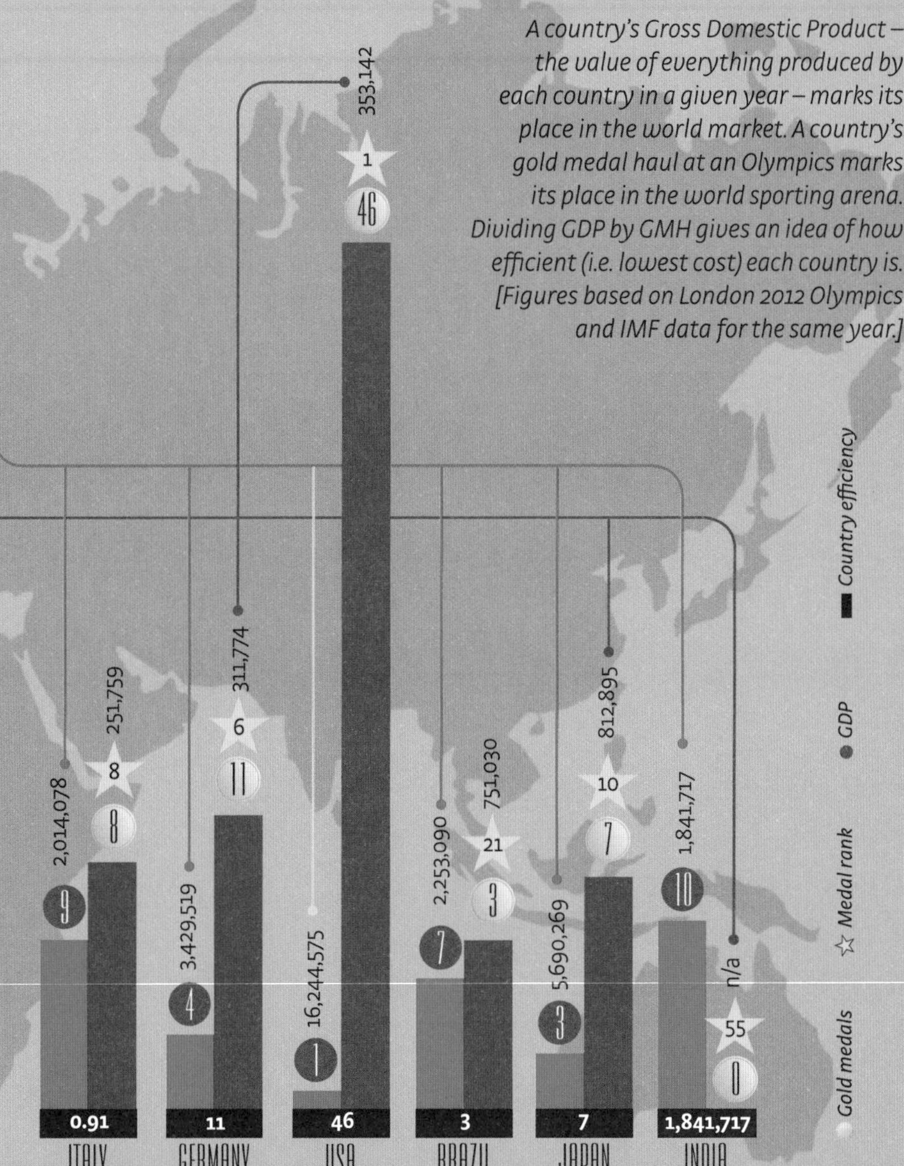

Country efficiency
GDP
Medal rank
Gold medals
353,142
1
46
2,014,078
251,759
8
8
9
0.91
ITALY
3,429,519
311,774
6
11
4
11
GERMANY
16,244,575
1
46
USA
2,253,090
751,030
21
3
7
3
BRAZIL
5,690,269
812,895
10
7
3
7
JAPAN
1,841,717
n/a
55
0
10
1,841,717
INDIA

STOP THAT **RACKET!**

The top ten loudest screamers and grunters on the women's professional tennis circuit tend to be winners, although it appears that you shouldn't exceed 101db if you want to make #1.

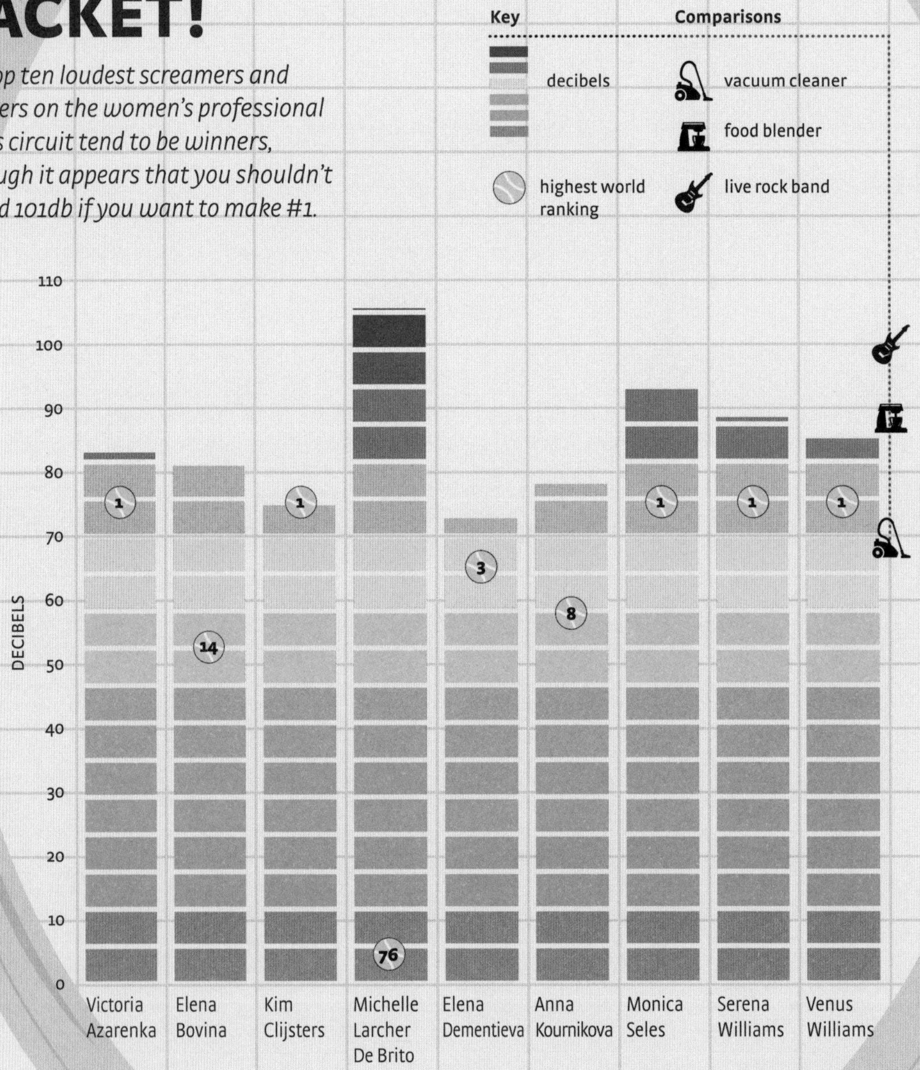

Key **Comparisons**

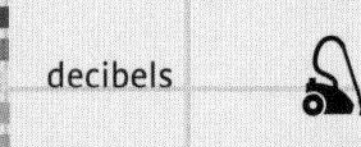

decibels

vacuum cleaner

food blender

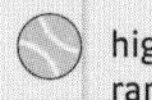

highest world ranking

live rock band

DECIBELS

110
100
90
80
70
60
50
40
30
20
10
0

	Highest world ranking
Victoria Azarenka	1
Elena Bovina	14
Kim Clijsters	1
Michelle Larcher De Brito	76
Elena Dementieva	3
Anna Kournikova	8
Monica Seles	1
Serena Williams	1
Venus Williams	1

telegraph.co.uk, dangerousdecibels.org, chchearing.org

WATT **POWER**

An athlete's body is capable of producing considerable power in short-burst activity. But which sports need the most power? It's an interesting comparison to note that the first cars built in the 1890s were powered by 4hp (2982 watt) engines, lower than some of the figures here. Results here are for bursts of power lasting between 2 and 5 seconds.

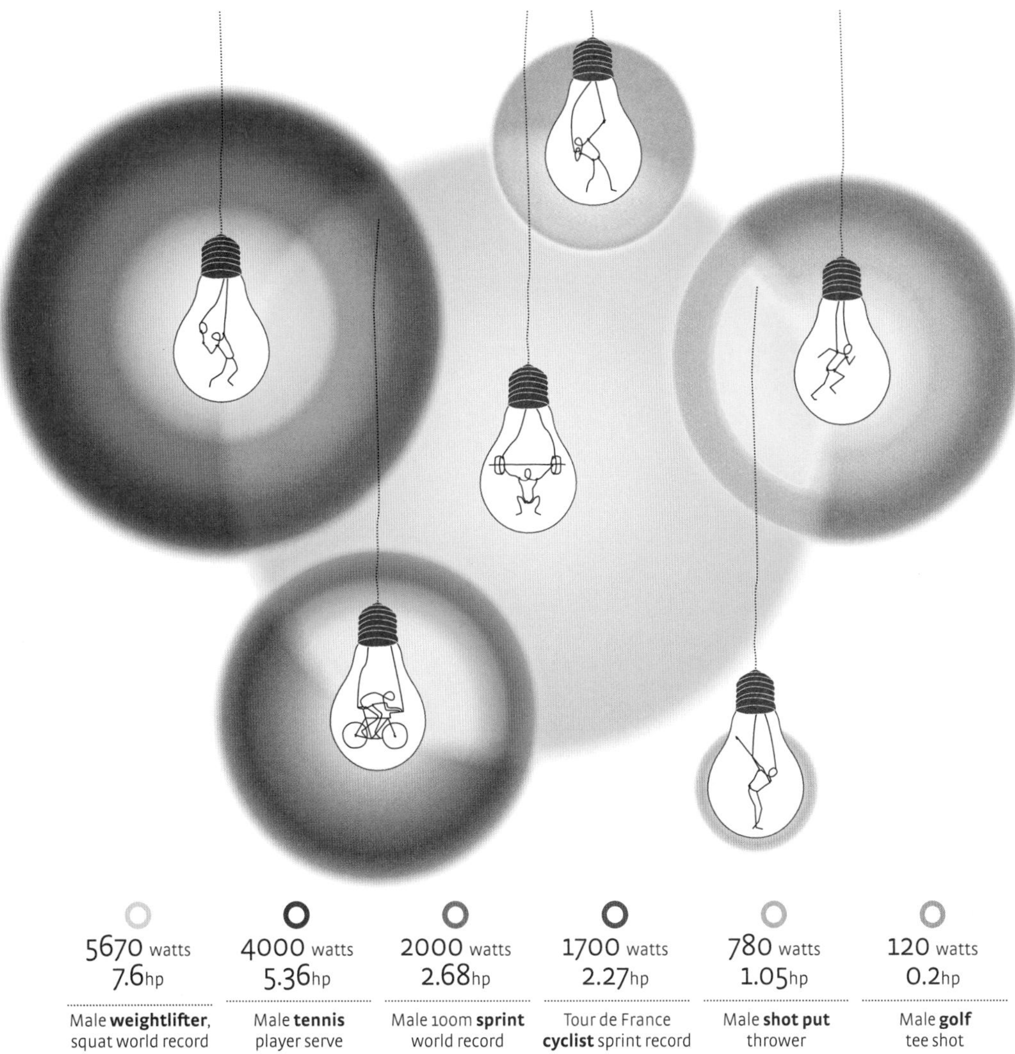
5670 watts
7.6hp
Male **weightlifter**, squat world record
4000 watts
5.36hp
Male **tennis** player serve
2000 watts
2.68hp
Male 100m **sprint** world record
1700 watts
2.27hp
Tour de France **cyclist** sprint record
780 watts
1.05hp
Male **shot put** thrower
120 watts
0.2hp
Male **golf** tee shot

wsj.com, totalrunning.com, wikipedia

HOLLYWOOD **BALLS**

Whenever a sports player attempts a spectacular play commentators invariably refer to it as a 'Hollywood pass/play/move'. That's because moviemakers and cinema goers have revelled in sporting stories of loss and triumph on the big screen. Unsurprisingly the biggest money-making sport is American football.

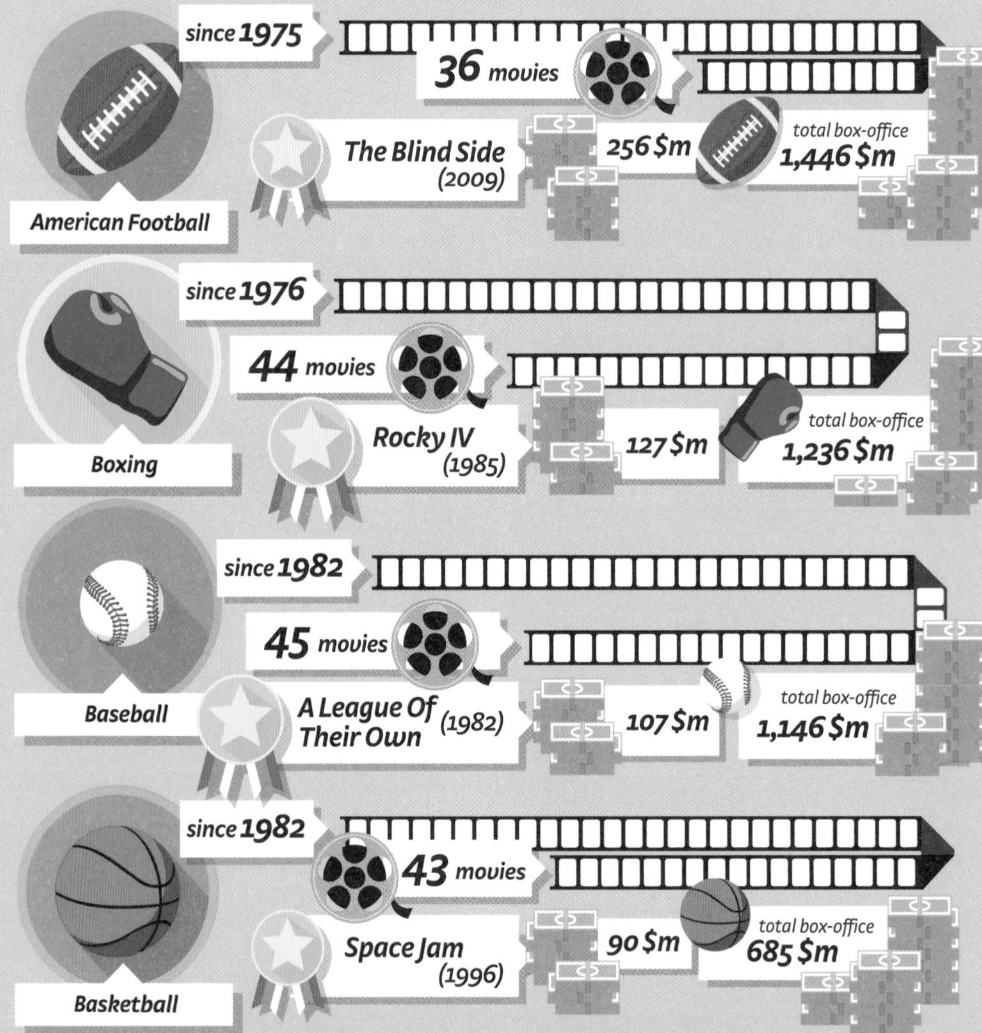

American Football
since 1975
36 movies
The Blind Side (2009)
256 $m
total box-office
1,446 $m
Boxing
since 1976
44 movies
Rocky IV (1985)
127 $m
total box-office
1,236 $m
Baseball
since 1982
45 movies
A League Of Their Own (1982)
107 $m
total box-office
1,146 $m
Basketball
since 1982
43 movies
Space Jam (1996)
90 $m
total box-office
685 $m

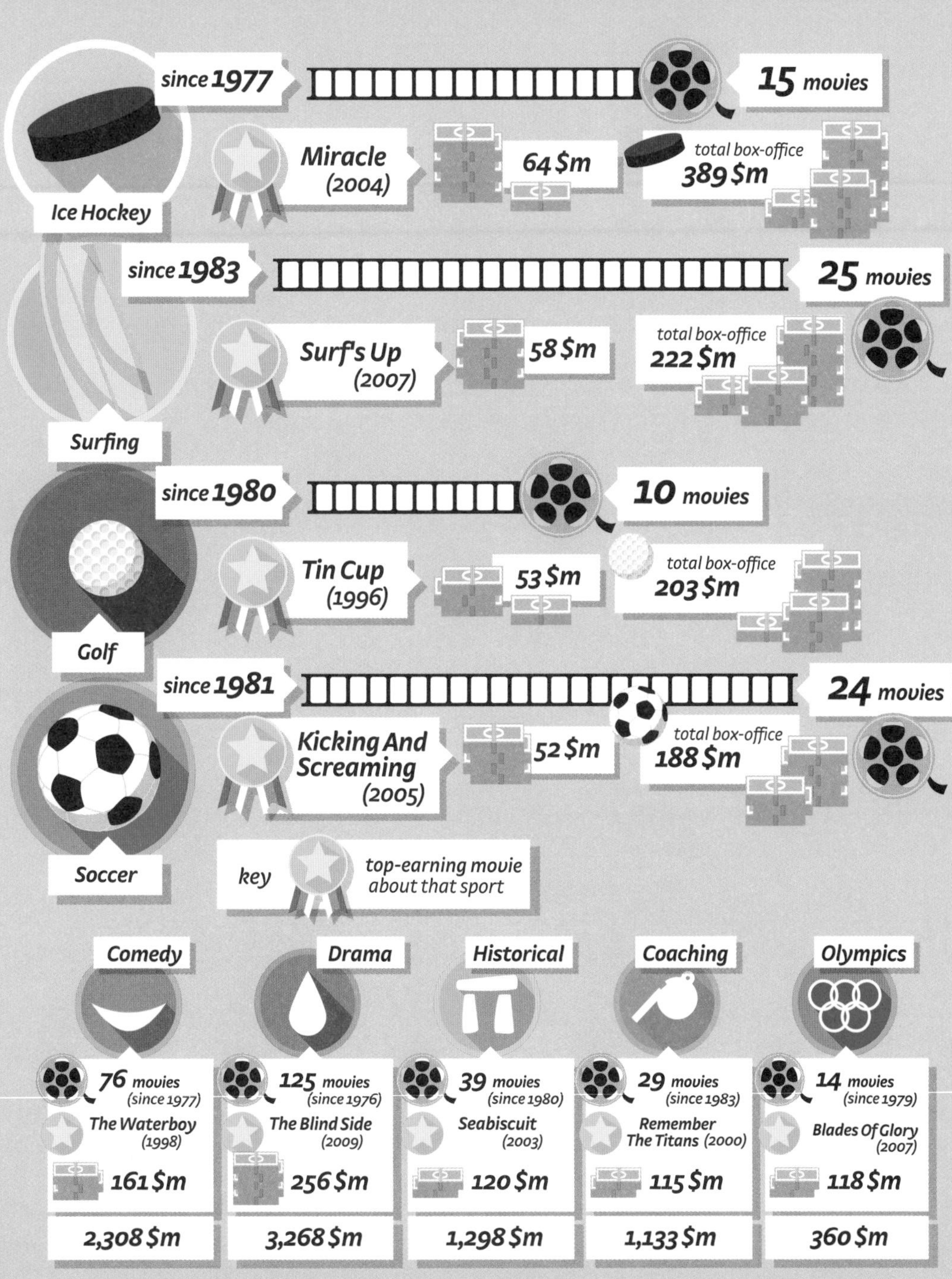

since 1977
15 movies
Miracle (2004)
64 $m
total box-office 389 $m
Ice Hockey
since 1983
25 movies
Surf's Up (2007)
58 $m
total box-office 222 $m
Surfing
since 1980
10 movies
Tin Cup (1996)
53 $m
total box-office 203 $m
Golf
since 1981
24 movies
Kicking And Screaming (2005)
52 $m
total box-office 188 $m
Soccer
key
top-earning movie about that sport
Comedy
76 movies (since 1977)
The Waterboy (1998)
161 $m
2,308 $m
Drama
125 movies (since 1976)
The Blind Side (2009)
256 $m
3,268 $m
Historical
39 movies (since 1980)
Seabiscuit (2003)
120 $m
1,298 $m
Coaching
29 movies (since 1983)
Remember The Titans (2000)
115 $m
1,133 $m
Olympics
14 movies (since 1979)
Blades Of Glory (2007)
118 $m
360 $m
boxofficemojo.com

SHUTTLECOCKS FASTER THAN **FERRARIS**

Hand-to-eye, or foot-to-eye, co-ordination is vital in most sports but how is it possible to hit something that is hurtling towards you at over 150kph? And which object comes at you fastest? It is not just the speed at which the object is travelling that is important, in a lot of cases it is how far away you are that will determine your reaction time.

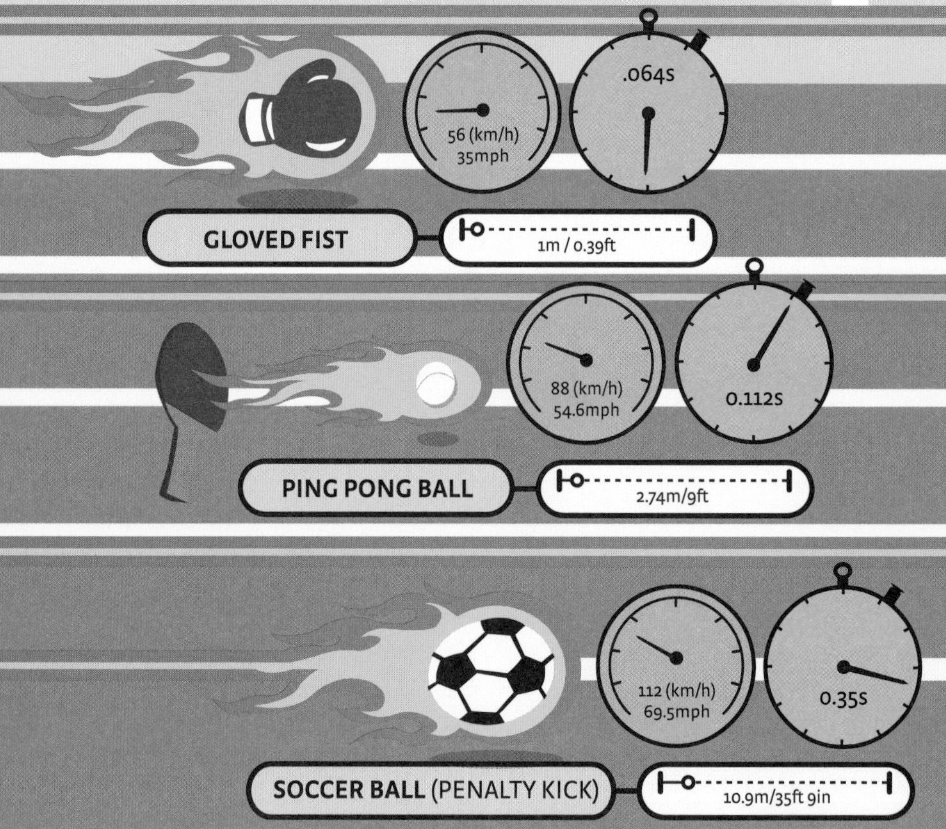

56 (km/h)
35mph
.064s
GLOVED FIST
1m / 0.39ft
88 (km/h)
54.6mph
0.112s
PING PONG BALL
2.74m/9ft
112 (km/h)
69.5mph
0.35s
SOCCER BALL (PENALTY KICK)
10.9m/35ft 9in

coxscorner.tripod.com, jayandwanda.com, hypertextbook.com/facts, thefootballknowledge.blogspot.co.uk, smh.com.au, Ferrari.com

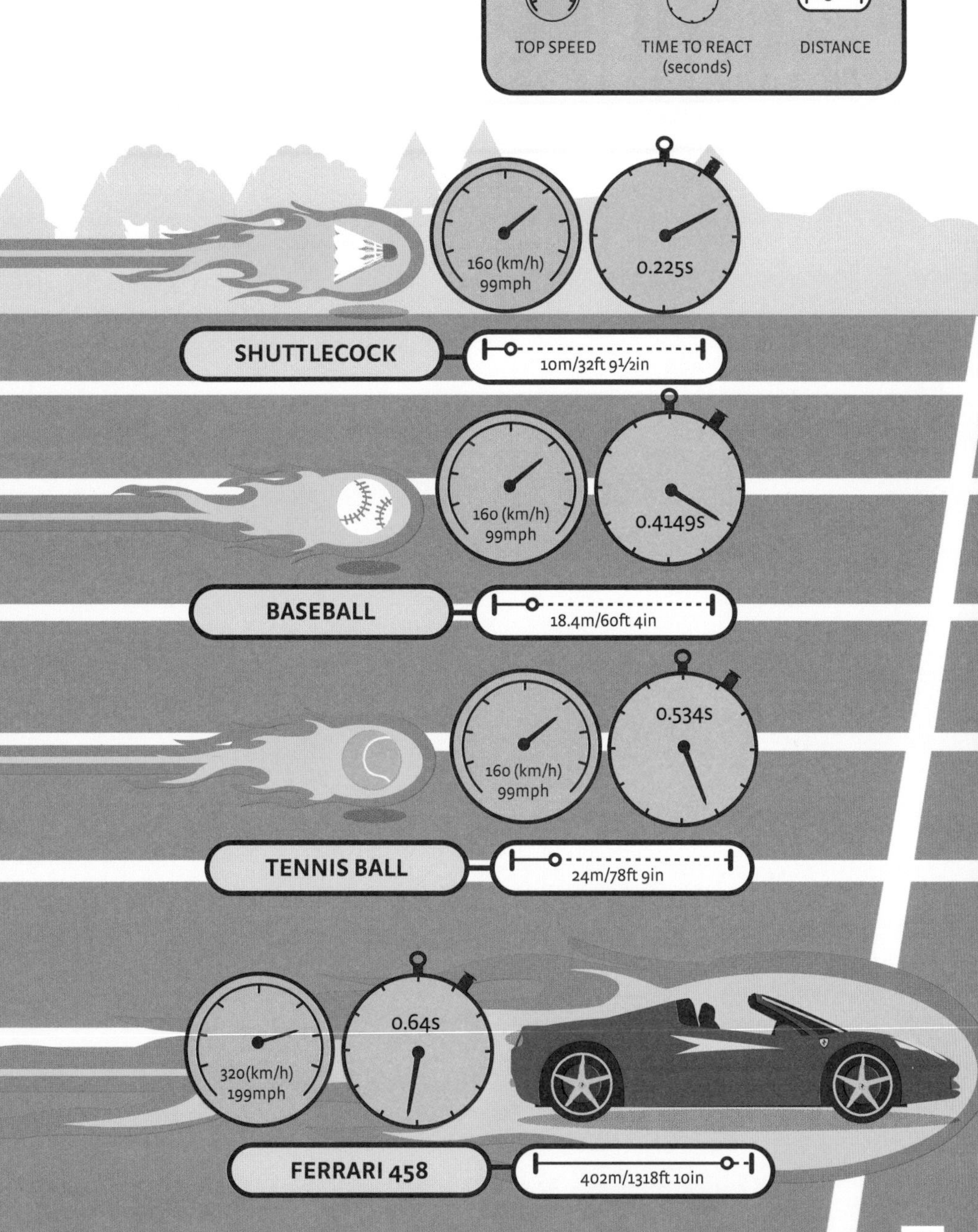
TOP SPEED
TIME TO REACT (seconds)
DISTANCE
160 (km/h) 99mph
0.225s
SHUTTLECOCK
10m/32ft 9½in
160 (km/h) 99mph
0.4149s
BASEBALL
18.4m/60ft 4in
160 (km/h) 99mph
0.534s
TENNIS BALL
24m/78ft 9in
320(km/h) 199mph
0.64s
FERRARI 458
402m/1318ft 10in

ALL HAIL **ALI DAEI**

These are the most famous footballers in the world, but Ali Daei – famous in Iran only – has played more international matches and scored more goals than them all. Here are the games and goals records of the ten best-known footballers in Europe, Africa and South America, and Ali Daei's.

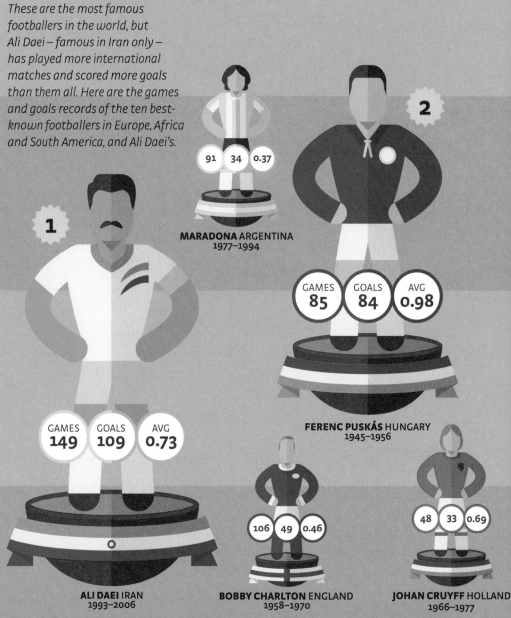

91
34
0.37
MARADONA ARGENTINA
1977–1994
2
GAMES 85
GOALS 84
AVG 0.98
FERENC PUSKÁS HUNGARY
1945–1956
106
49
0.46
48
33
0.69

1

GAMES 149

GOALS 109

AVG 0.73

ALI DAEI IRAN
1993–2006

BOBBY CHARLTON ENGLAND
1958–1970

JOHAN CRUYFF HOLLAND
1966–1977

76
75
0.99
KUNISHIGE KAMAMOTO JAPAN
1964–1977
38
52
1.37
POUL NIELSEN DENMARK
1910–1925
64
41
0.64
EUSEBIO PORTUGAL
1961–1973
92
77
0.84
PELÉ BRAZIL
1957–1971
3
68
75
1.10
SÁNDOR KOCSIS HUNGARY
1948–1956
GAMES
108
GOALS
0.72
AVG
78
GODFREY CHITALU ZAMBIA
1968–1980
62
68
1.09
GERD MÜLLER WEST GERMANY
1966–1974

SURF'S **UP**

Surfers love to beat the waves and each other, the bigger the wave the bigger the thrill. Here's how the highest wave ever surfed stacks up against the highest leaps and rides of other sports.

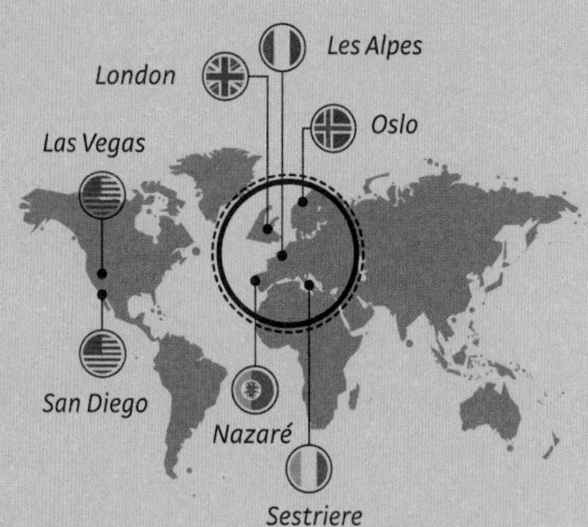

London
Les Alpes
Oslo
Las Vegas
San Diego
Nazaré
Sestriere

352

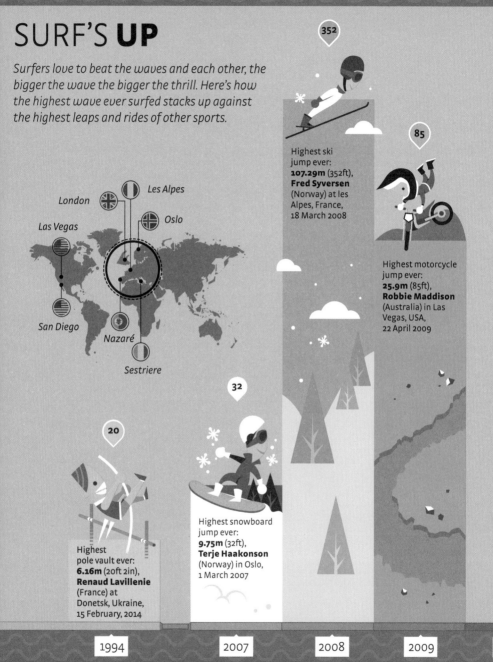

Highest ski jump ever: **107.29m** (352ft), **Fred Syversen** (Norway) at les Alpes, France, 18 March 2008

85

Highest motorcycle jump ever: **25.9m** (85ft), **Robbie Maddison** (Australia) in Las Vegas, USA, 22 April 2009

20

Highest pole vault ever: **6.16m** (20ft 2in), **Renaud Lavillenie** (France) at Donetsk, Ukraine, 15 February, 2014

32

Highest snowboard jump ever: **9.75m** (32ft), **Terje Haakonson** (Norway) in Oslo, 1 March 2007

1994

2007

2008

2009

201

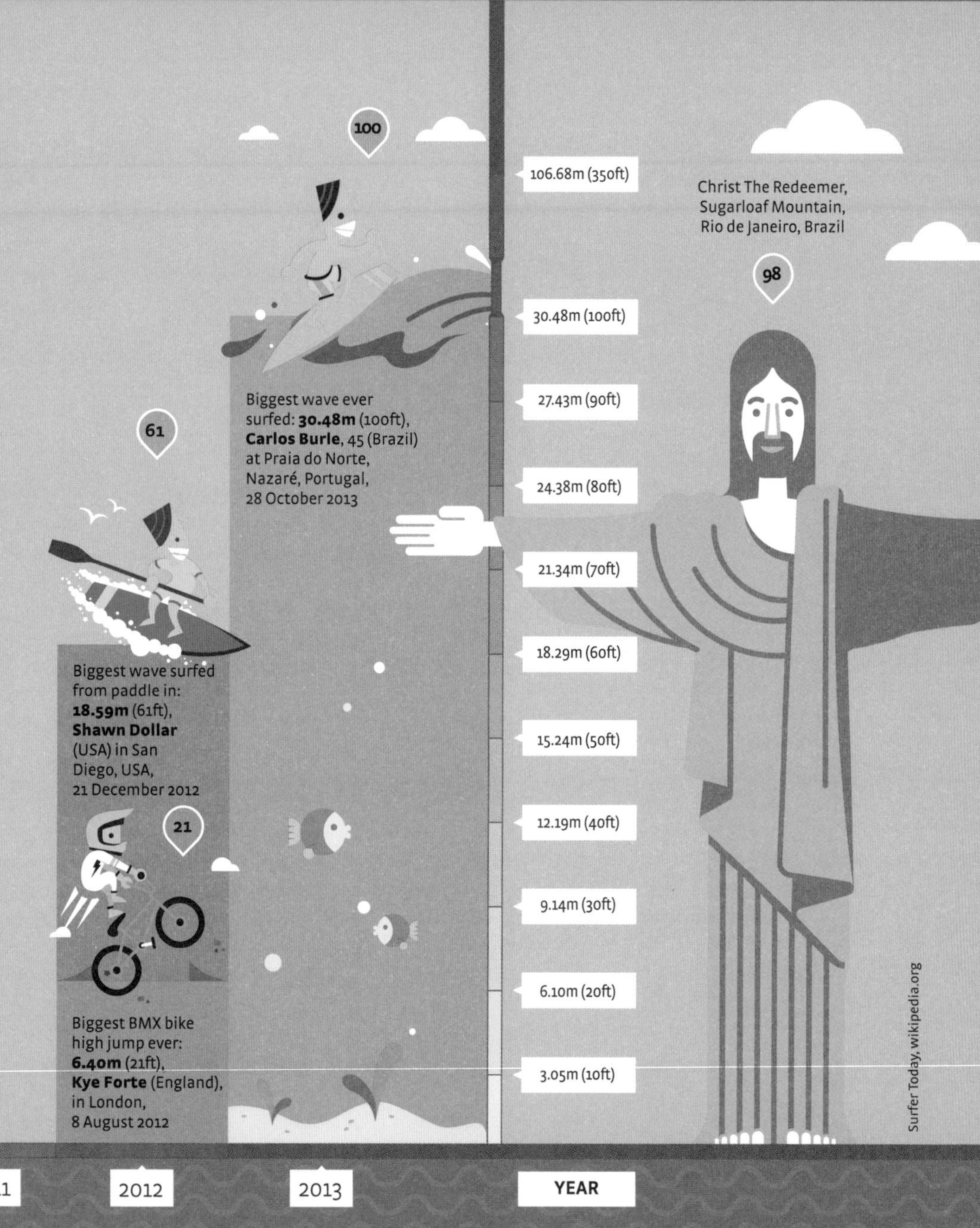
100
106.68m (350ft)
Christ The Redeemer,
Sugarloaf Mountain,
Rio de Janeiro, Brazil
98
30.48m (100ft)
Biggest wave ever
surfed: **30.48m** (100ft),
Carlos Burle, 45 (Brazil)
at Praia do Norte,
Nazaré, Portugal,
28 October 2013
27.43m (90ft)
61
24.38m (80ft)
21.34m (70ft)
18.29m (60ft)
Biggest wave surfed
from paddle in:
18.59m (61ft),
Shawn Dollar
(USA) in San
Diego, USA,
21 December 2012
15.24m (50ft)
21
12.19m (40ft)
9.14m (30ft)
6.10m (20ft)
Biggest BMX bike
high jump ever:
6.40m (21ft),
Kye Forte (England),
in London,
8 August 2012
3.05m (10ft)
Surfer Today, wikipedia.org
2011
2012
2013
YEAR

WORLD **TENNIS**

The nationalities of the world's top 10 tennis players since 1989 and the fall of Communism.

FEMALE CHAMPIONSHIP

		1988	1989	1994	1999	2004	2009	2013
Eastern Europe	Russia					2	5	1
	Czech Republic	1	1	1	1			1
	Poland						1	1
	Serbia						2	
Western Europe	Belarus		1					1
	Spain			2	2			
	France				2	1		
	Denmark							1
	Germany	2	1	2	1			1
	Switzerland	1	1		1			
	Belgium					2		
	Italy							1
	Argentina	1	1	1				
	Japan					1		
	China							1
	Australia	1						1
	USA	4	5	4	3	4	2	1

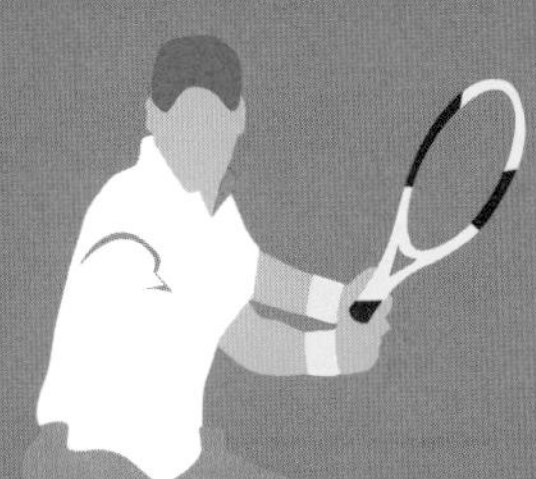

before the fall of the Berlin Wall
aftere the fall of the Berlin Wall

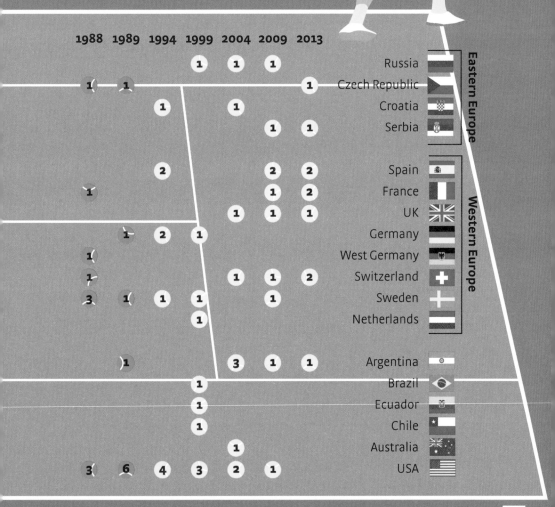

MALE CHAMPIONSHIP

	1988	1989	1994	1999	2004	2009	2013	Country
Eastern Europe				1	1	1		Russia
Eastern Europe	1	1					1	Czech Republic
Eastern Europe			1		1			Croatia
Eastern Europe						1	1	Serbia
Western Europe			2			2	2	Spain
Western Europe	1					1	2	France
Western Europe					1	1	1	UK
Western Europe		1	2	1				Germany
Western Europe	1							West Germany
Western Europe	1				1	1	2	Switzerland
Western Europe	3	1	1	1		1		Sweden
Western Europe				1				Netherlands
		1			3	1	1	Argentina
				1				Brazil
				1				Ecuador
				1				Chile
					1			Australia
	3	6	4	3	2	1		USA

LIKE FATHER, **LIKE SON**

Pitting yourself against an world medal-winning parent can't be easy, but here are men who have done just that in order to compare their trophy hauls.

FATHER

VS SON

Nascar racing US
DALE EARNHARDT SNR

76 race wins, 7 Winston Cups

Water Polo Hungary
ISTVÁN SZÍVÓS SNR

1948 1952 1956

Sailing US
JERRY KIRBY

1992

Nascar racing US
DALE EARNHARDT JNR

18 race wins

Water Polo Hungary
ISTVÁN SZÍVÓS JNR

1968 1972 1976 1980

Sailing US
ROME KIRBY

2003

Swimming US
GARY HALL SNR

1968 1972 1976

Shooting Sweden
OSCAR SWAHN

1908 1912 1920

Gymnastics USSR
ALBERT AZARYAN

1956 1960

Swimming US
GARY HALL JNR

1996 2000 2004

Shooting Sweden
ALFRED SWAHN

1908 1912 1920 1924

Gymnastics Armenia
EDUARD AZARYAN

1980

	GRANDFATHER	FATHER
	VS FATHER	VS SON
	VS SON	VS SON

Rowing UK
CHARLES BURNELL
1908

Rowing UK
DICKIE BURNELL
1948

Athletics US
CHARLES JENKINS
1956

Athletics US
CHIP JENKINS
1992

Skating US
JACK SHEA
1932

Skating US
JIM SHEA
1964

Skating US
JIMMY SHEA
2002

Dog Sledding US
DICK MACKEY
1978

Dog Sledding US
RICK MACKEY

1983 1997

Dog Sledding US
LANCE MACKEY

2005 2006 2007 2008 2009 2010

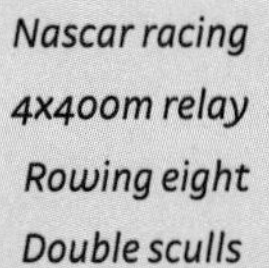

gold *silver* *bronze*

Nascar racing
4x400m relay
Rowing eight
Double sculls

Olympics
Winter Olympics
America's Cup
Iditarod Trail Sled Dog Race
Yukon Quest

COST OVER **DISTANCE**

Do the earnings of different sports stars for key events bear any relation to the amount of work that they put into competing?

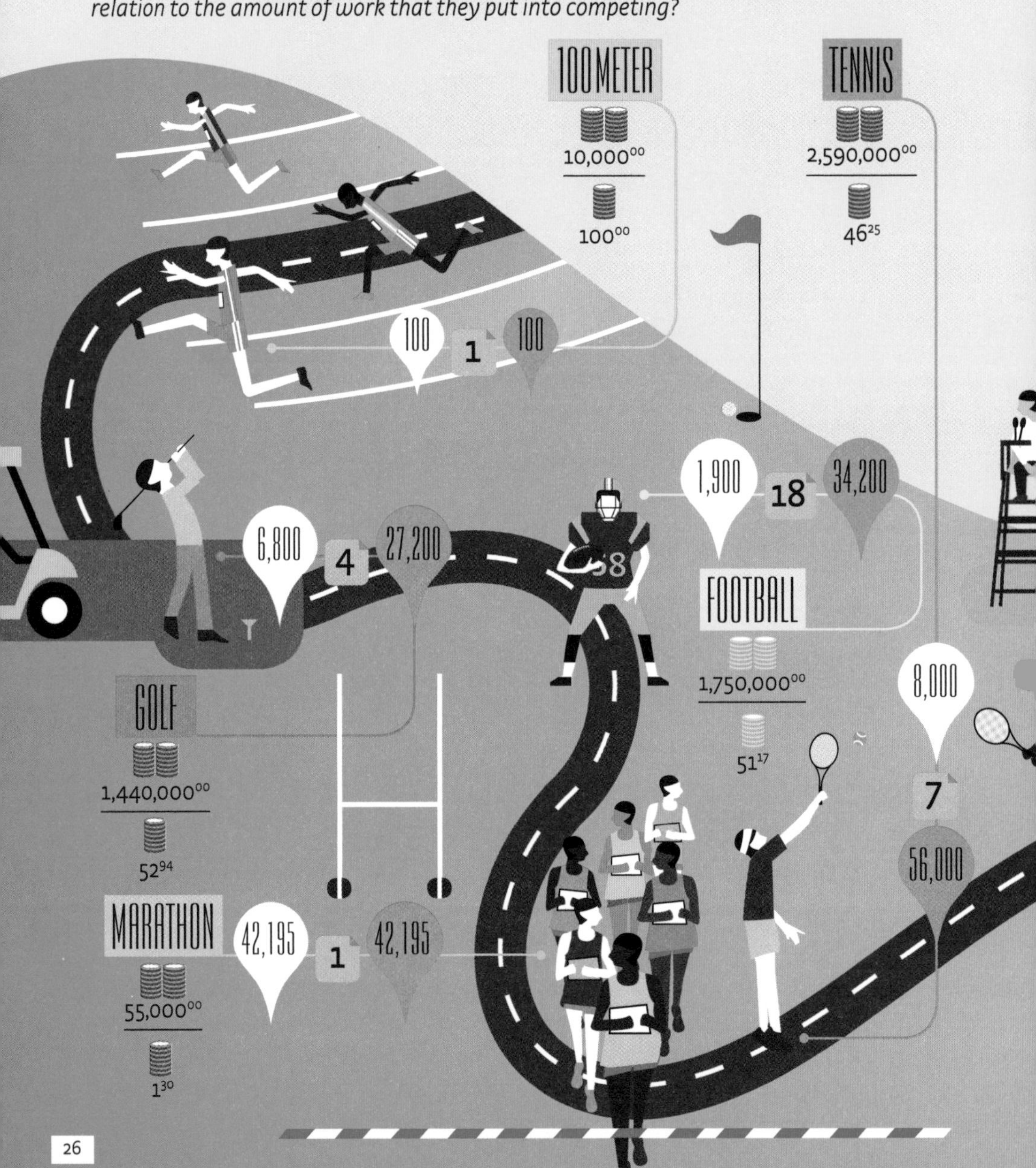

100 METER
10,000⁰⁰
100⁰⁰
100
1
100
TENNIS
2,590,000⁰⁰
46²⁵
1,900
18
34,200
6,800
4
27,200
FOOTBALL
1,750,000⁰⁰
51¹⁷
8,000
7
56,000
GOLF
1,440,000⁰⁰
52⁹⁴
MARATHON
42,195
1
42,195
55,000⁰⁰
1³⁰

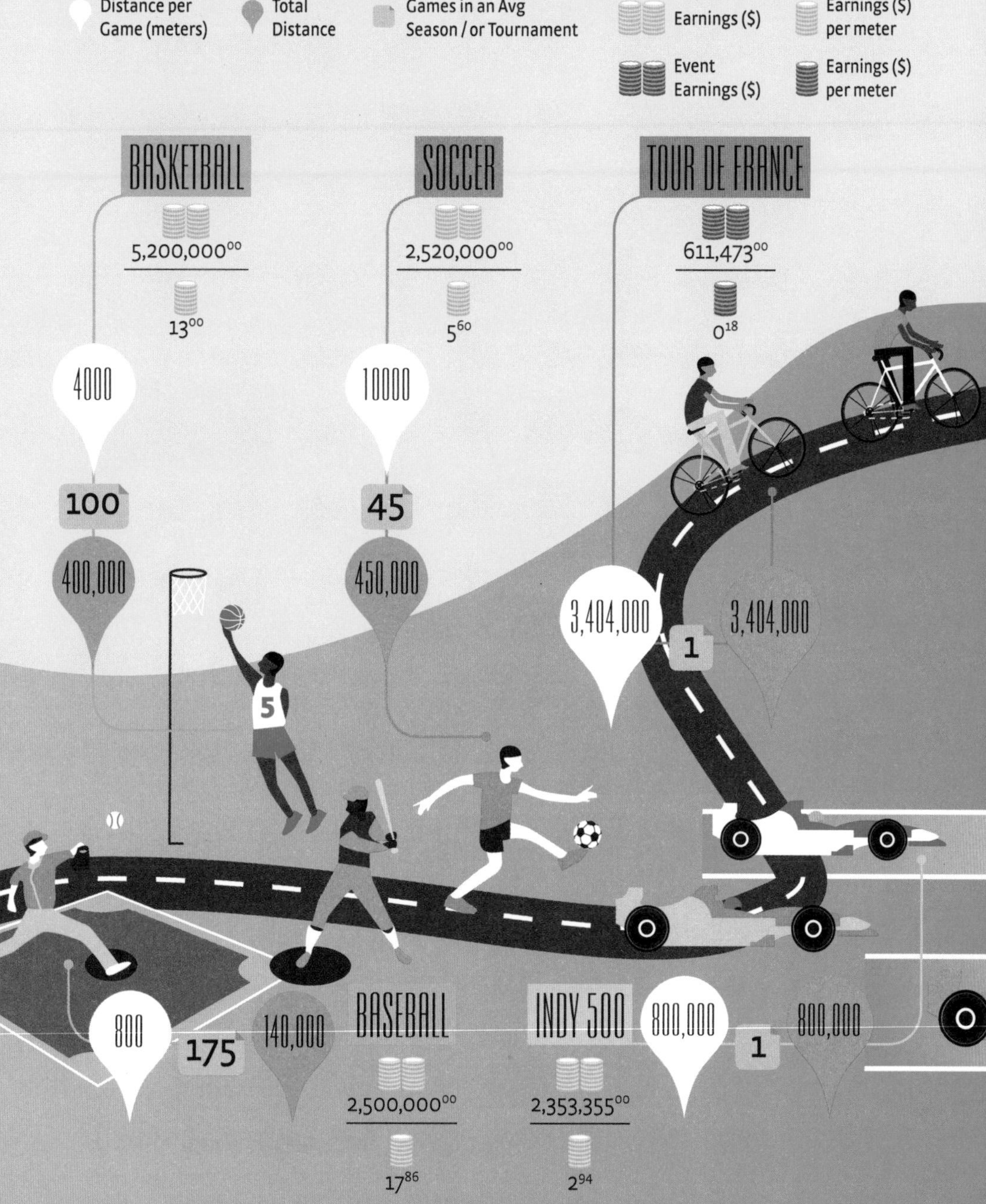

Distance per Game (meters)
Total Distance
Games in an Avg Season / or Tournament
Earnings ($)
Earnings ($) per meter
Event Earnings ($)
Earnings ($) per meter
BASKETBALL
5,200,000.00
13.00
4000
100
400,000
SOCCER
2,520,000.00
5.60
10000
45
450,000
TOUR DE FRANCE
611,473.00
0.18
3,404,000
1
3,404,000
5
800
175
140,000
BASEBALL
2,500,000.00
17.86
INDY 500
2,353,355.00
2.94
800,000
1
800,000

tribesports.com, statisticbrain.com, diamondleague.com, static.london.marathon.co.uk, wimbledon.com, augusta.com, bbc.co.uk/sport, indianapolismotorspeedway.com

ZORBING THE GEEK

Want to walk on water? Try Zorbing; inside a waterproof, inflated sphere you can walk as it floats. That's not much fun though. Real Zorbers get pushed over hills, wear no harness and have soapy water inside their sphere. It all began in England, but the Kiwis made it a 'sport'.

OXFORD DICTIONARY DESCRIPTION (2001)
'Zorbing is a sport in which a participant is secured inside an inner capsule in a large, transparent ball which is then rolled along the ground or downhill.'

CONSTRUCTION
double-sectioned, with one ball inside the other with an air layer between as a cushion

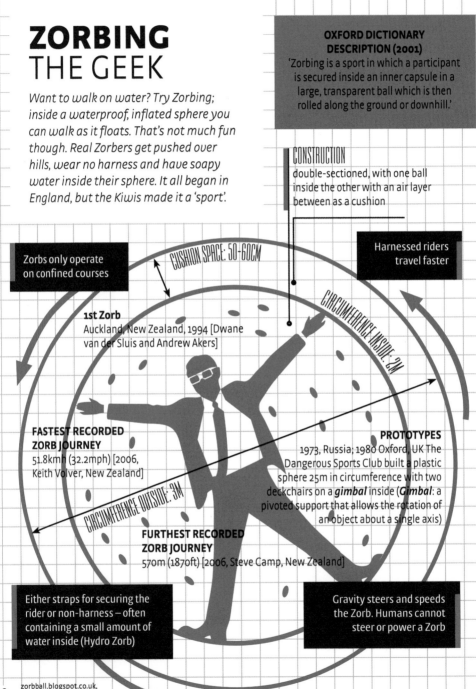

Zorbs only operate on confined courses

CUSHION SPACE: 50-60CM

Harnessed riders travel faster

CIRCUMFERENCE INSIDE: 2M

1st Zorb
Auckland, New Zealand, 1994 [Dwane van der Sluis and Andrew Akers]

FASTEST RECORDED ZORB JOURNEY
51.8kmh (32.2mph) [2006, Keith Volver, New Zealand]

PROTOTYPES
1973, Russia; 1980 Oxford, UK The Dangerous Sports Club built a plastic sphere 25m in circumference with two deckchairs on a ***gimbal*** inside (***Gimbal***: a pivoted support that allows the rotation of an object about a single axis)

CIRCUMFERENCE OUTSIDE: 3M

FURTHEST RECORDED ZORB JOURNEY
570m (1870ft) [2006, Steve Camp, New Zealand]

Either straps for securing the rider or non-harness – often containing a small amount of water inside (Hydro Zorb)

Gravity steers and speeds the Zorb. Humans cannot steer or power a Zorb

zorbball.blogspot.co.uk, Zorb.com, wikipedia.org

PLAY **ZONES**

The word arena comes from the latin for sand – which was strewn on the ground to soak up the blood during gladiatorial bouts. The area of 'play' had to be determined to give the combatants an equal chance. For modern sports that area can be as small as 1.525 meters by 2.74 meters.

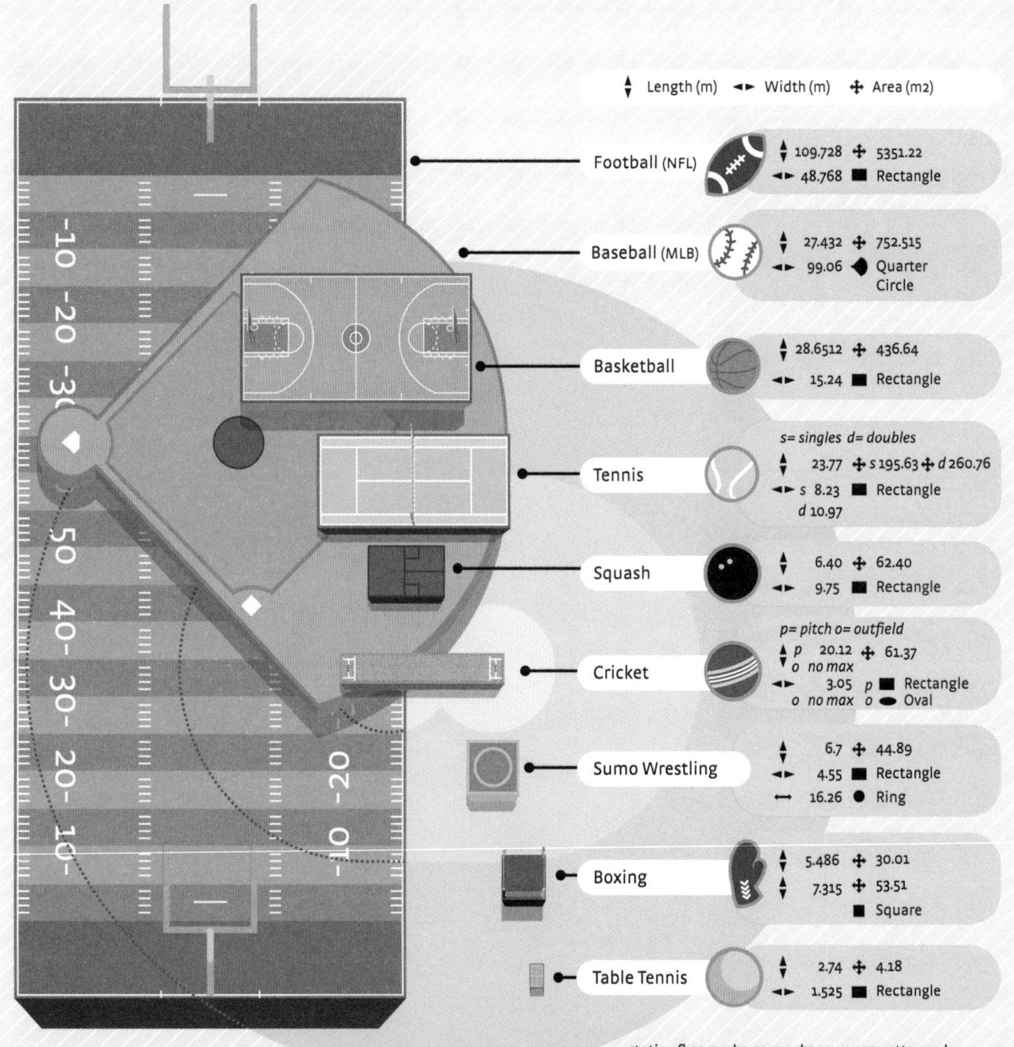

Length (m) Width (m) Area (m2)
Football (NFL)
109.728 5351.22
48.768 Rectangle
Baseball (MLB)
27.432 752.515
99.06 Quarter Circle
Basketball
28.6512 436.64
15.24 Rectangle
s= singles d= doubles
Tennis
23.77 s 195.63 d 260.76
s 8.23 Rectangle
d 10.97
Squash
6.40 62.40
9.75 Rectangle
p= pitch o= outfield
Cricket
p 20.12 61.37
o no max
3.05 p Rectangle
o no max o Oval
Sumo Wrestling
6.7 44.89
4.55 Rectangle
16.26 Ring
Boxing
5.486 30.01
7.315 53.51
Square
Table Tennis
2.74 4.18
1.525 Rectangle

static.nfl.com, nba.com, wbanews.com, etta.co.uk, itftennis.com, worldsquash.org, mlb.com, lords.org

IMPROVING **WITH AGE**

Tracy Austin won her first US Open when she was 16, and won it again two years later – yet once out of her teens she never won another Grand Slam. At the other end of the spectrum, George Foreman regained the world heavyweight boxing title at the age of 45. In some sports age can be an advantage.

19
Age Turned Pro

39
Age Finally Lost No. 1 Rank

22
Age Ranked No. 1

40
Age of Retirement

Muhammad Ali
Boxing
17/01/1942
19 – 22 – 39 – 40

Wayne Gretzky
Ice Hockey
26/01/1961
17 – 19 – 38 – 38

Asashōryū Akinori
Sumo Wrestler
27/09/1980
18 – 22 – 29 – 29

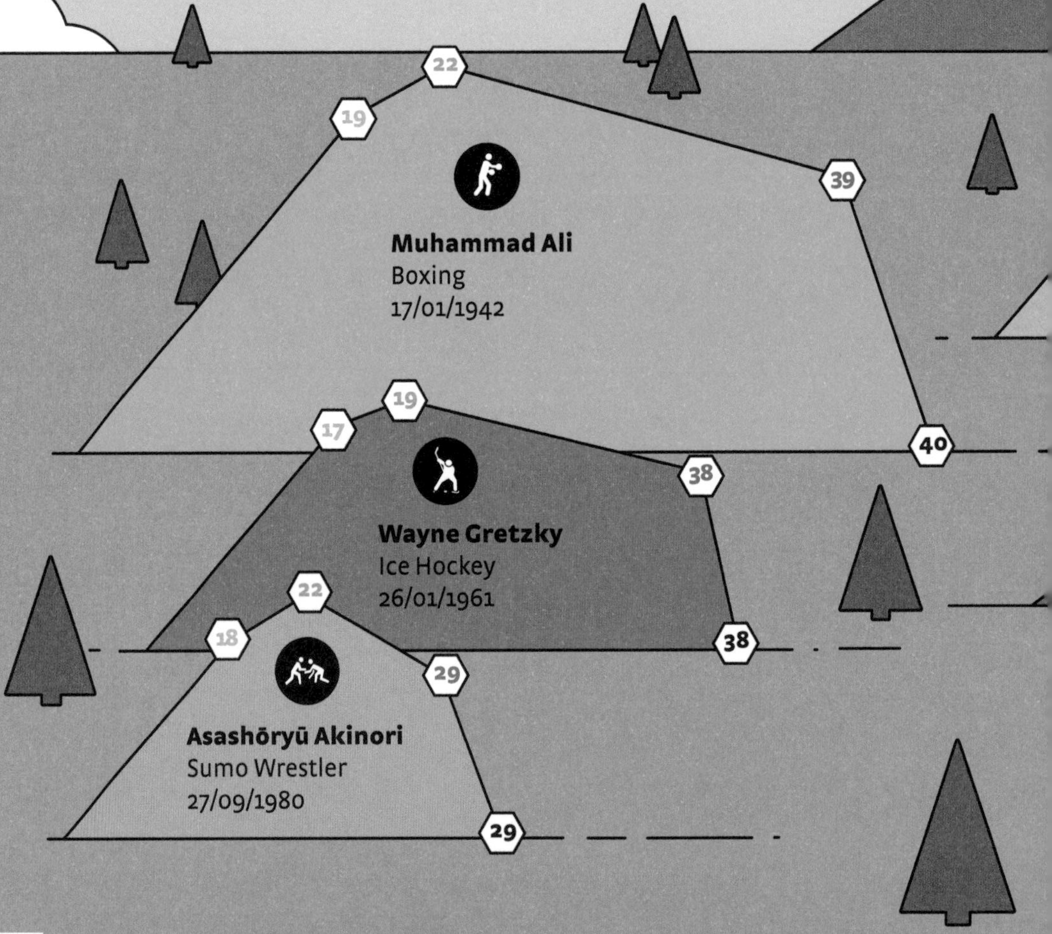

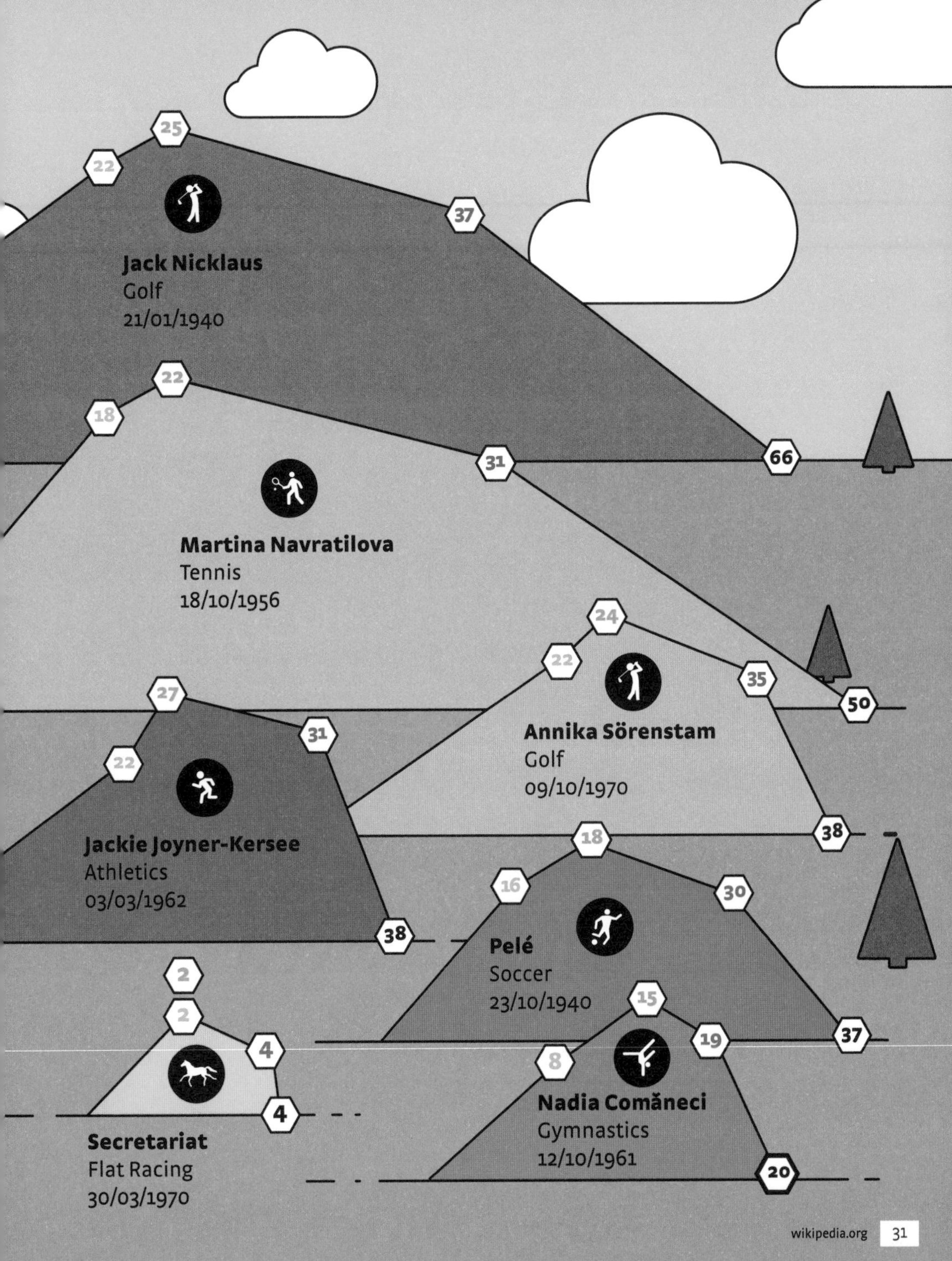
25
22
37
Jack Nicklaus
Golf
21/01/1940
22
18
31
66
Martina Navratilova
Tennis
18/10/1956
24
22
35
50
27
31
22
Annika Sörenstam
Golf
09/10/1970
Jackie Joyner-Kersee
Athletics
03/03/1962
38
18
16
30
38
Pelé
Soccer
23/10/1940
2
2
15
4
19
37
8
4
Nadia Comăneci
Gymnastics
12/10/1961
Secretariat
Flat Racing
30/03/1970
20

ADVANTAGE **SURFACE**

Each of the four major tennis grand slam tournaments are played on different surfaces. Here's how artificial grass or clay, acrylic, grass and red clay affect the game, using the longest matches played on each as a comparison.

Slam

Longest Match

Surface Type

Lloyd (UK) *vs* McNamee (AUS)

1979

63

232

54

Roddick (USA) *vs* El Aynaoui (MOR)

2003

83

229

71

USA

AUSTRALIA

Artificial Grass and Artificial Clay

1. Geotextile membrane and drainage system.
2. Carboniferous limestone or granite.
3. Base course porous asphalt.
4. Aggregate porous asphalt.
5. Sand-filled artificial grass-wearing course.
6. Artificial grass is supplied on rolls. Outside, it needs to be laid over a porous base of concrete or asphalt to allow drainage.

Acrylic

1. Geotextile membrane.
2. Foundation.
3. Base course asphalt.
4. Wearing course asphalt.
5. Cushion system
6. Acrylic (PMMA) or polyurethan (PU) based coating with aggregate.

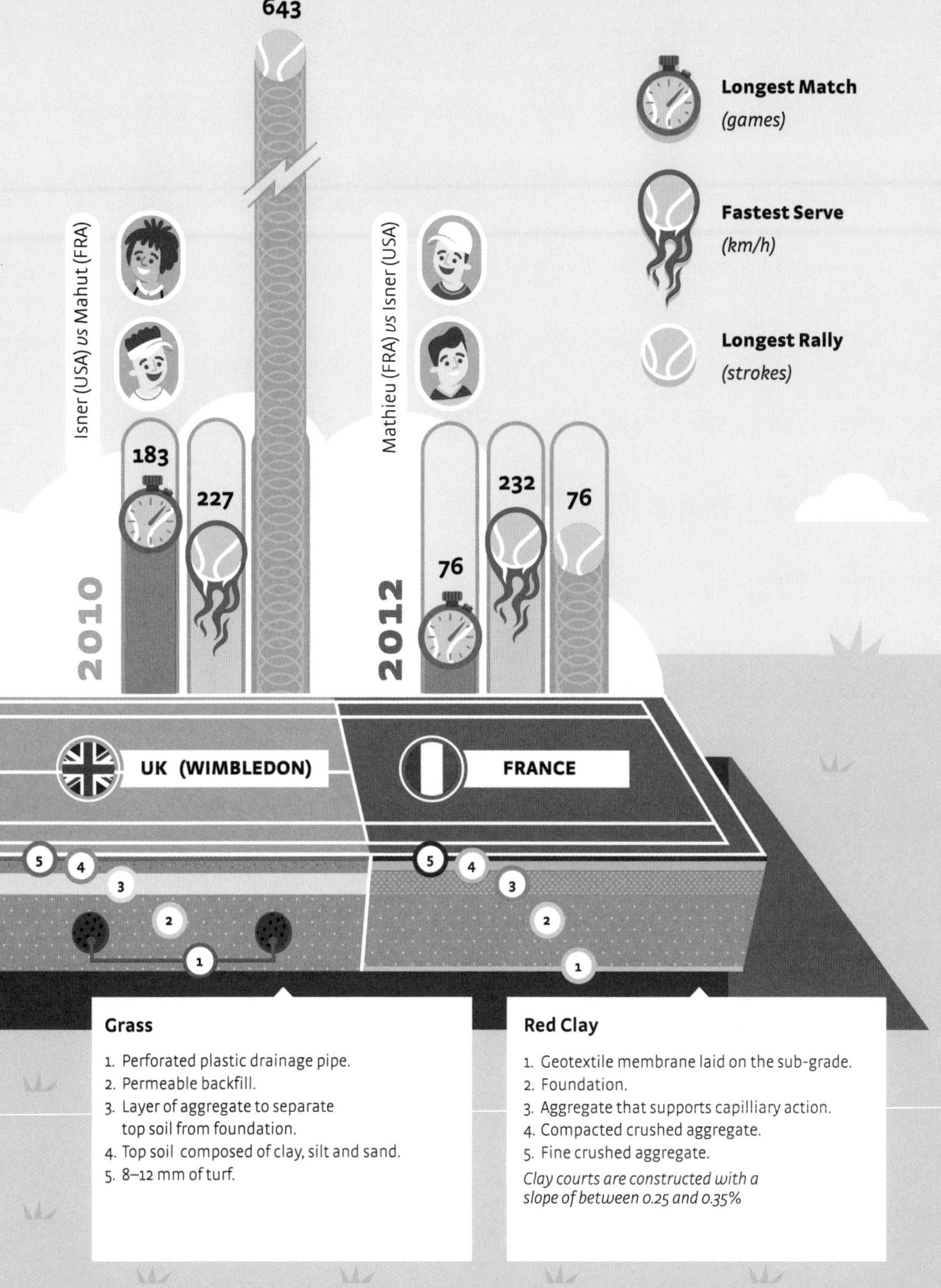
643
Longest Match
(games)
Fastest Serve
(km/h)
Longest Rally
(strokes)
Isner (USA) vs Mahut (FRA)
Mathieu (FRA) vs Isner (USA)
183
227
76
232
76
2010
2012
UK (WIMBLEDON)
FRANCE
5
4
3
2
1
5
4
3
2
1

Grass

1. Perforated plastic drainage pipe.
2. Permeable backfill.
3. Layer of aggregate to separate top soil from foundation.
4. Top soil composed of clay, silt and sand.
5. 8–12 mm of turf.

Red Clay

1. Geotextile membrane laid on the sub-grade.
2. Foundation.
3. Aggregate that supports capilliary action.
4. Compacted crushed aggregate.
5. Fine crushed aggregate.

Clay courts are constructed with a slope of between 0.25 and 0.35%

itftennis.com, telegraph.co.uk, wikipedia.org

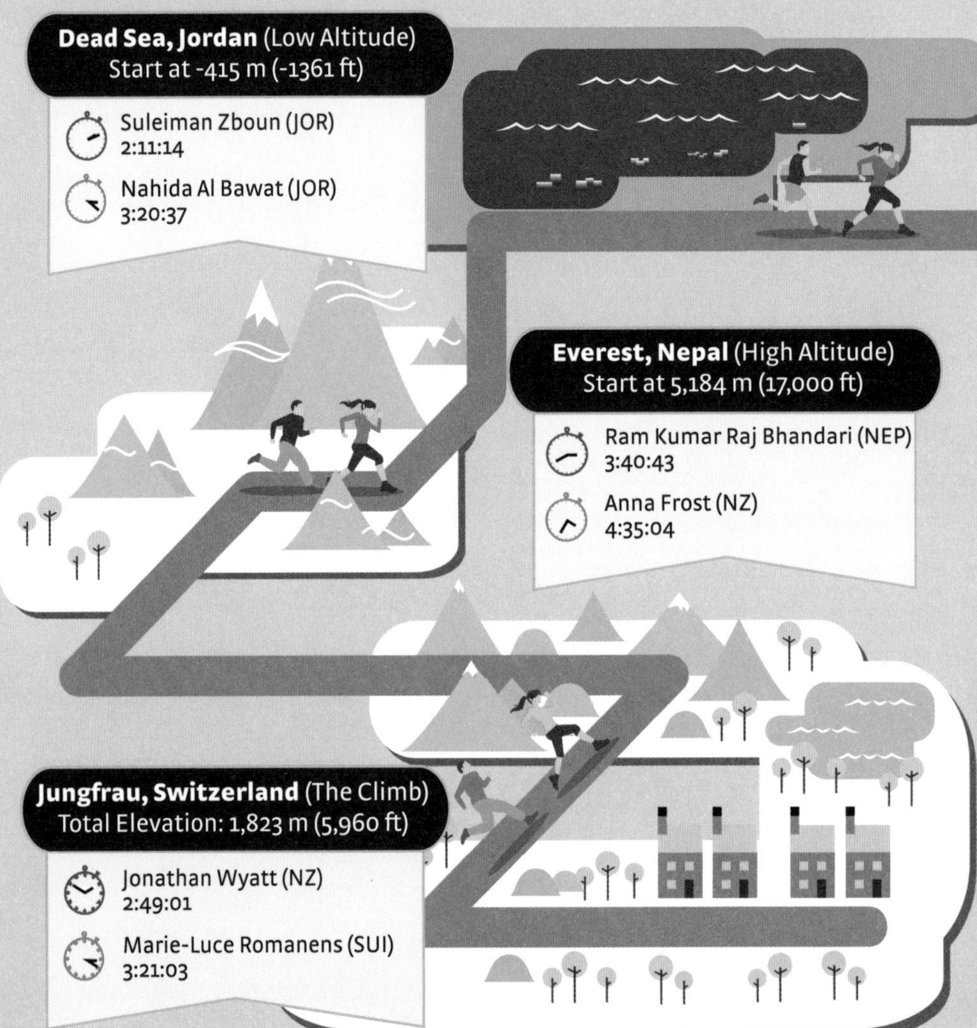
Dead Sea, Jordan (Low Altitude)
Start at -415 m (-1361 ft)
Suleiman Zboun (JOR)
2:11:14
Nahida Al Bawat (JOR)
3:20:37
Everest, Nepal (High Altitude)
Start at 5,184 m (17,000 ft)
Ram Kumar Raj Bhandari (NEP)
3:40:43
Anna Frost (NZ)
4:35:04
Jungfrau, Switzerland (The Climb)
Total Elevation: 1,823 m (5,960 ft)
Jonathan Wyatt (NZ)
2:49:01
Marie-Luce Romanens (SUI)
3:21:03

THE **TOUGHEST** MARATHONS

Marathon running is hard enough on the flat, in mild weather, but when the terrain, altitude and weather are extreme, the competitors need to be as resilient as a sherpa crossed with a mountain goat or polar bear.

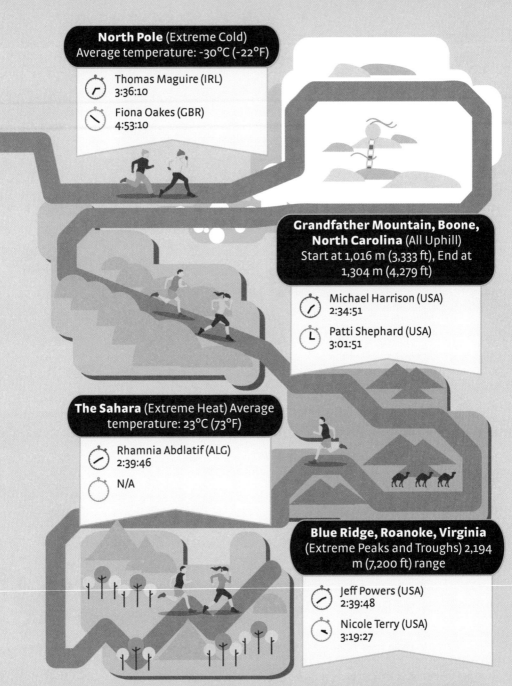

North Pole (Extreme Cold)
Average temperature: -30°C (-22°F)

Thomas Maguire (IRL)
3:36:10

Fiona Oakes (GBR)
4:53:10

Grandfather Mountain, Boone, North Carolina (All Uphill)
Start at 1,016 m (3,333 ft), End at 1,304 m (4,279 ft)

Michael Harrison (USA)
2:34:51

Patti Shephard (USA)
3:01:51

The Sahara (Extreme Heat) Average temperature: 23°C (73°F)

Rhamnia Abdlatif (ALG)
2:39:46

N/A

Blue Ridge, Roanoke, Virginia (Extreme Peaks and Troughs) 2,194 m (7,200 ft) range

Jeff Powers (USA)
2:39:48

Nicole Terry (USA)
3:19:27

jordantimes.com, hopeformarrow.org, northpolemarathon.com, saharamarathon.org, marathonguide.com, blueridgemarathon.com, nepalnews.com

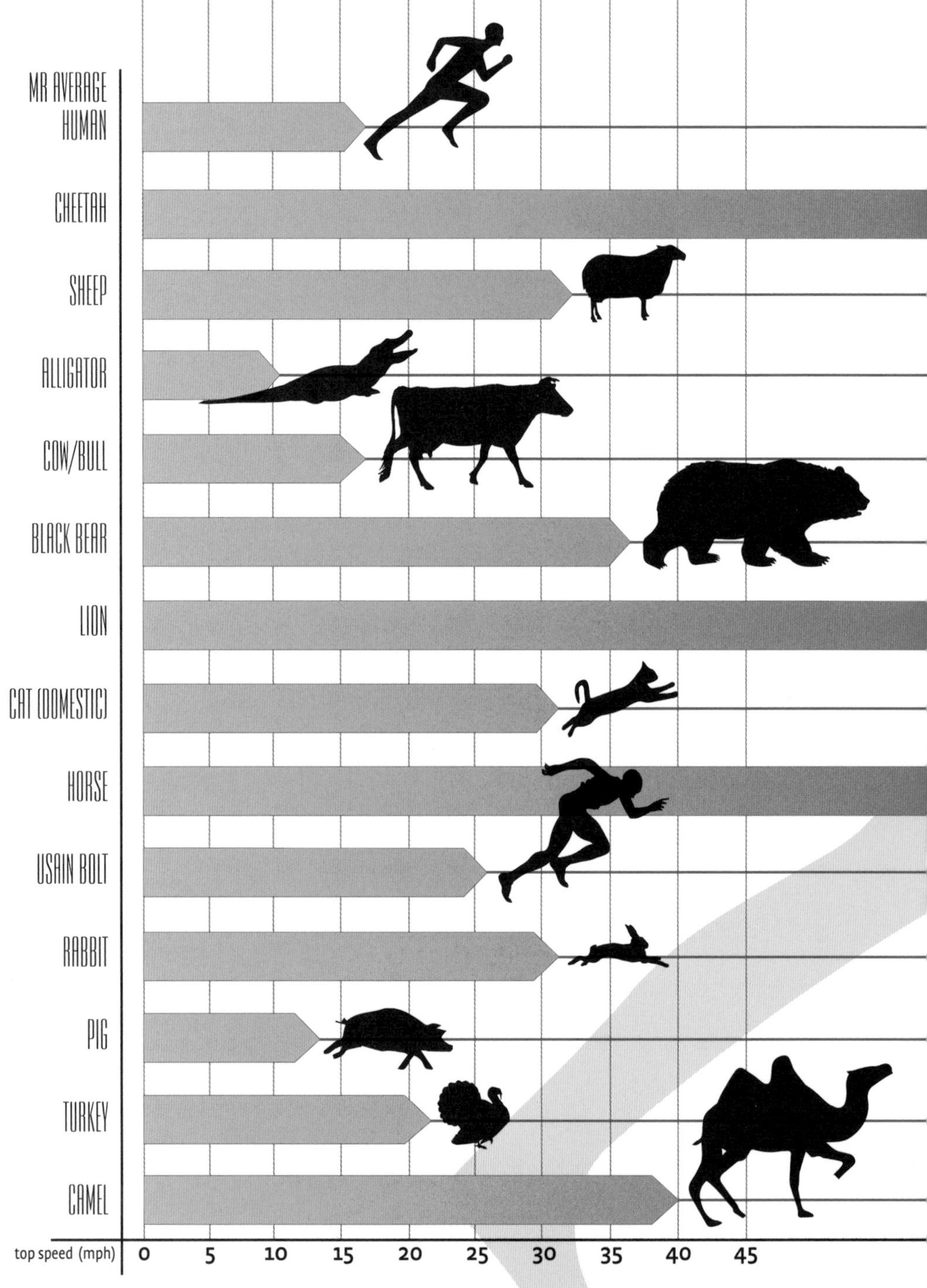
MR AVERAGE HUMAN
CHEETAH
SHEEP
ALLIGATOR
COW/BULL
BLACK BEAR
LION
CAT (DOMESTIC)
HORSE
USAIN BOLT
RABBIT
PIG
TURKEY
CAMEL
top speed (mph)
0
5
10
15
20
25
30
35
40
45

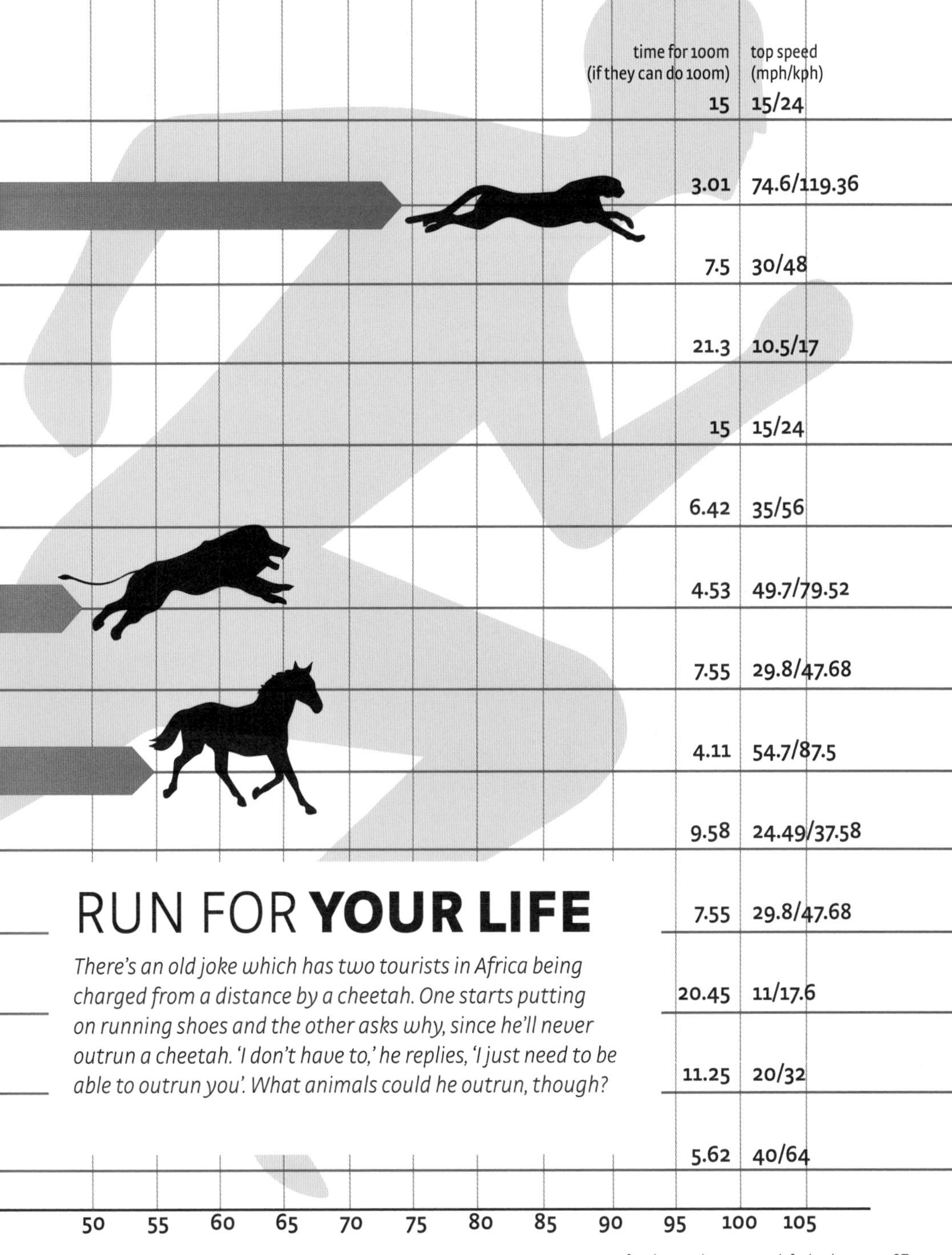
time for 100m
(if they can do 100m)
top speed
(mph/kph)
15 15/24
3.01 74.6/119.36
7.5 30/48
21.3 10.5/17
15 15/24
6.42 35/56
4.53 49.7/79.52
7.55 29.8/47.68
4.11 54.7/87.5
9.58 24.49/37.58
7.55 29.8/47.68
20.45 11/17.6
11.25 20/32
5.62 40/64
50 55 60 65 70 75 80 85 90 95 100 105

RUN FOR **YOUR LIFE**

There's an old joke which has two tourists in Africa being charged from a distance by a cheetah. One starts putting on running shoes and the other asks why, since he'll never outrun a cheetah. 'I don't have to,' he replies, 'I just need to be able to outrun you'. What animals could he outrun, though?

sanfermin.pamplona.es, speedofanimals.com

WHEN IS A SPORT **NOT A SPORT?**

The Council of Europe's European Sports Charter 1992 might disagree with us, but we think sport should involve a physical skill, be competitive and the result decided quantitatively, not qualitatively. Which is why we think some Olympic 'sports' really shouldn't be in the competition at all...

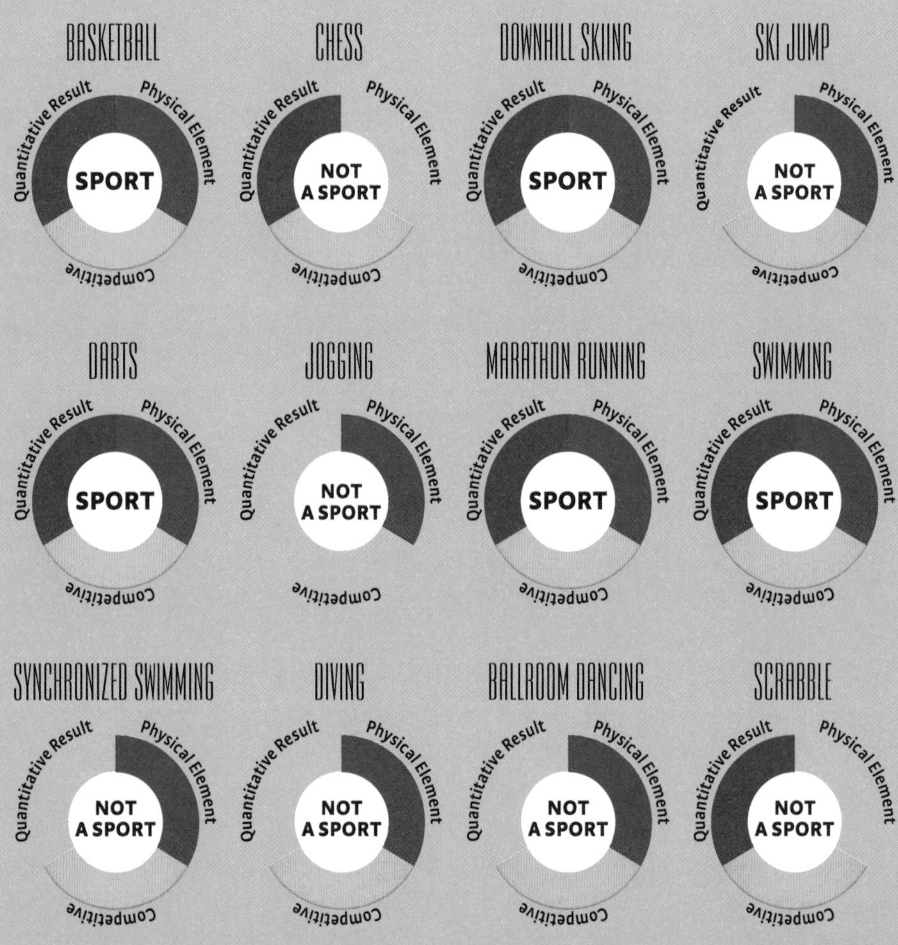
BASKETBALL
Quantitative Result
Physical Element
Competitive
SPORT
CHESS
Quantitative Result
Physical Element
Competitive
NOT A SPORT
DOWNHILL SKIING
Quantitative Result
Physical Element
Competitive
SPORT
SKI JUMP
Quantitative Result
Physical Element
Competitive
NOT A SPORT
DARTS
Quantitative Result
Physical Element
Competitive
SPORT
JOGGING
Quantitative Result
Physical Element
Competitive
NOT A SPORT
MARATHON RUNNING
Quantitative Result
Physical Element
Competitive
SPORT
SWIMMING
Quantitative Result
Physical Element
Competitive
SPORT
SYNCHRONIZED SWIMMING
Quantitative Result
Physical Element
Competitive
NOT A SPORT
DIVING
Quantitative Result
Physical Element
Competitive
NOT A SPORT
BALLROOM DANCING
Quantitative Result
Physical Element
Competitive
NOT A SPORT
SCRABBLE
Quantitative Result
Physical Element
Competitive
NOT A SPORT

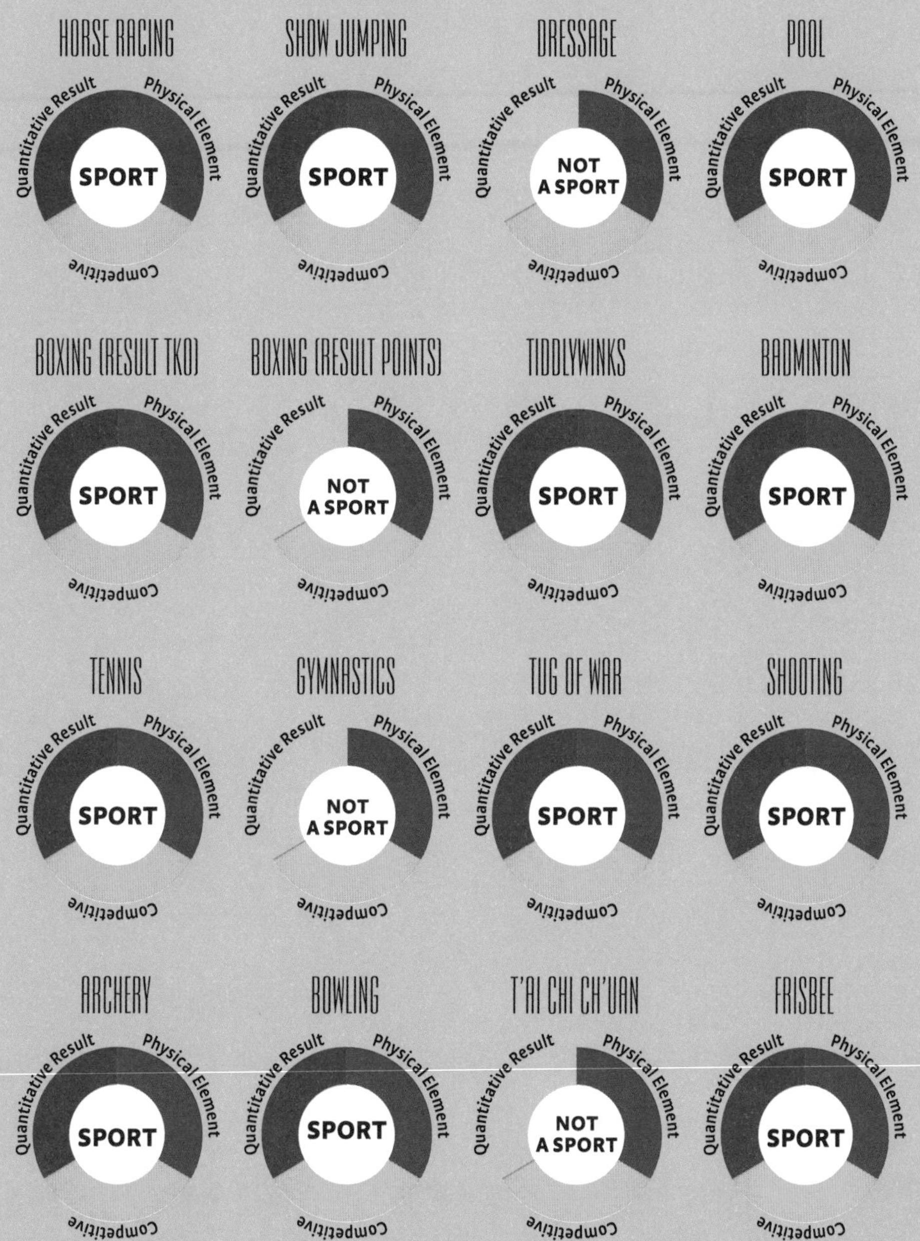
HORSE RACING
Quantitative Result
Physical Element
Competitive
SPORT
SHOW JUMPING
Quantitative Result
Physical Element
Competitive
SPORT
DRESSAGE
Quantitative Result
Physical Element
Competitive
NOT A SPORT
POOL
Quantitative Result
Physical Element
Competitive
SPORT
BOXING (RESULT TKO)
Quantitative Result
Physical Element
Competitive
SPORT
BOXING (RESULT POINTS)
Quantitative Result
Physical Element
Competitive
NOT A SPORT
TIDDLYWINKS
Quantitative Result
Physical Element
Competitive
SPORT
BADMINTON
Quantitative Result
Physical Element
Competitive
SPORT
TENNIS
Quantitative Result
Physical Element
Competitive
SPORT
GYMNASTICS
Quantitative Result
Physical Element
Competitive
NOT A SPORT
TUG OF WAR
Quantitative Result
Physical Element
Competitive
SPORT
SHOOTING
Quantitative Result
Physical Element
Competitive
SPORT
ARCHERY
Quantitative Result
Physical Element
Competitive
SPORT
BOWLING
Quantitative Result
Physical Element
Competitive
SPORT
T'AI CHI CH'UAN
Quantitative Result
Physical Element
Competitive
NOT A SPORT
FRISBEE
Quantitative Result
Physical Element
Competitive
SPORT

FALLING TO **VICTORY**

A basic reading of the laws of gravity would suggest that a heavier object would fall to earth at a faster rate than a lighter one. Downhill skiing is to all intents and purposes controlled falling, so you'd expect heavier skiers to win. But as the results from the last five World Championships prove, that's far from the case in the Men's competition (where 3 out of 5 were lighter) but is true in the Women's (only 1 out of 5 were lighter).

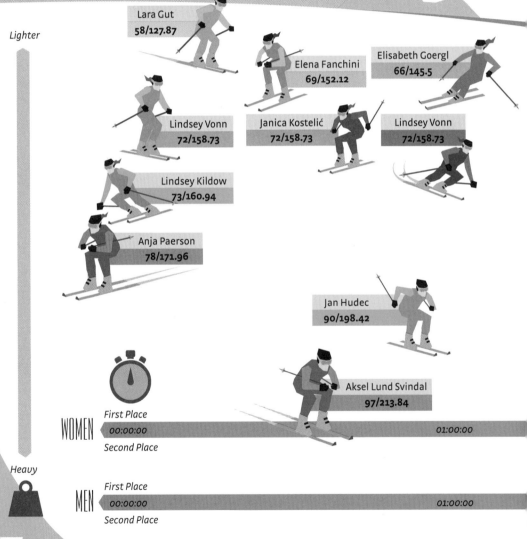

Lighter

Lara Gut
58/127.87

Elena Fanchini
69/152.12

Elisabeth Goergl
66/145.5

Lindsey Vonn
72/158.73

Janica Kostelić
72/158.73

Lindsey Vonn
72/158.73

Lindsey Kildow
73/160.94

Anja Paerson
78/171.96

Jan Hudec
90/198.42

Aksel Lund Svindal
97/213.84

WOMEN
First Place
00:00:00 *01:00:00*
Second Place

Heavy

MEN
First Place
00:00:00 *01:00:00*
Second Place

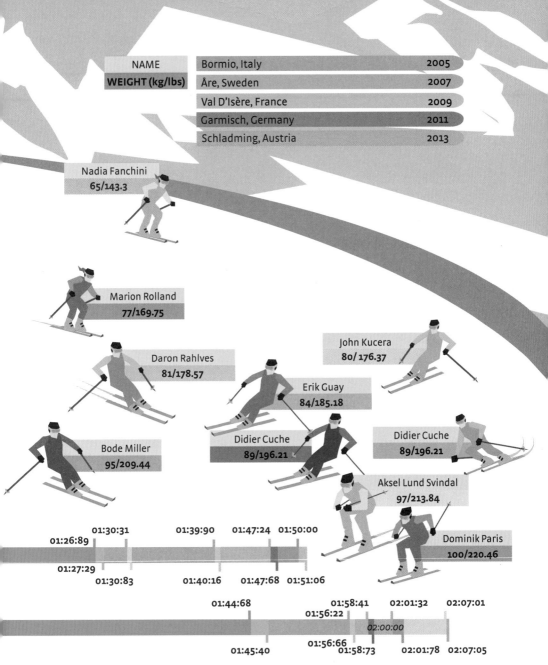

NAME	
WEIGHT (kg/lbs)	
Bormio, Italy	2005
Åre, Sweden	2007
Val D'Isère, France	2009
Garmisch, Germany	2011
Schladming, Austria	2013

Nadia Fanchini
65/143.3

Marion Rolland
77/169.75

John Kucera
80/ 176.37

Daron Rahlves
81/178.57

Erik Guay
84/185.18

Bode Miller
95/209.44

Didier Cuche
89/196.21

Didier Cuche
89/196.21

Aksel Lund Svindal
97/213.84

Dominik Paris
100/220.46

01:26:89
01:27:29
01:30:31
01:30:83
01:39:90
01:40:16
01:47:24
01:47:68
01:50:00
01:51:06

01:44:68
01:45:40
01:56:22
01:56:66
01:58:41
01:58:73
02:00:00
02:01:32
02:01:78
02:07:01
02:07:05

BREAK A **LEG**

Cheerleading began as a way for females to be a part of US high school all-male football games, and now 29 US state high schools recognize cheerleading as a sport. The International Cheer Union has offices in 103 countries and claims an annual growth rate of 18% for each of the past five years in the USA. It's also very dangerous...

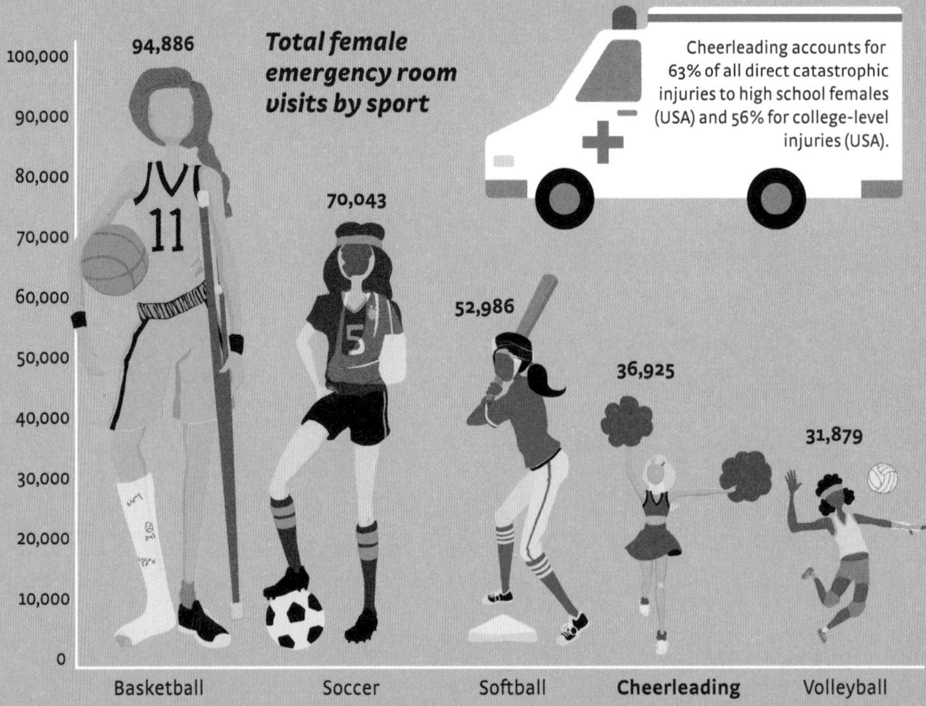

Total female emergency room visits by sport

Basketball	94,886
Soccer	70,043
Softball	52,986
Cheerleading	36,925
Volleyball	31,879

Cheerleading accounts for 63% of all direct catastrophic injuries to high school females (USA) and 56% for college-level injuries (USA).

Shields BJ, Smith GA. "Cheerleading-Related Injuries in the United States: A Prospective Surveillance Study." J Athl Train., 44.6 (2009), pp. 567–577.
Foley, E., Bird, H. "Extreme" or tariff sports: their injuries and their prevention (with particular reference to diving, cheerleading, gymnastics, and figure skating). Clinical Rheumatology, 32.4 (2013), pp. 463–467.

The most common injuries for cheerleaders are:

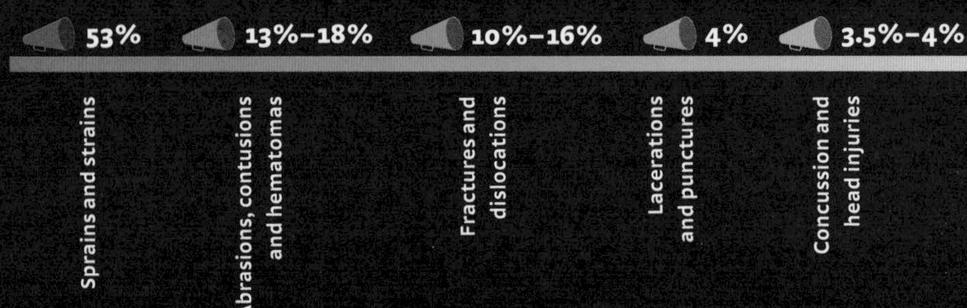
53%
Sprains and strains
13%–18%
Abrasions, contusions and hematomas
10%–16%
Fractures and dislocations
4%
Lacerations and punctures
3.5%–4%
Concussion and head injuries

WHY PING WHEN **YOU** **CAN PONG?**

Spin may be a dirty word in the world of politics but in Table Tennis it is a vital weapon. Power can win you points but spin is the artist's way of winning. This is how to get the 3 types of spin working for you.

1. TOP SPIN

Use an upward stroking movement, above the center axis of the ball. Top spin takes the ball higher over the net but as it hits the table the ball will accelerate and keep low.

Rafael Nadal's top spin averages 3200 rpm (>53 per second)

2. BACK SPIN

A downward stroking movement below the center axis. The ball will fly low over the net and decelerate as it hits the table. The bounce will be higher than top spin. Makes it difficult for the opponent to return with pace as they have to create lift to get it over the net.

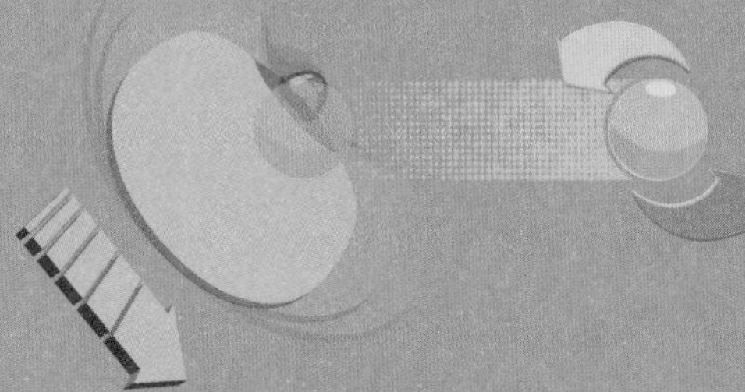

Baseball: top pitcher averages 1200 rpm on a Slider (>20 per sec)

3. SIDE SPIN

A stroking movement on the left hand side of the ball will create spin that, on bouncing, will cause the ball to move to the right. This can be used with either top spin or back spin.

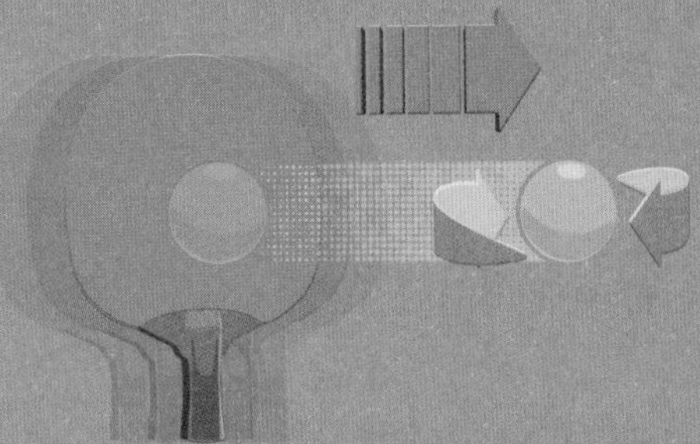

American football: top quarterback spiral pass averages 500 rpm (>8 per sec)

4. SURPRISE

The element of surprise or disguise is crucial. If you can send the ball back with top spin that your opponent has not noticed, the return is usually overhit. With disguised backspin, the return will hit the net.

Table Tennis: ball spins at 9000 rpm (>133 per sec)

tabletennis.about.com, iweb.tms.org

THE **GREATEST** SPORTING ANIMALS

Some animals compete carrying humans, others have no need of two-legged assistance. Horse racing is the Sport of Kings, but what is snail racing? They're both great spectator sports and like all other animal-related sports have thrown up some truly great champions. These are the pick of the bunch.

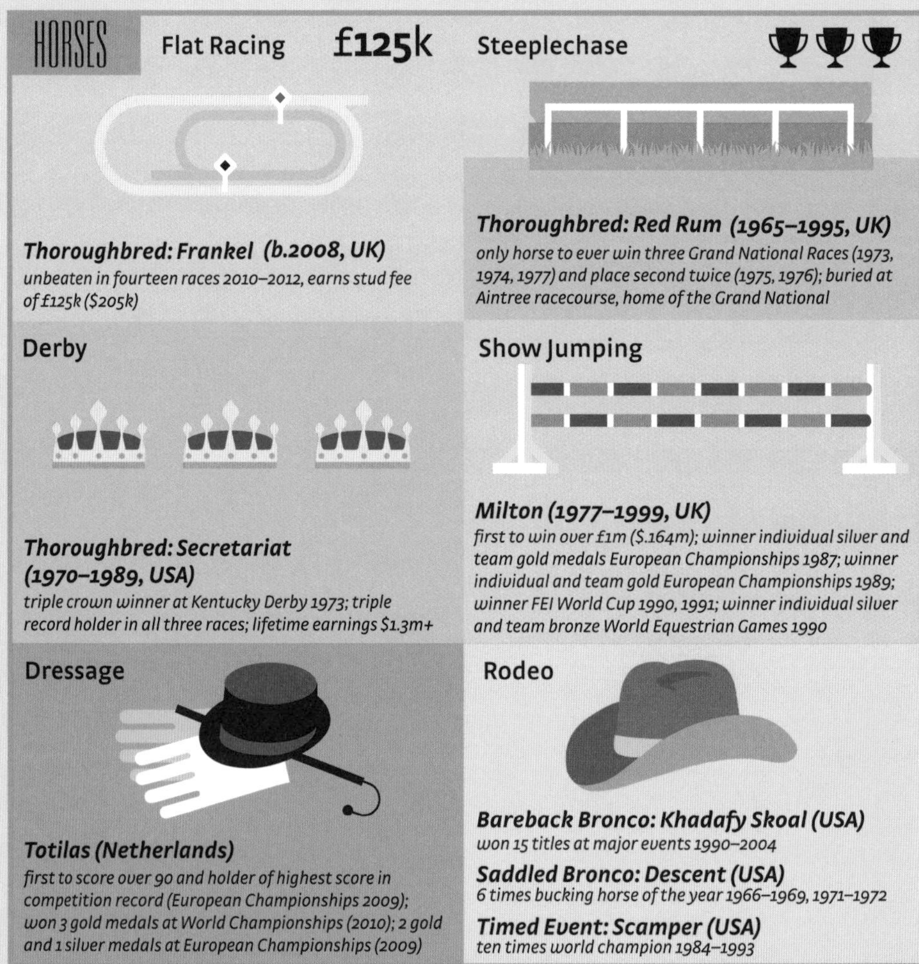

HORSES
Flat Racing
£125k
Steeplechase
Thoroughbred: Frankel (b.2008, UK)
unbeaten in fourteen races 2010–2012, earns stud fee of £125k ($205k)
Thoroughbred: Red Rum (1965–1995, UK)
only horse to ever win three Grand National Races (1973, 1974, 1977) and place second twice (1975, 1976); buried at Aintree racecourse, home of the Grand National
Derby
Thoroughbred: Secretariat (1970–1989, USA)
triple crown winner at Kentucky Derby 1973; triple record holder in all three races; lifetime earnings $1.3m+
Show Jumping
Milton (1977–1999, UK)
first to win over £1m ($.164m); winner individual silver and team gold medals European Championships 1987; winner individual and team gold European Championships 1989; winner FEI World Cup 1990, 1991; winner individual silver and team bronze World Equestrian Games 1990
Dressage
Totilas (Netherlands)
first to score over 90 and holder of highest score in competition record (European Championships 2009); won 3 gold medals at World Championships (2010); 2 gold and 1 silver medals at European Championships (2009)
Rodeo
Bareback Bronco: Khadafy Skoal (USA)
won 15 titles at major events 1990–2004
Saddled Bronco: Descent (USA)
6 times bucking horse of the year 1966–1969, 1971–1972
Timed Event: Scamper (USA)
ten times world champion 1984–1993

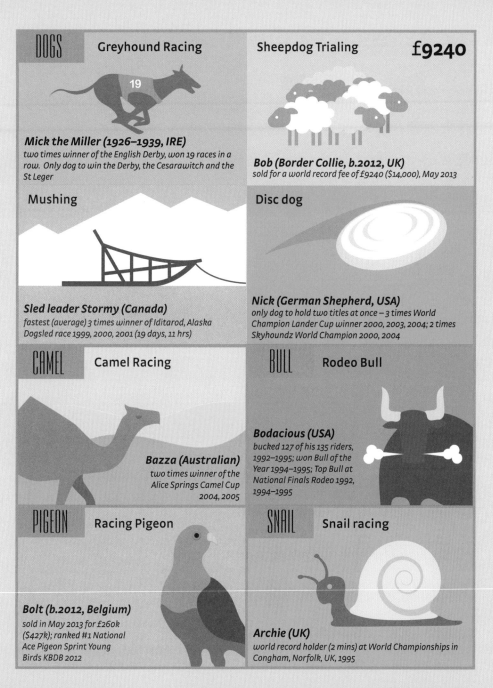

DOGS

Greyhound Racing

19

Mick the Miller (1926–1939, IRE)

two times winner of the English Derby, won 19 races in a row. Only dog to win the Derby, the Cesarawitch and the St Leger

Sheepdog Trialing

£9240

Bob (Border Collie, b.2012, UK)

sold for a world record fee of £9240 ($14,000), May 2013

Mushing

Sled leader Stormy (Canada)

fastest (average) 3 times winner of Iditarod, Alaska Dogsled race 1999, 2000, 2001 (19 days, 11 hrs)

Disc dog

Nick (German Shepherd, USA)

only dog to hold two titles at once – 3 times World Champion Lander Cup winner 2000, 2003, 2004; 2 times Skyhoundz World Champion 2000, 2004

CAMEL

Camel Racing

Bazza (Australian)

two times winner of the Alice Springs Camel Cup 2004, 2005

BULL

Rodeo Bull

Bodacious (USA)

bucked 127 of his 135 riders, 1992–1995; won Bull of the Year 1994–1995; Top Bull at National Finals Rodeo 1992, 1994–1995

PIGEON

Racing Pigeon

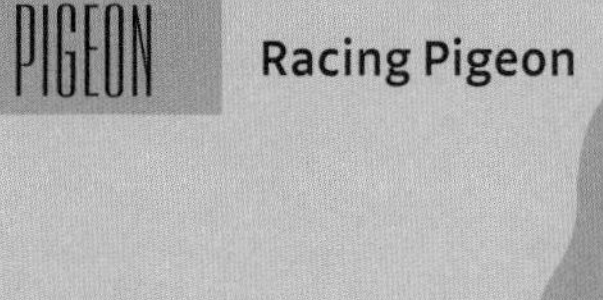

Bolt (b.2012, Belgium)

sold in May 2013 for £260k ($427k); ranked #1 National Ace Pigeon Sprint Young Birds KBDB 2012

SNAIL

Snail racing

Archie (UK)

world record holder (2 mins) at World Championships in Congham, Norfolk, UK, 1995

guardian.com, bbc.co.uk/sport, horsecarecourses.com, skyhoundz.com, wikipedia.org, prorodeohalloffame.com, camelcup.com.au, snailracing.net

BOSSABALL

Equipment required
A trampoline, volleyball net, volleyball, teams 3–5 players.
How to play One player bounces, rest of the team surround the trampoline, the object is to hit the ground opposite, not the trampoline. Any part of the body can be used to keep the ball in the air.

WORLD BEARD AND MUSTACHE CHAMPIONSHIPS

Equipment required
Exotic facial hair.
How to play In the two years between competitions, grow and groom facial hair in order to enter one of 18 categories.

HAKA PEI

Equipment required
Two banana tree trunks, 120m long, 45° hill.
How to play Wearing no protective clothing, lay on the banana tree trunks lashed together and push off downhill (at up to 80mph). Staying on until the bottom earns extra points.

CHEESE ROLLING

Equipment required
A round of double Gloucester cheese, a hill.
How to play Roll your cheese down a hill, chase it down and first across the finish line wins. Extra prizes given for catching the cheese.

VINKENSPORT

Equipment required
A birdcage, a male chaffinch, a stool.
How to play Write down the number of chirps your bird makes in 60 mins.

WIFE CARRYING

Equipment required
A wife, an obstacle course, a sense of humor.
How to play
Competitors must carry their wives through an obstacle course in the fastest time possible without dropping her.

SILLY GAMES

Some people are not satisfied with playing the same sports as everyone else, so they take a ball and add silly extras in order to create a new sport. In Belgium they add a trampoline to volleyball. In Finland they add carrying a wife to the 100m sprint. Here are the dozen silliest games in the world.

RADBALL AKA CYCLEBALL

Equipment required
Fixed wheel bicycles with no brakes, 5 players per team, a soccer ball, goals.
How to play The ball can be kicked, headed or nudged with the bicycle into the opponents' goal. Goalkeepers can use their hands.

GIANT PUMPKIN KAYAKING

Equipment required
A giant pumpkin carved into a kayak, a paddle, a life vest
How to play
Race to the finish line.

PALANT

Equipment required
A baseball bat, a baseball, a fool.
How to play Pitch the baseball at the fool with the bat, score points by hitting the fool.

WATER JOUSTING

Equipment required
A boat with platform, wooden shield, jousting pole, team of 8–10 rowers.
How to play The jousters stand on separate boats and are rowed toward each other in order to knock their opponent into the water.

INUIT MOUTH PULL

Equipment required
Fingers, a mouth, high pain threshold.
How to play Players kneel opposite one another or side by side, hook a finger into their opponent's mouth-cheek and pull. The first to give in loses.

BUZKASHI

Equipment required
Horses, a dead goat (decapitated), goals (3.5m × 1.5m), pitch 400m sq.
How to play Teams of 10, but only 5 on the pitch at any one time play two 45-minute halves per game.The riders must not deliberately whip their opponents. The object is to drag or throw the goat carcass into the opponents' goal.

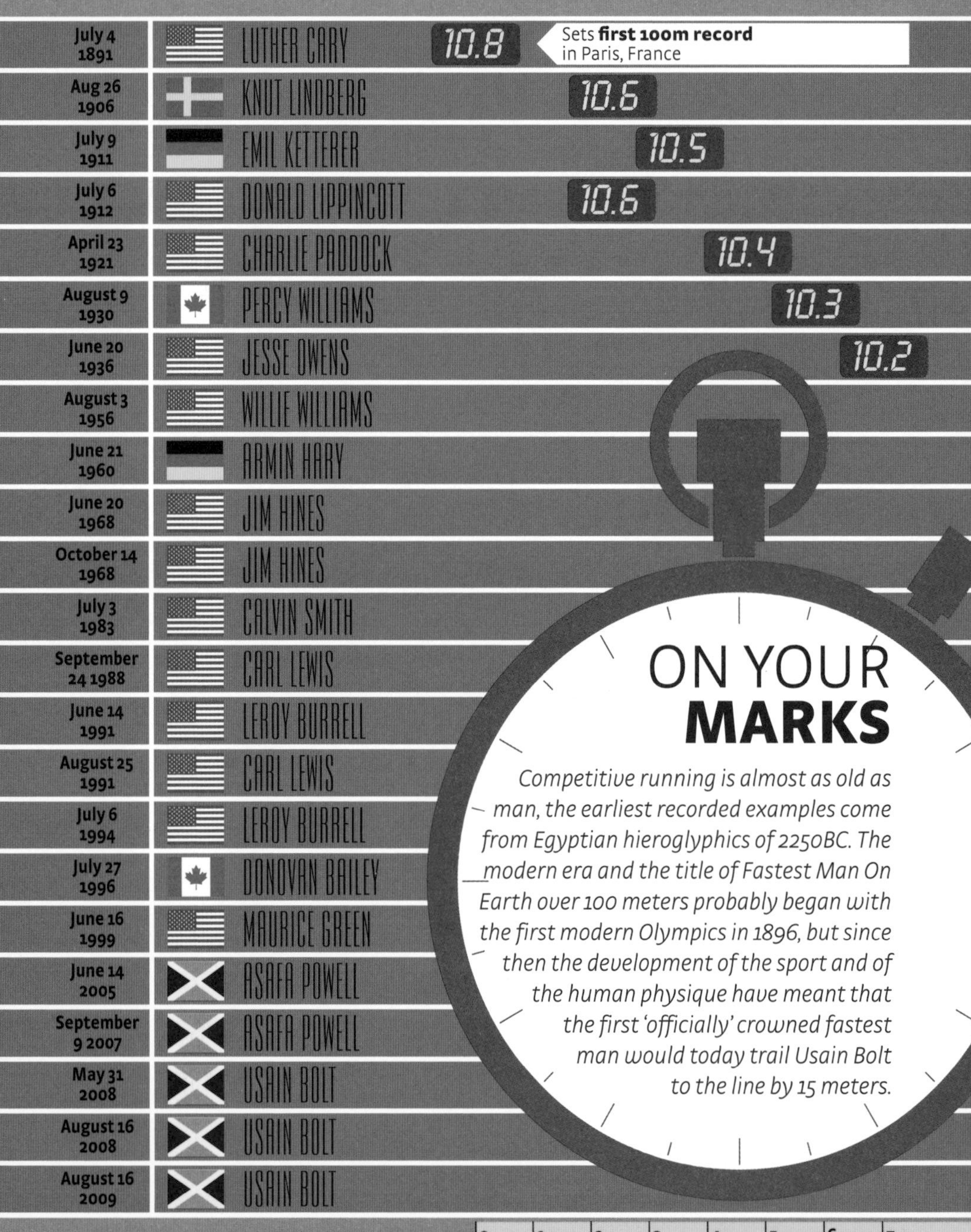
July 4 1891
LUTHER CARY
10.8
Sets **first 100m record** in Paris, France
Aug 26 1906
KNUT LINDBERG
10.6
July 9 1911
EMIL KETTERER
10.5
July 6 1912
DONALD LIPPINCOTT
10.6
April 23 1921
CHARLIE PADDOCK
10.4
August 9 1930
PERCY WILLIAMS
10.3
June 20 1936
JESSE OWENS
10.2
August 3 1956
WILLIE WILLIAMS
June 21 1960
ARMIN HARY
June 20 1968
JIM HINES
October 14 1968
JIM HINES
July 3 1983
CALVIN SMITH
September 24 1988
CARL LEWIS
June 14 1991
LEROY BURRELL
August 25 1991
CARL LEWIS
July 6 1994
LEROY BURRELL
July 27 1996
DONOVAN BAILEY
June 16 1999
MAURICE GREEN
June 14 2005
ASAFA POWELL
September 9 2007
ASAFA POWELL
May 31 2008
USAIN BOLT
August 16 2008
USAIN BOLT
August 16 2009
USAIN BOLT
ON YOUR MARKS
Competitive running is almost as old as man, the earliest recorded examples come from Egyptian hieroglyphics of 2250BC. The modern era and the title of Fastest Man On Earth over 100 meters probably began with the first modern Olympics in 1896, but since then the development of the sport and of the human physique have meant that the first 'officially' crowned fastest man would today trail Usain Bolt to the line by 15 meters.
0
1
2
3
4
5
6
7

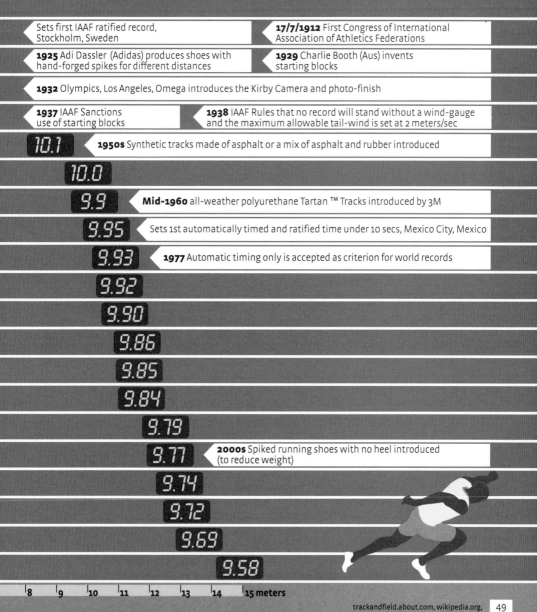

1896 First modern Olympic Games held in Athens, Greece

Late 1890s JW Foster and Sons (now Reebok) introduced spikes – running pumps

Sets first IAAF ratified record, Stockholm, Sweden

17/7/1912 First Congress of International Association of Athletics Federations

1925 Adi Dassler (Adidas) produces shoes with hand-forged spikes for different distances

1929 Charlie Booth (Aus) invents starting blocks

1932 Olympics, Los Angeles, Omega introduces the Kirby Camera and photo-finish

1937 IAAF Sanctions use of starting blocks

1938 IAAF Rules that no record will stand without a wind-gauge and the maximum allowable tail-wind is set at 2 meters/sec

10.1

1950s Synthetic tracks made of asphalt or a mix of asphalt and rubber introduced

10.0

9.9

Mid-1960 all-weather polyurethane Tartan ™ Tracks introduced by 3M

9.95

Sets 1st automatically timed and ratified time under 10 secs, Mexico City, Mexico

9.93

1977 Automatic timing only is accepted as criterion for world records

9.92

9.90

9.86

9.85

9.84

9.79

9.77

2000s Spiked running shoes with no heel introduced (to reduce weight)

9.74

9.72

9.69

9.58

8 9 10 11 12 13 14 **15 meters**

trackandfield.about.com, wikipedia.org, webarchive.org, runblogrun.com

SPORTING **SUPERWOMAN**

If a super sportswoman could be constructed from the separate parts of successful sports stars, this is how she'd look.

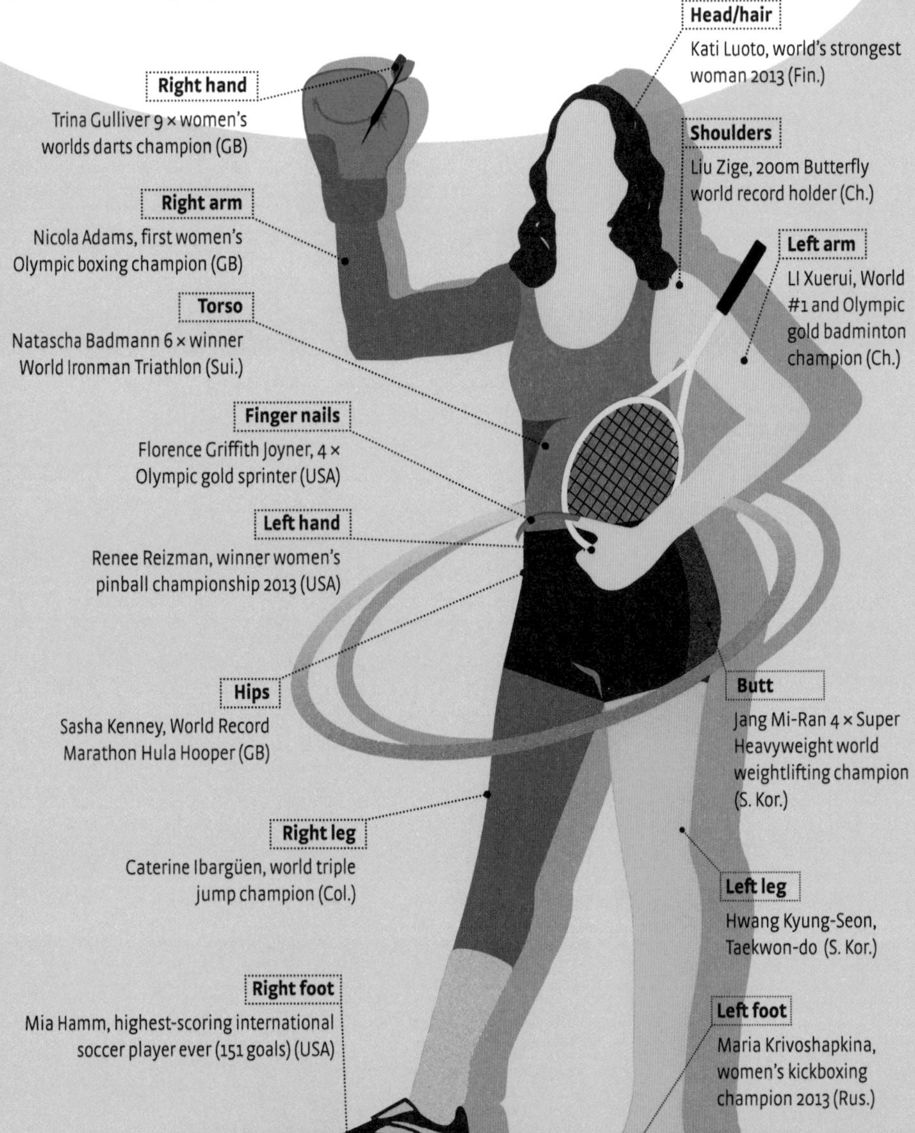

Head/hair
Kati Luoto, world's strongest woman 2013 (Fin.)
Right hand
Trina Gulliver 9 × women's worlds darts champion (GB)
Shoulders
Liu Zige, 200m Butterfly world record holder (Ch.)
Right arm
Nicola Adams, first women's Olympic boxing champion (GB)
Left arm
LI Xuerui, World #1 and Olympic gold badminton champion (Ch.)
Torso
Natascha Badmann 6 × winner World Ironman Triathlon (Sui.)
Finger nails
Florence Griffith Joyner, 4 × Olympic gold sprinter (USA)
Left hand
Renee Reizman, winner women's pinball championship 2013 (USA)
Hips
Sasha Kenney, World Record Marathon Hula Hooper (GB)
Butt
Jang Mi-Ran 4 × Super Heavyweight world weightlifting champion (S. Kor.)
Right leg
Caterine Ibargüen, world triple jump champion (Col.)
Left leg
Hwang Kyung-Seon, Taekwon-do (S. Kor.)
Right foot
Mia Hamm, highest-scoring international soccer player ever (151 goals) (USA)
Left foot
Maria Krivoshapkina, women's kickboxing champion 2013 (Rus.)

SPORTING **SUPERMAN**

If a super sportsman could be constructed from the separate parts of successful sports stars, this is how he'd look.

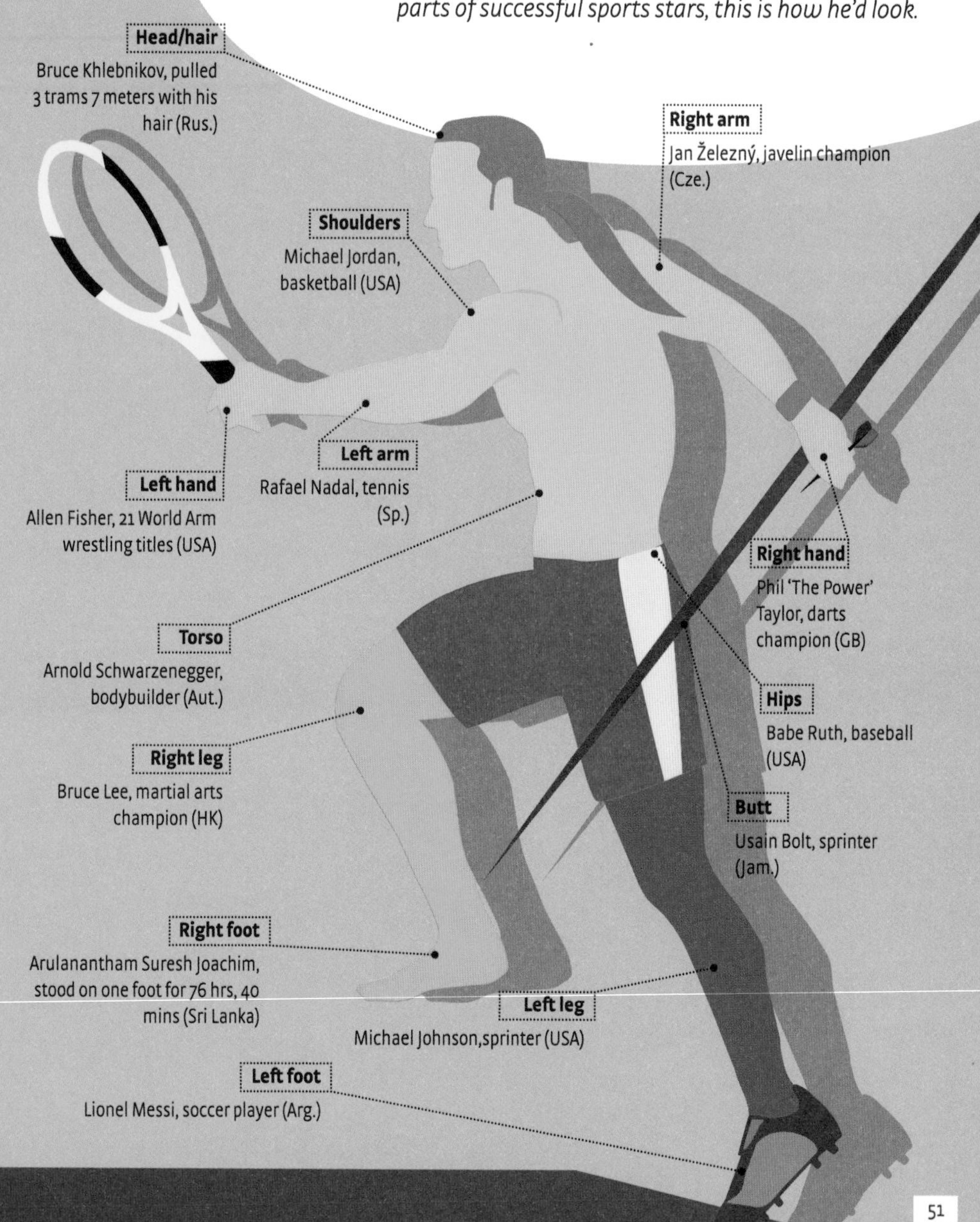

Head/hair
Bruce Khlebnikov, pulled 3 trams 7 meters with his hair (Rus.)
Right arm
Jan Železný, javelin champion (Cze.)
Shoulders
Michael Jordan, basketball (USA)
Left arm
Rafael Nadal, tennis (Sp.)
Left hand
Allen Fisher, 21 World Arm wrestling titles (USA)
Right hand
Phil 'The Power' Taylor, darts champion (GB)
Torso
Arnold Schwarzenegger, bodybuilder (Aut.)
Hips
Babe Ruth, baseball (USA)
Right leg
Bruce Lee, martial arts champion (HK)
Butt
Usain Bolt, sprinter (Jam.)
Right foot
Arulanantham Suresh Joachim, stood on one foot for 76 hrs, 40 mins (Sri Lanka)
Left leg
Michael Johnson, sprinter (USA)
Left foot
Lionel Messi, soccer player (Arg.)

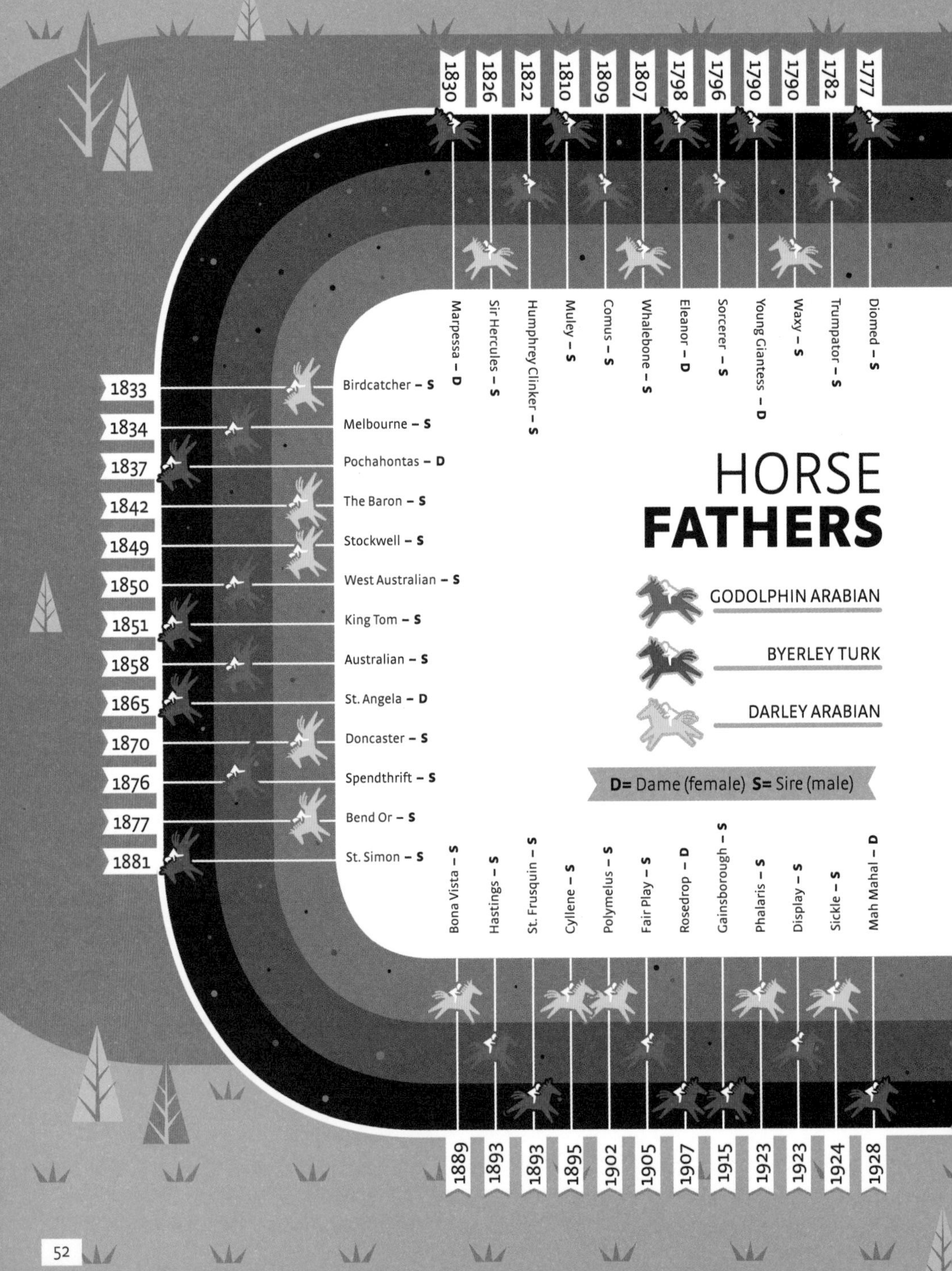

HORSE
FATHERS
GODOLPHIN ARABIAN
BYERLEY TURK
DARLEY ARABIAN
D= Dame (female) S= Sire (male)
1777 Diomed – S
1782 Trumpator – S
1790 Waxy – S
1790 Young Giantess – D
1796 Sorcerer – S
1798 Eleanor – D
1807 Whalebone – S
1809 Comus – S
1810 Muley – S
1822 Humphrey Clinker – S
1826 Sir Hercules – S
1830 Marpessa – D
1833 Birdcatcher – S
1834 Melbourne – S
1837 Pochahontas – D
1842 The Baron – S
1849 Stockwell – S
1850 West Australian – S
1851 King Tom – S
1858 Australian – S
1865 St. Angela – D
1870 Doncaster – S
1876 Spendthrift – S
1877 Bend Or – S
1881 St. Simon – S
1889 Bona Vista – S
1893 Hastings – S
1893 St. Frusquin – S
1895 Cyllene – S
1902 Polymelus – S
1905 Fair Play – S
1907 Rosedrop – D
1915 Gainsborough – S
1923 Phalaris – S
1923 Display – S
1924 Sickle – S
1928 Mah Mahal – D

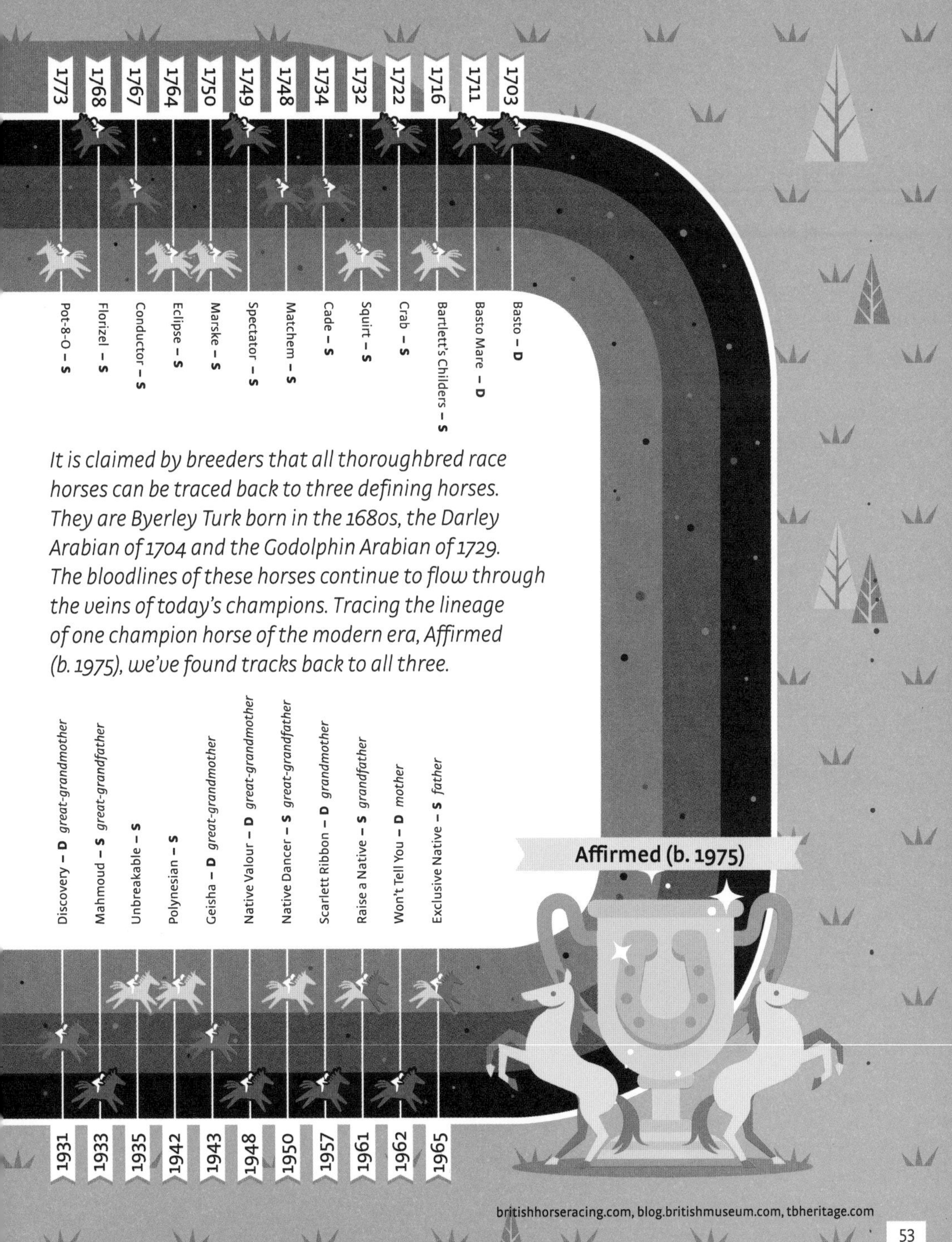
1703
1711
1716
1722
1732
1734
1748
1749
1750
1764
1767
1768
1773
Basto – **D**
Basto Mare – **D**
Bartlett's Childers – **S**
Crab – **S**
Squirt – **S**
Cade – **S**
Matchem – **S**
Spectator – **S**
Marske – **S**
Eclipse – **S**
Conductor – **S**
Florizel – **S**
Pot-8-O – **S**
Discovery – **D** *great-grandmother*
Mahmoud – **S** *great-grandfather*
Unbreakable – **S**
Polynesian – **S**
Geisha – **D** *great-grandmother*
Native Valour – **D** *great-grandmother*
Native Dancer – **S** *great-grandfather*
Scarlett Ribbon – **D** *grandmother*
Raise a Native – **S** *grandfather*
Won't Tell You – **D** *mother*
Exclusive Native – **S** *father*
1931
1933
1935
1942
1943
1948
1950
1957
1961
1962
1965
Affirmed (b. 1975)

It is claimed by breeders that all thoroughbred race horses can be traced back to three defining horses. They are Byerley Turk born in the 1680s, the Darley Arabian of 1704 and the Godolphin Arabian of 1729. The bloodlines of these horses continue to flow through the veins of today's champions. Tracing the lineage of one champion horse of the modern era, Affirmed (b. 1975), we've found tracks back to all three.

britishhorseracing.com, blog.britishmuseum.com, tbheritage.com

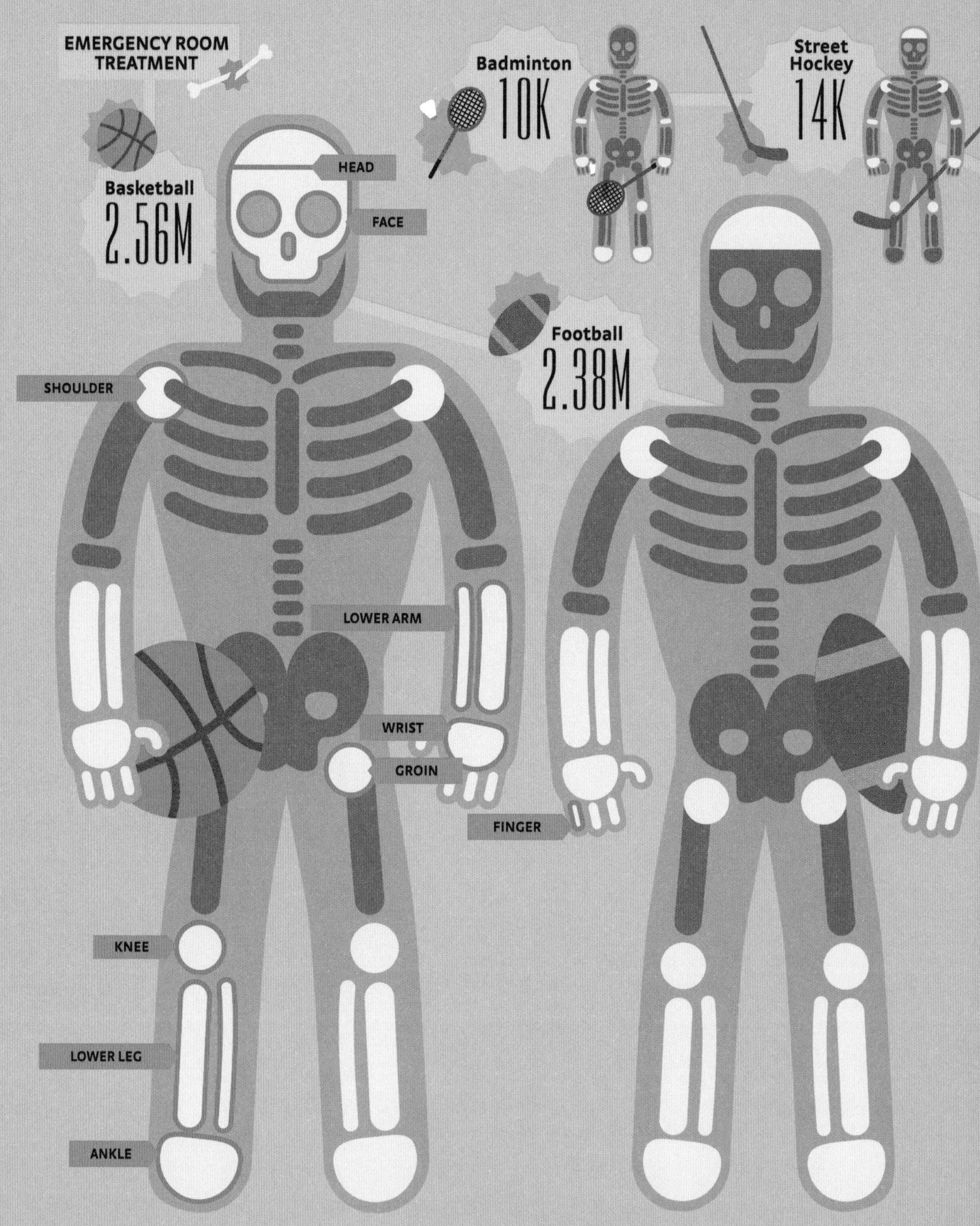
EMERGENCY ROOM TREATMENT
Basketball
2.56M
Badminton
10K
Street Hockey
14K
Football
2.38M
HEAD
FACE
SHOULDER
LOWER ARM
WRIST
GROIN
FINGER
KNEE
LOWER LEG
ANKLE

DANGER **BALLS**

Data from American ER room admissions for one year suggests that the most dangerous sports involve balls of differing sizes, from tiny (golf) to cigar-shaped (American football) and feathered (badminton). Here's which balls do most damage, and where.

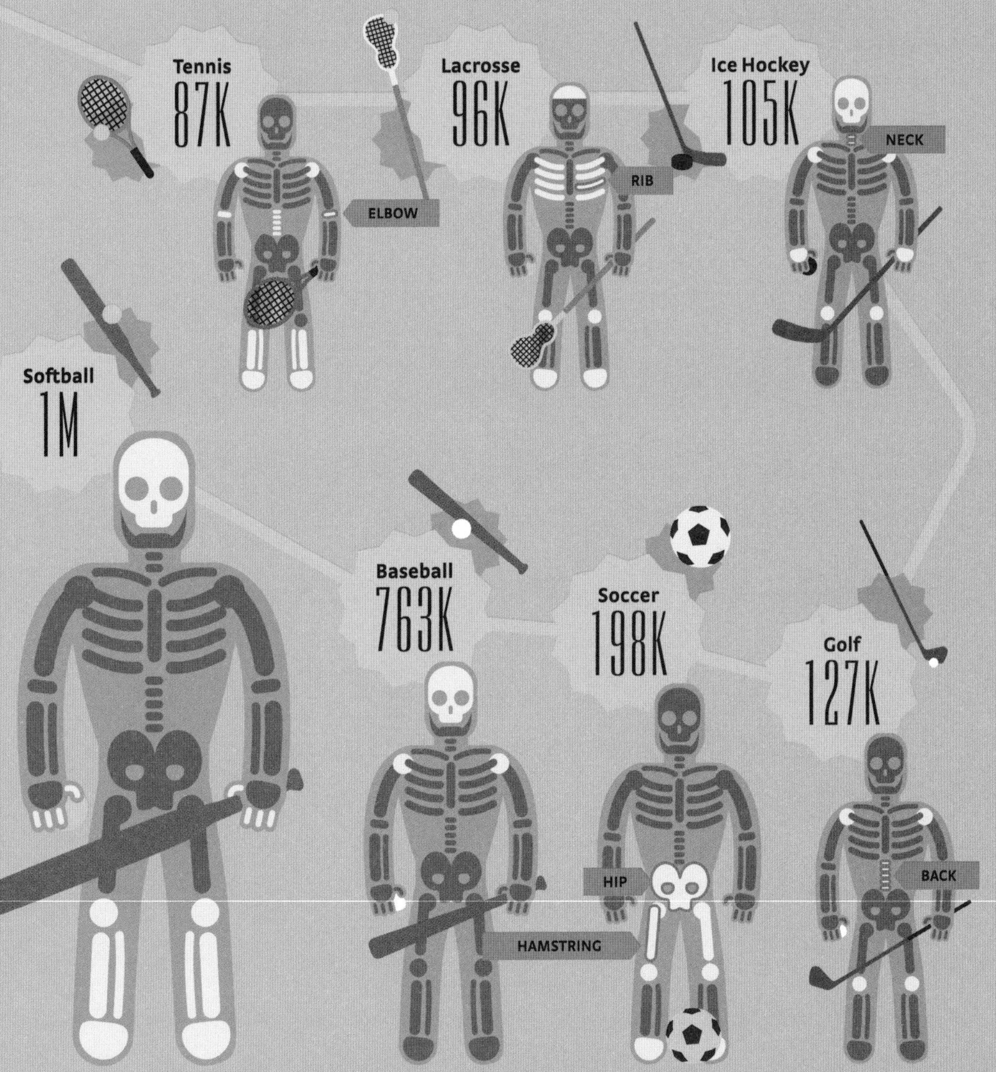

Tennis
87K
ELBOW
Lacrosse
96K
RIB
Ice Hockey
105K
NECK
Softball
1M
Baseball
763K
HAMSTRING
Soccer
198K
HIP
Golf
127K
BACK

upmc.com, physioroom.com, advancedphysicalmedecine.org, cpcs.gov, nsga.org, sportsinjurybulletin.com

TESTS

Matches

200

(Next Highest Steve Waugh/ Ricky Ponting 168)

Career Runs 15,921
Ricky Ponting 13,378

Centuries 51
Jacques Kallis 45

Fifties* 68
Raul Dravid/Allan Border 63
*(*That didn't become 100s)*

6s – 69

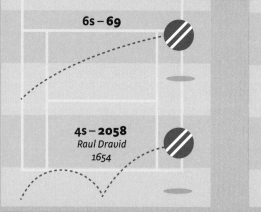

4s – 2058
Raul Dravid 1654

ONE DAY INTERNATIONALS

Matches

463

(Next Highest Sanath Jayasuria 445)

Career Runs 18,426
Ricky Ponting 13,704

Centuries 49
Ricky Ponting 30

Fifties* 96
Jacques Kallis 86
*(*That didn't become 100s)*

6s – 195

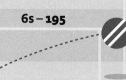

4s – 2016
Sanath Jayasuria 1500

TENDULKAR 10

THE **MOST POPULAR** SPORTSMAN IN THE WORLD

Because he plays cricket, a sport never heard of in some parts of the USA, Sachin Tendulkar is an unknown entity there. But in India he has, it is estimated, more than 1.2 billion fans. These figures show why his countrymen love him, and how far he has to go to eclipse the social media fame of other major sports stars.

TWITTER'S MOST FOLLOWED SPORTSMEN		FACEBOOK'S MOST 'LIKED' SPORTSMEN
24.0m	**Cristiano Ronaldo** *soccer*	71.5m
0.4m	**David Beckham** *soccer*	33.6m
4.2m	**Kobe Bryant** *basketball*	17.8m
11.4m	**LeBron James** *basketball*	15.7m
1.3m	**Roger Federer** *tennis*	13.8m
4.0m	**Sachin Tendulkar** *cricket*	13.2m
3.7m	**Tiger Woods** *golf*	12.9m
4.6m	**Floyd Mayweather** *boxing*	3.9m
3.2m	**Usain Bolt** *sprinter*	2.9m
0.1m	**Alex Rodriguez (A-Rod)** *baseball*	1.2m

bbc.co.uk/news/world-asia-india-24910411, wikipedia.org, twitter.com, facebook.com

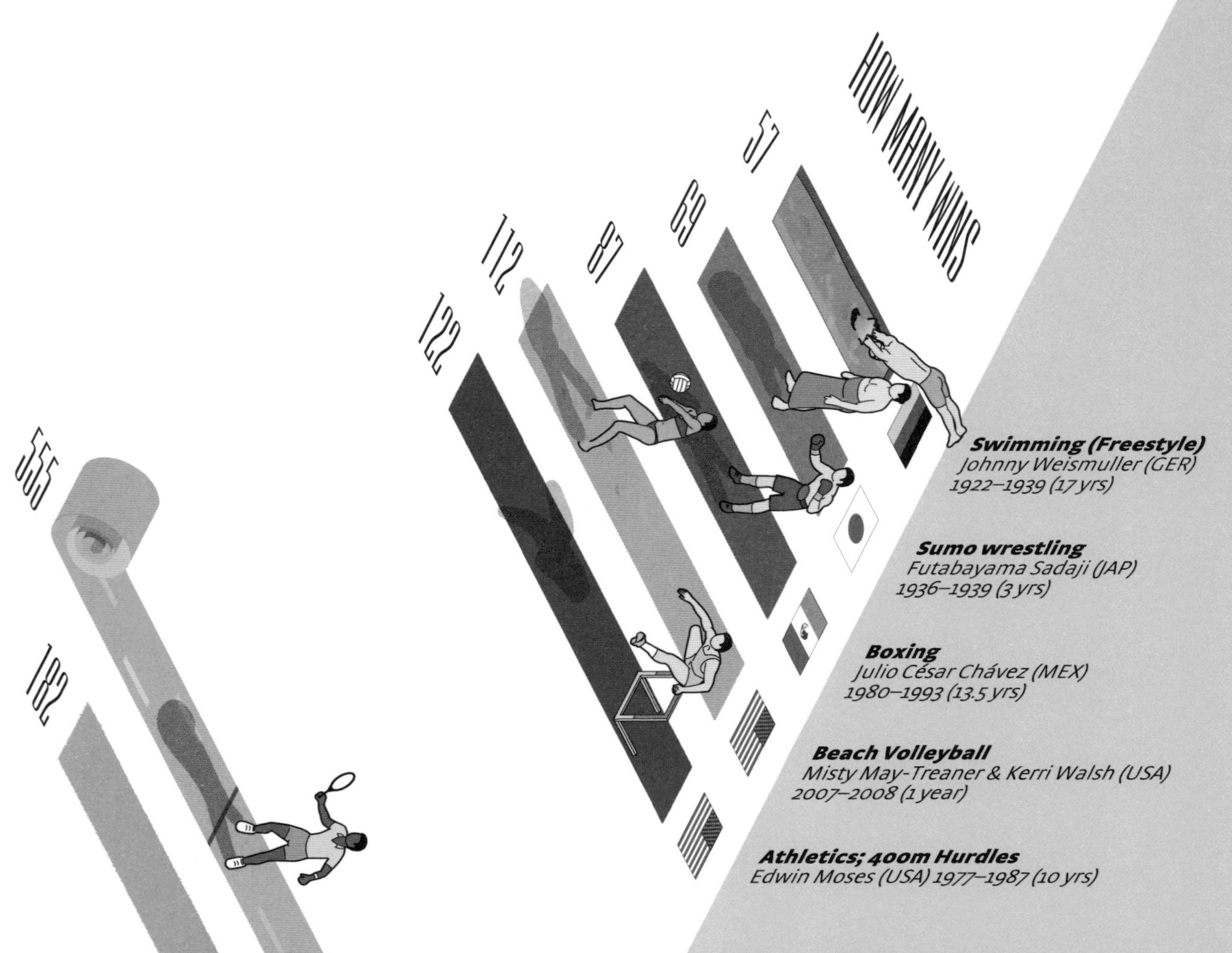
HOW MANY WINS
57
69
87
112
122
555
182
Swimming (Freestyle)
Johnny Weismuller (GER)
1922–1939 (17 yrs)
Sumo wrestling
Futabayama Sadaji (JAP)
1936–1939 (3 yrs)
Boxing
Julio César Chávez (MEX)
1980–1993 (13.5 yrs)
Beach Volleyball
Misty May-Treaner & Kerri Walsh (USA)
2007–2008 (1 year)
Athletics; 400m Hurdles
Edwin Moses (USA) 1977–1987 (10 yrs)

LONGEST **WINNING** STREAKS

What's the longest winning streak in any professional sport? And how do different sports measure up to each other in the length and dates of those winning streaks.

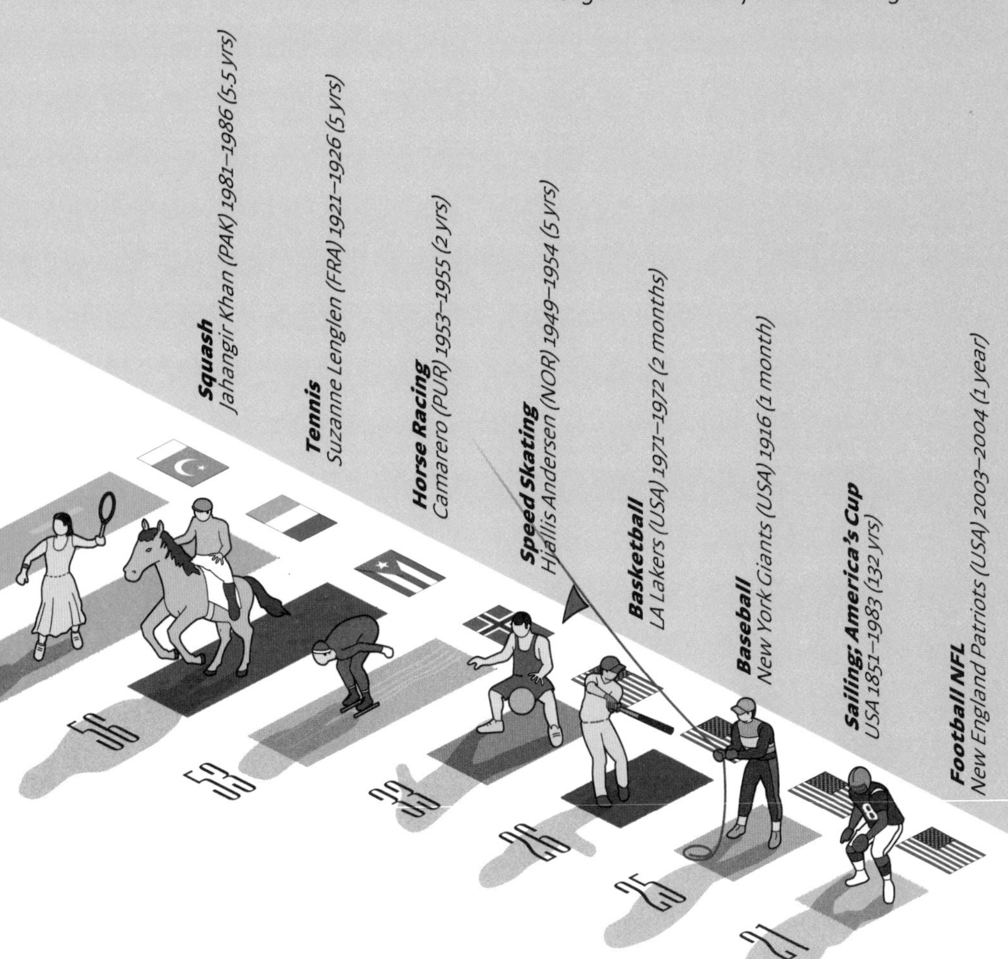

Squash
Jahangir Khan (PAK) 1981–1986 (5.5 yrs)
Tennis
Suzanne Lenglen (FRA) 1921–1926 (5 yrs)
Horse Racing
Camarero (PUR) 1953–1955 (2 yrs)
Speed Skating
Hjallis Andersen (NOR) 1949–1954 (5 yrs)
Basketball
LA Lakers (USA) 1971–1972 (2 months)
Baseball
New York Giants (USA) 1916 (1 month)
Sailing: America's Cup
USA 1851–1983 (132 yrs)
Football NFL
New England Patriots (USA) 2003–2004 (1 year)
56
53
33
26
25
21

TIMELINE OF
OLYMPIC TORCHES

The Olympic flame was introduced to the modern era of Olympics in 1936 by the Germans. After the next two series of games were cancelled due to WWII, it was again used in London in 1948 and has persisted as a tradition ever since, being lit in the last host city and carried, ever alight, to the next host city of both the summer and winter games. Here's how the torch has changed in shape since 1936.

1936
Berlin, Germany
designed by Walter Lenke
1948
London, England
designed by Ralph Lavers
1952
Oslo, Sweden
lit in the hearth of skier Sondre Norheim
1952
Helsinki, Finland
only 22 made
1956
Cortina d'Amprezzo, Italy
lit in Rome and blessed by the Pope
1956
Melbourne, Australia
design echoed the Sydney Opera House
1960
Squaw Valley, USA
designed by Disney Studios artist John Hench
1960
Rome, Italy
designed in a Roman style
1964
Innsbruck, Austria
1964
Tokyo, Japan
1968
Grenoble, France
made of bronzed steel and had a protective shield for the flame
1968
Mexico City, Mexico
the logo was represented in 3D
1972
Sapporo, Japan
designed by Sori Yanagi
1972
Munich, West Germany

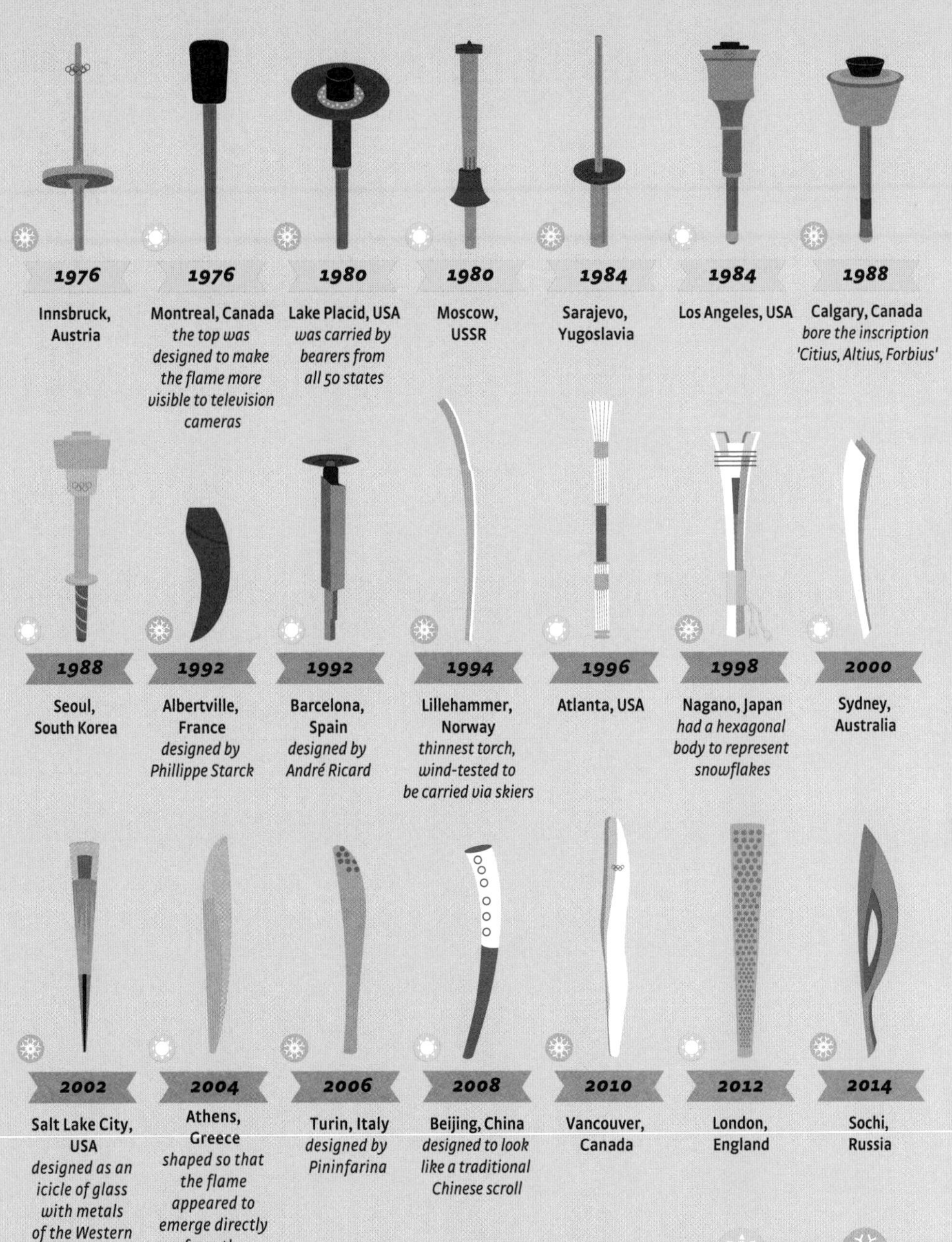
1976
Innsbruck, Austria
1976
Montreal, Canada
the top was designed to make the flame more visible to television cameras
1980
Lake Placid, USA
was carried by bearers from all 50 states
1980
Moscow, USSR
1984
Sarajevo, Yugoslavia
1984
Los Angeles, USA
1988
Calgary, Canada
bore the inscription 'Citius, Altius, Forbius'
1988
Seoul, South Korea
1992
Albertville, France
designed by Phillippe Starck
1992
Barcelona, Spain
designed by André Ricard
1994
Lillehammer, Norway
thinnest torch, wind-tested to be carried via skiers
1996
Atlanta, USA
1998
Nagano, Japan
had a hexagonal body to represent snowflakes
2000
Sydney, Australia
2002
Salt Lake City, USA
designed as an icicle of glass with metals of the Western US, copper and bronze
2004
Athens, Greece
shaped so that the flame appeared to emerge directly from the bearer's hand
2006
Turin, Italy
designed by Pininfarina
2008
Beijing, China
designed to look like a traditional Chinese scroll
2010
Vancouver, Canada
2012
London, England
2014
Sochi, Russia
Summer Olympics
Winter Olympics

WOMEN AT THE OLYMPICS

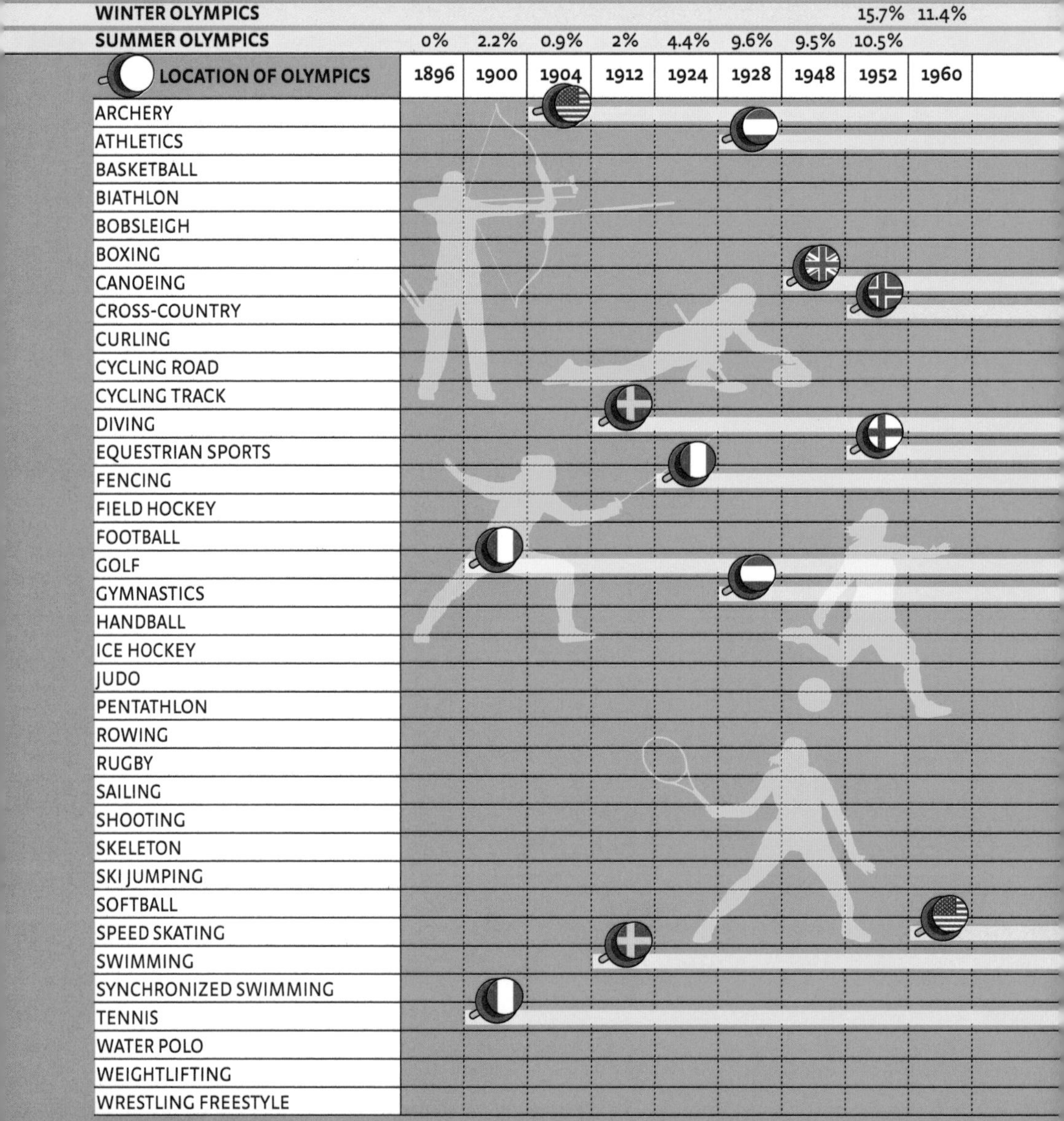

WINTER OLYMPICS								15.7%	11.4%	
SUMMER OLYMPICS	0%	2.2%	0.9%	2%	4.4%	9.6%	9.5%	10.5%		
LOCATION OF OLYMPICS	1896	1900	1904	1912	1924	1928	1948	1952	1960	
ARCHERY										
ATHLETICS										
BASKETBALL										
BIATHLON										
BOBSLEIGH										
BOXING										
CANOEING										
CROSS-COUNTRY										
CURLING										
CYCLING ROAD										
CYCLING TRACK										
DIVING										
EQUESTRIAN SPORTS										
FENCING										
FIELD HOCKEY										
FOOTBALL										
GOLF										
GYMNASTICS										
HANDBALL										
ICE HOCKEY										
JUDO										
PENTATHLON										
ROWING										
RUGBY										
SAILING										
SHOOTING										
SKELETON										
SKI JUMPING										
SOFTBALL										
SPEED SKATING										
SWIMMING										
SYNCHRONIZED SWIMMING										
TENNIS										
WATER POLO										
WEIGHTLIFTING										
WRESTLING FREESTYLE										

Women have had to fight to be allowed to compete at the Olympics. These are the Olympics at which women were first allowed to compete in each sport, plus the percentage of female competitors overall at each.

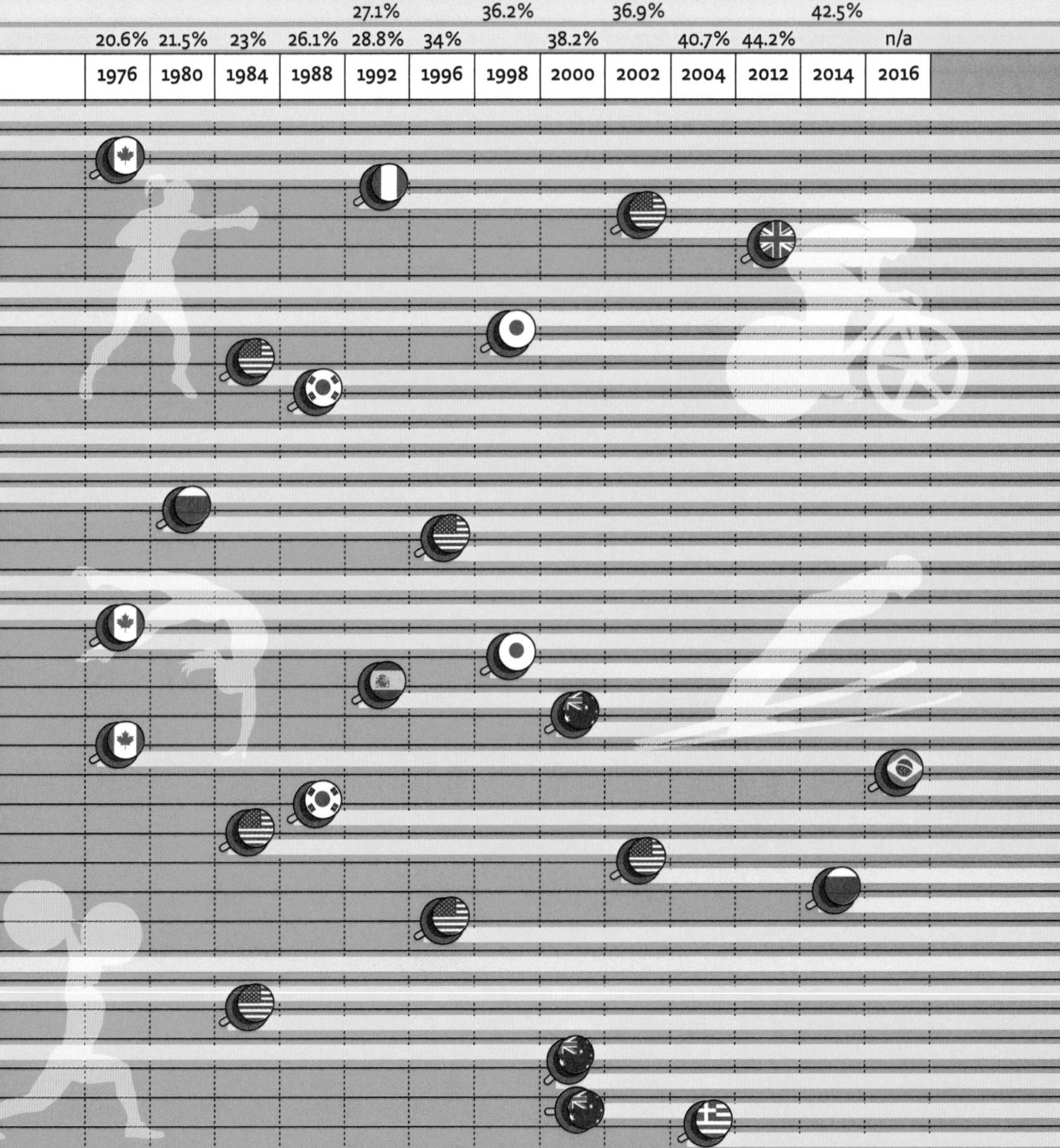

20.6%
21.5%
23%
26.1%
27.1%
28.8%
34%
36.2%
38.2%
36.9%
40.7%
44.2%
42.5%
n/a
1976
1980
1984
1988
1992
1996
1998
2000
2002
2004
2012
2014
2016

THE *SPORTS ILLUSTRATED* **JINX**

America's best-loved weekly sports magazine Sports Illustrated *has a long and deserved reputation for its reportage and punditry. However, because some cover stars have unfortunately gone on to suffer a change in their fortunes following their appearance, the urban legend that there's a jinx attached to appearing on the cover has grown. The claim is groundless though, as these stats show.*

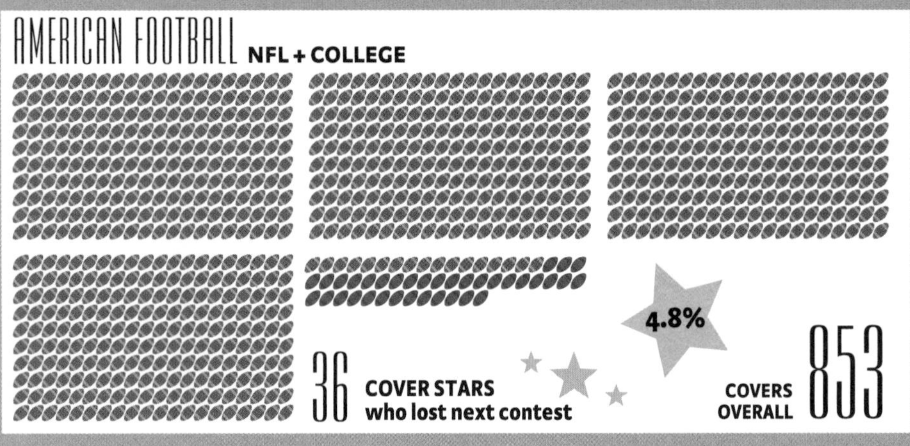

AMERICAN FOOTBALL NFL + COLLEGE
4.8%
36 COVER STARS who lost next contest
COVERS OVERALL 853

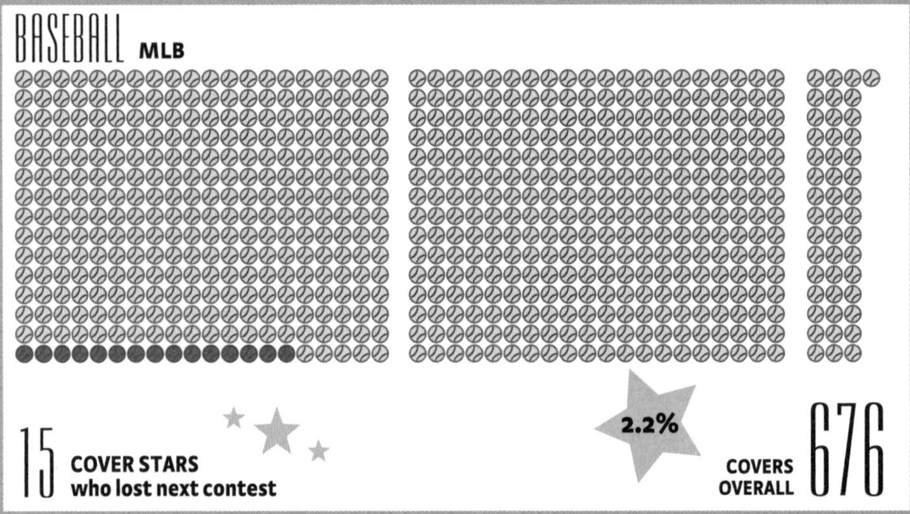

BASEBALL MLB
2.2%
15 COVER STARS who lost next contest
COVERS OVERALL 676

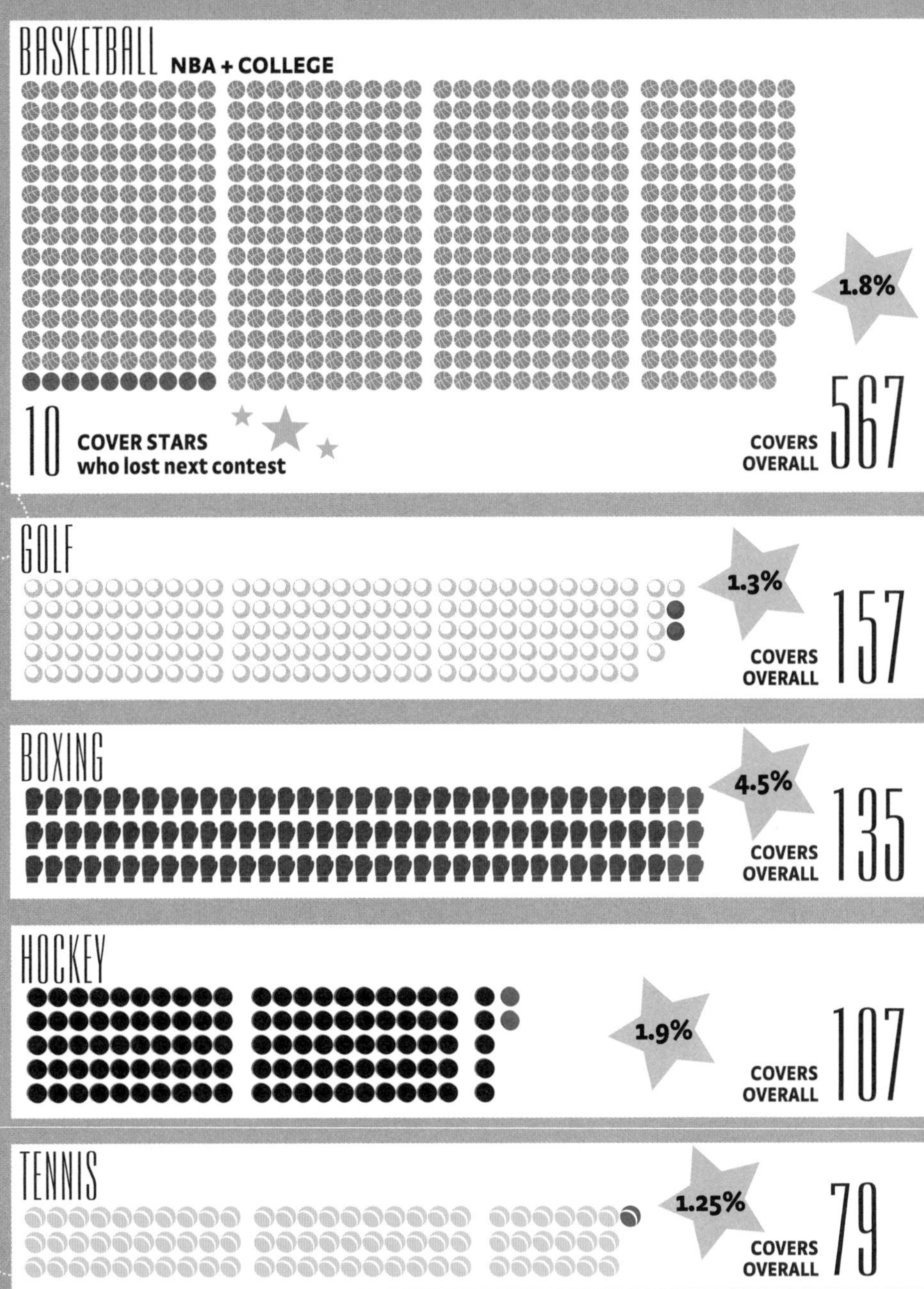
BASKETBALL NBA + COLLEGE
1.8%
10
COVER STARS
who lost next contest
COVERS
OVERALL
567
GOLF
1.3%
COVERS
OVERALL
157
BOXING
4.5%
COVERS
OVERALL
135
HOCKEY
1.9%
COVERS
OVERALL
107
TENNIS
1.25%
COVERS
OVERALL
79

THE **TOUGHEST** GOLF COURSES IN THE WORLD

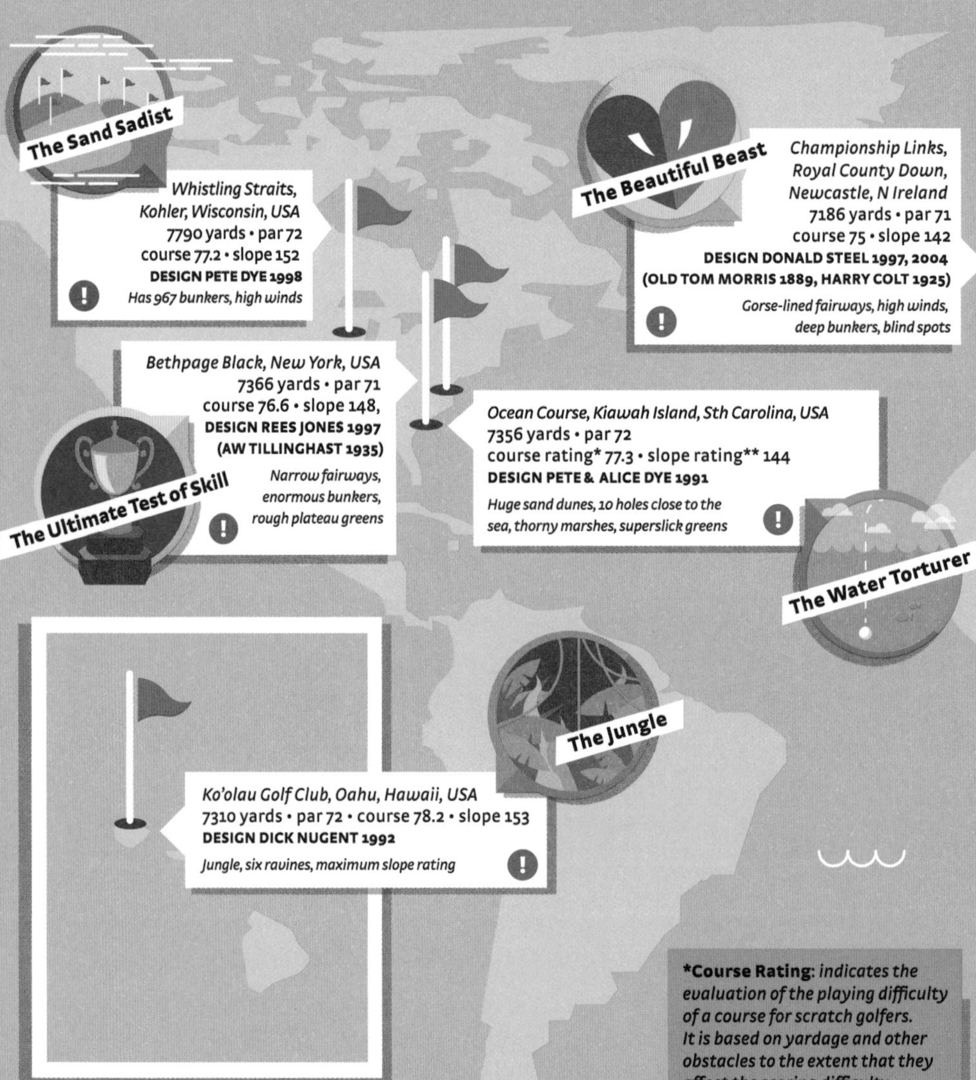

The Sand Sadist
Whistling Straits, Kohler, Wisconsin, USA
7790 yards • par 72
course 77.2 • slope 152
DESIGN PETE DYE 1998
Has 967 bunkers, high winds

The Beautiful Beast
Championship Links, Royal County Down, Newcastle, N Ireland
7186 yards • par 71
course 75 • slope 142
DESIGN DONALD STEEL 1997, 2004
(OLD TOM MORRIS 1889, HARRY COLT 1925)
Gorse-lined fairways, high winds, deep bunkers, blind spots

The Ultimate Test of Skill
Bethpage Black, New York, USA
7366 yards • par 71
course 76.6 • slope 148,
DESIGN REES JONES 1997
(AW TILLINGHAST 1935)
Narrow fairways, enormous bunkers, rough plateau greens

The Water Torturer
Ocean Course, Kiawah Island, Sth Carolina, USA
7356 yards • par 72
course rating* 77.3 • slope rating** 144
DESIGN PETE & ALICE DYE 1991
Huge sand dunes, 10 holes close to the sea, thorny marshes, superslick greens

The Jungle
Ko'olau Golf Club, Oahu, Hawaii, USA
7310 yards • par 72 • course 78.2 • slope 153
DESIGN DICK NUGENT 1992
Jungle, six ravines, maximum slope rating

***Course Rating**: *indicates the evaluation of the playing difficulty of a course for scratch golfers. It is based on yardage and other obstacles to the extent that they affect the scoring difficulty.*

CNN, usga.org, worldgolf.com

They're the courses that make champions despair, with ravines, jungle, swamps and bunkers so small they can fool seasoned pros. They're also the most dangerous places to attempt a round, according to CNN.

The Perfect Storm

Carnoustie Medal, Dundee, Scotland UK
7421 yards • par 71 • course 75.1 • slope 145,
DESIGN JAMES BRAID 1926 (OLD TOM MORRIS 1840)
Stormy weather, holes close to the sea, pot bunkers, high winds !

The Green Cobra

Palm Course, Saujana Golf Club, Kuala Lumpur, Malaysia
6992 yards • par 72
course 75.1 • slope 142
DESIGN RON FREAM, 1986
Jungle, super-fast undulating greens !

The Wind Tunnel

Jade Dragon Snow Mountain Golf Club, Lijiang, Yunnan, China
8548 yards • par 72 • course 73.4 • slope 140
DESIGN ROBIN NELSON/NEIL HAYWORTH
Extreme altitude making breathing difficult, high winds, long travel in thin air

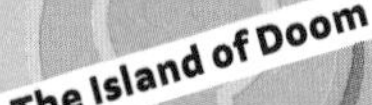
The Island of Doom

Le Touessrok Golf Course, Ile aux Cerfs, Mauritius
7056 yards • par 72 • course 79 • slope 155
DESIGN BERNHARD LANGER 2003
Long carries to tees and greens over mangrove swamps, water hazards and 200-yard long bunkers !

Cape Kidnapper's, Hawke's Bay, New Zealand
7119 yards • par 71 • course 76.6 • slope 145,
DESIGN TOM DOAK 2004
! *High sea winds, ravines. 183-metre drops off narrow fairways*

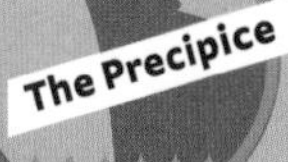
The Precipice

****Slope Rating:** *a single number indicating the difficulty of a golf course to an expert or 'par golfer'. The figure is used when calculating handicaps.*

BECAUSE THEY'RE **WORTH IT**

Major sports stars are no longer measured just by the success they have in their chosen sport, but also by the size of their sponsorship deal. If you were to build a composite most valuable player by sponsorship he would look like this:

Headband
Derrick Rose (basketball), sponsor adidas, worth **$260m**

Hat
Rory McIlroy (golfer), sponsor Nike, worth **$250m**

Arm
Derek Jeter (Baseball), worth **$35m** per annum (wages as a pitcher)

Watch
Roger Federer (tennis), sponsor Rolex, worth **$10m**

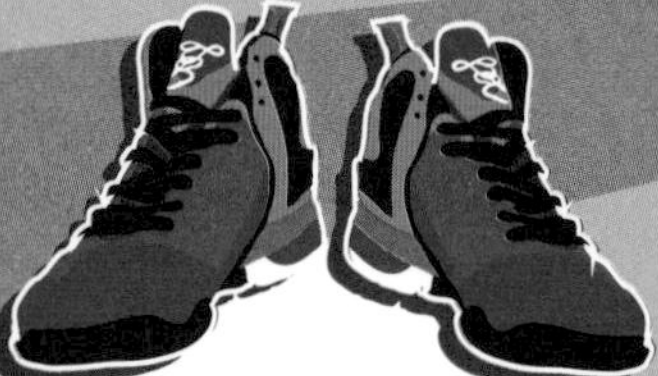

Shoes
LeBron James (basketball), sponsor Nike, worth **$13.3m**

Shirt
Manchester United (soccer), sponsor Chevrolet, worth **$80m** per annum

Underwear
Cristiano Ronaldo (soccer), sponsor Armani, worth **$18m**

wikipedia.org, yahoo.sports.com, opendorse,com

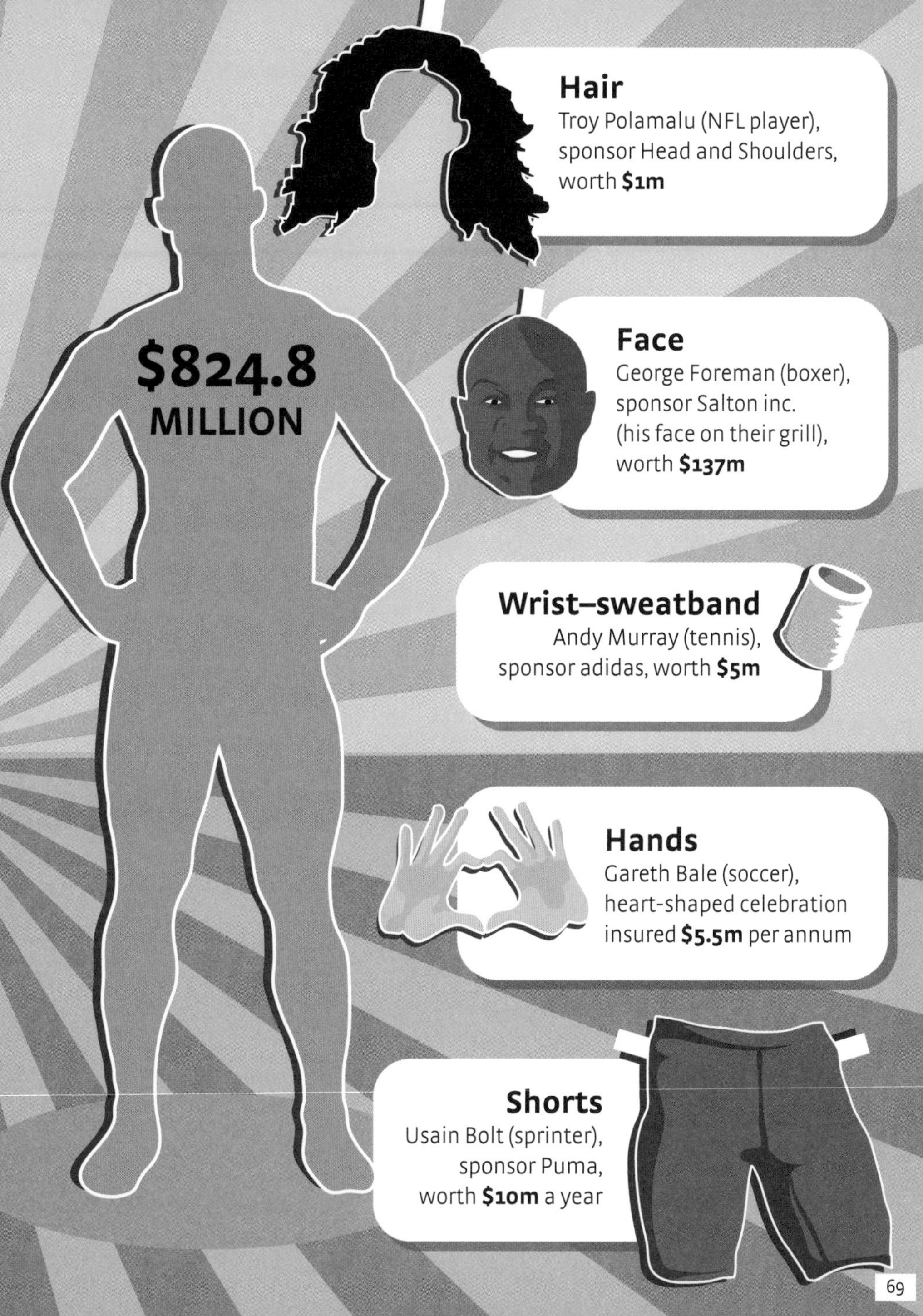
Hair
Troy Polamalu (NFL player),
sponsor Head and Shoulders,
worth $1m
$824.8
MILLION
Face
George Foreman (boxer),
sponsor Salton inc.
(his face on their grill),
worth $137m
Wrist–sweatband
Andy Murray (tennis),
sponsor adidas, worth $5m
Hands
Gareth Bale (soccer),
heart-shaped celebration
insured $5.5m per annum
Shorts
Usain Bolt (sprinter),
sponsor Puma,
worth $10m a year

WORLD-BEATING **GRUDGE MATCHES**

Sporting competition between nations or individuals who are at war – figuratively and literally – may be intended to ease tensions between them. But it doesn't always happen, as these world-beating grudge matches demonstrate.

NATIONS

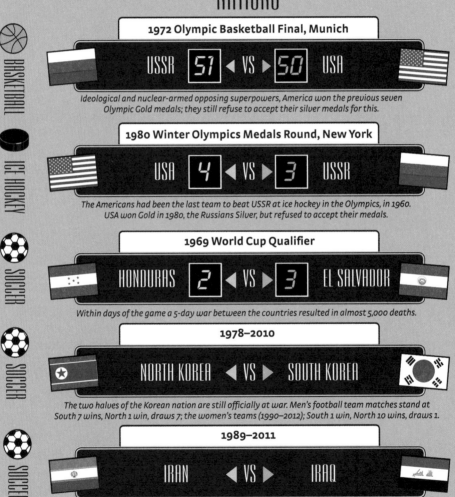

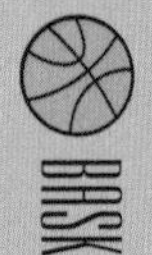

BASKETBALL

1972 Olympic Basketball Final, Munich

USSR
51
VS
50
USA

Ideological and nuclear-armed opposing superpowers, America won the previous seven Olympic Gold medals; they still refuse to accept their silver medals for this.

ICE HOCKEY

1980 Winter Olympics Medals Round, New York

USA
4
VS
3
USSR

The Americans had been the last team to beat USSR at ice hockey in the Olympics, in 1960. USA won Gold in 1980, the Russians Silver, but refused to accept their medals.

SOCCER

1969 World Cup Qualifier

HONDURAS
2
VS
3
EL SALVADOR

Within days of the game a 5-day war between the countries resulted in almost 5,000 deaths.

SOCCER

1978–2010

NORTH KOREA
VS
SOUTH KOREA

The two halves of the Korean nation are still officially at war. Men's football team matches stand at South 7 wins, North 1 win, draws 7; the women's teams (1990–2012); South 1 win, North 10 wins, draws 1.

SOCCER

1989–2011

IRAN
VS
IRAQ

The Iran-Iraq war lasted from 1980 to 1988, the last prisoners of war were exchanged in 2003. In 1989 their first match since 1976, The Islamic Peace trophy, was a draw. The following 13 games stand at Iraq 3 wins, Iran 7 wins, draws 3.

INDIVIDUALS

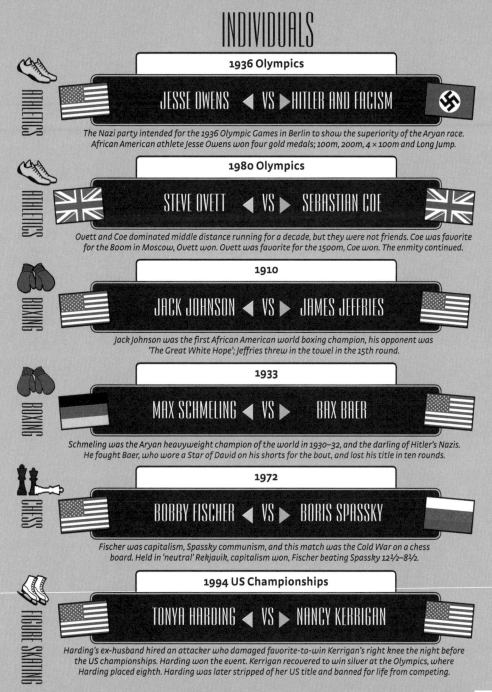

ATHLETICS

1936 Olympics

JESSE OWENS ◀ VS ▶ HITLER AND FACISM

The Nazi party intended for the 1936 Olympic Games in Berlin to show the superiority of the Aryan race. African American athlete Jesse Owens won four gold medals; 100m, 200m, 4 × 100m and Long Jump.

ATHLETICS

1980 Olympics

STEVE OVETT ◀ VS ▶ SEBASTIAN COE

Ovett and Coe dominated middle distance running for a decade, but they were not friends. Coe was favorite for the 800m in Moscow, Ovett won. Ovett was favorite for the 1500m, Coe won. The enmity continued.

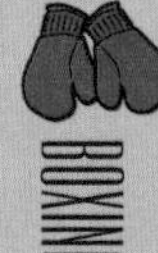

BOXING

1910

JACK JOHNSON ◀ VS ▶ JAMES JEFFRIES

Jack Johnson was the first African American world boxing champion, his opponent was 'The Great White Hope'; Jeffries threw in the towel in the 15th round.

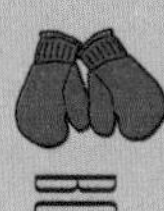

BOXING

1933

MAX SCHMELING ◀ VS ▶ BAX BAER

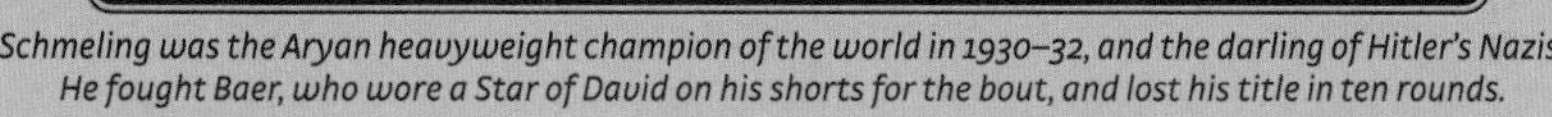

Schmeling was the Aryan heavyweight champion of the world in 1930–32, and the darling of Hitler's Nazis. He fought Baer, who wore a Star of David on his shorts for the bout, and lost his title in ten rounds.

CHESS

1972

BOBBY FISCHER ◀ VS ▶ BORIS SPASSKY

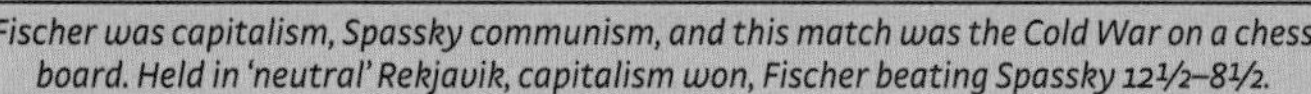

Fischer was capitalism, Spassky communism, and this match was the Cold War on a chess board. Held in 'neutral' Rekjavik, capitalism won, Fischer beating Spassky 12½–8½.

FIGURE SKATING

1994 US Championships

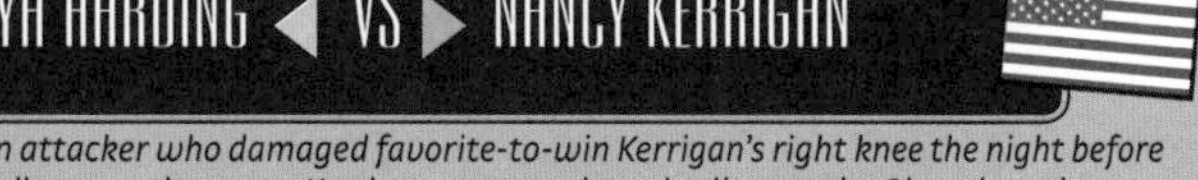

TONYA HARDING ◀ VS ▶ NANCY KERRIGAN

Harding's ex-husband hired an attacker who damaged favorite-to-win Kerrigan's right knee the night before the US championships. Harding won the event. Kerrigan recovered to win silver at the Olympics, where Harding placed eighth. Harding was later stripped of her US title and banned for life from competing.

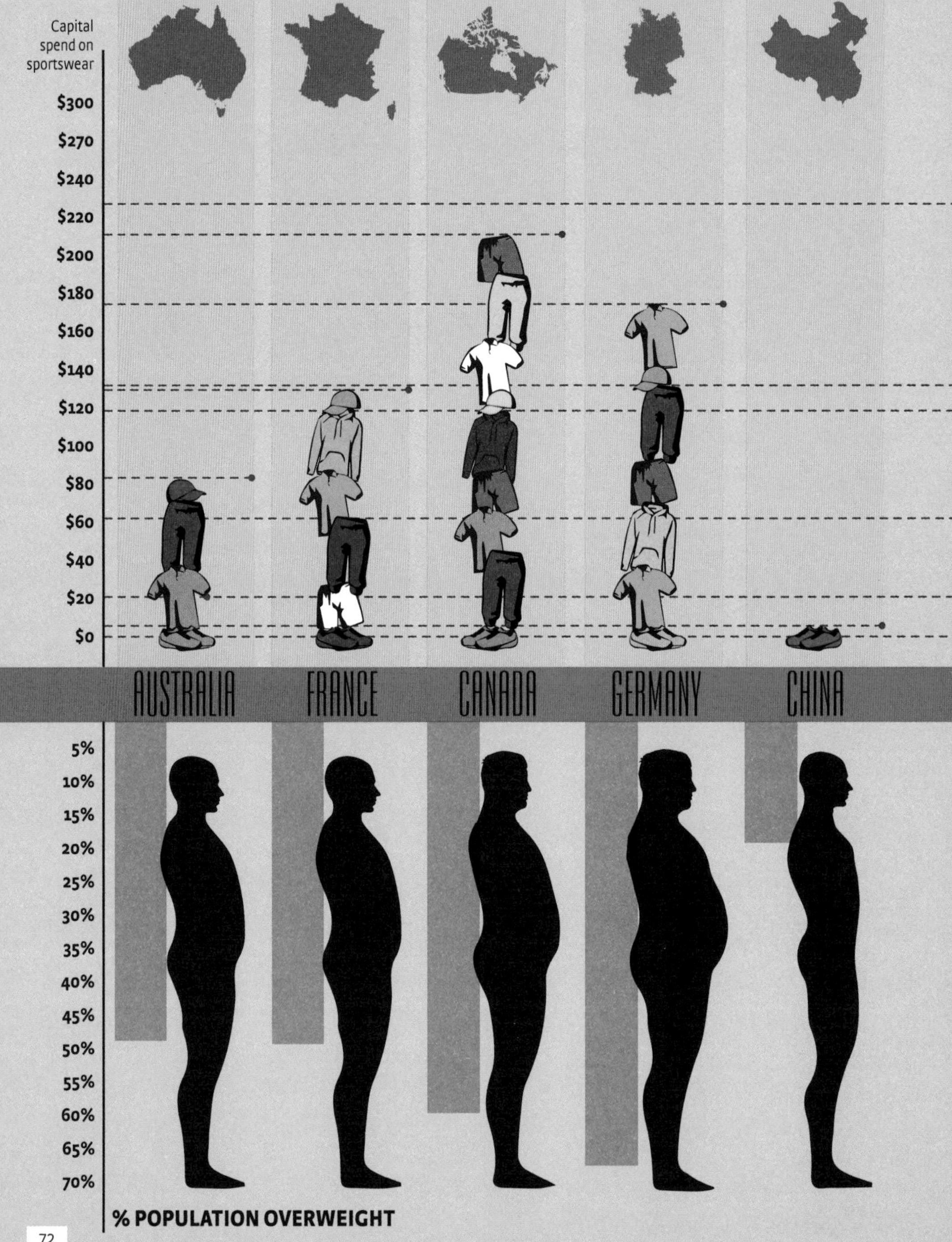

Capital spend on sportswear
$300
$270
$240
$220
$200
$180
$160
$140
$120
$100
$80
$60
$40
$20
$0
AUSTRALIA
FRANCE
CANADA
GERMANY
CHINA
5%
10%
15%
20%
25%
30%
35%
40%
45%
50%
55%
60%
65%
70%
% POPULATION OVERWEIGHT

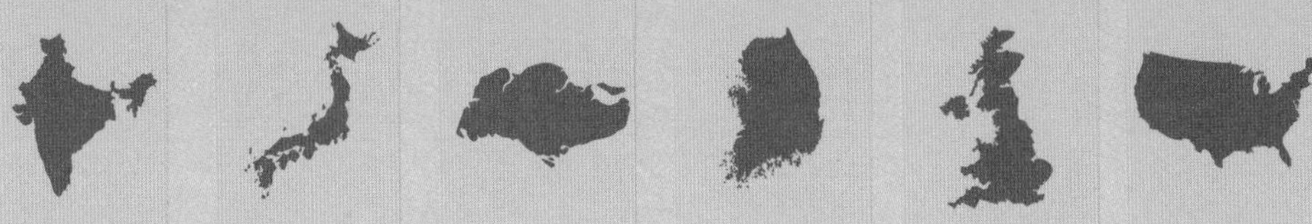

FIT NATION?

Major sports brands spend millions of dollars getting major sports stars to wear their logo, in order that non-superstar sports people will want to buy their wares. But it seems that the sportswear isn't being worn for sporting activities, at least according to this comparison of overweight populations and spend on sportswear.

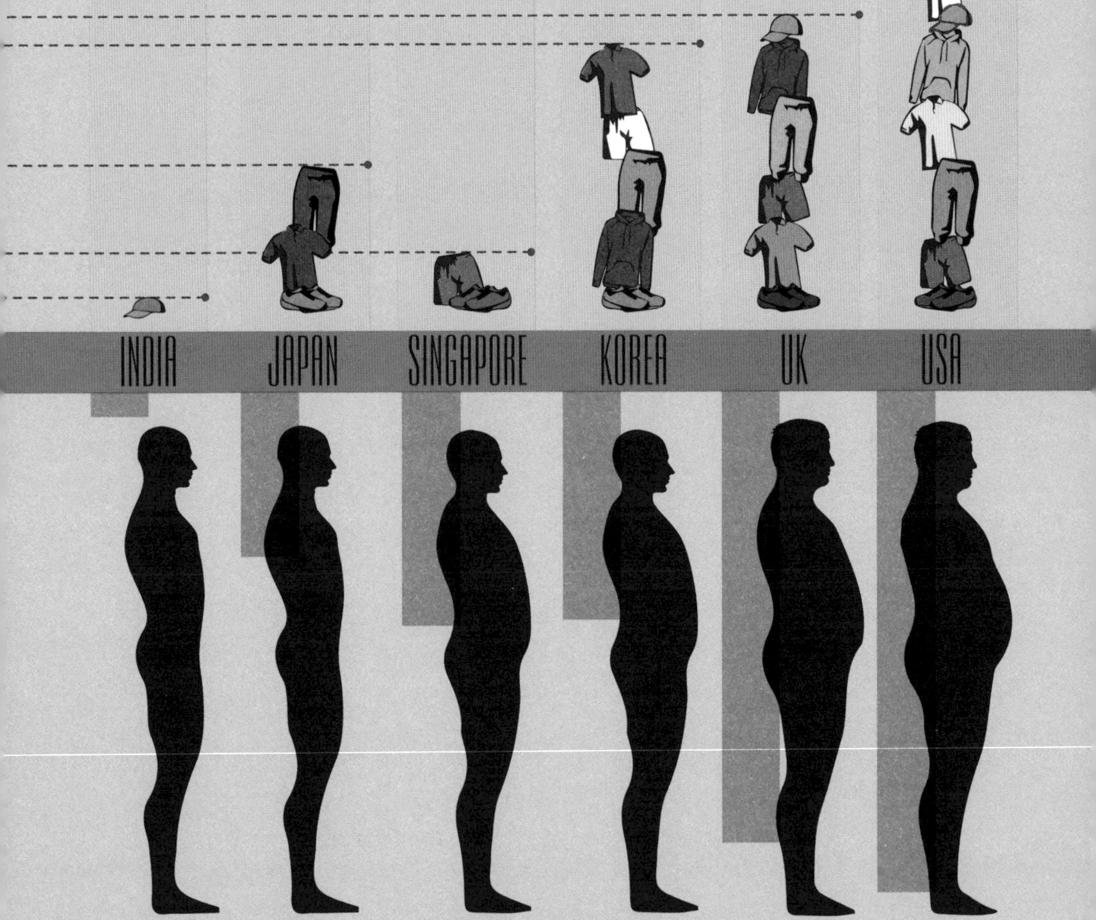

INDIA JAPAN SINGAPORE KOREA UK USA

apps.who.int/bmi, getfilings.com

KOBE BRYANT

JERSEY #24

AGE: **31** *HEIGHT:* **6ft 6in 1.98m** *WEIGHT:* **205lbs / 93kg**

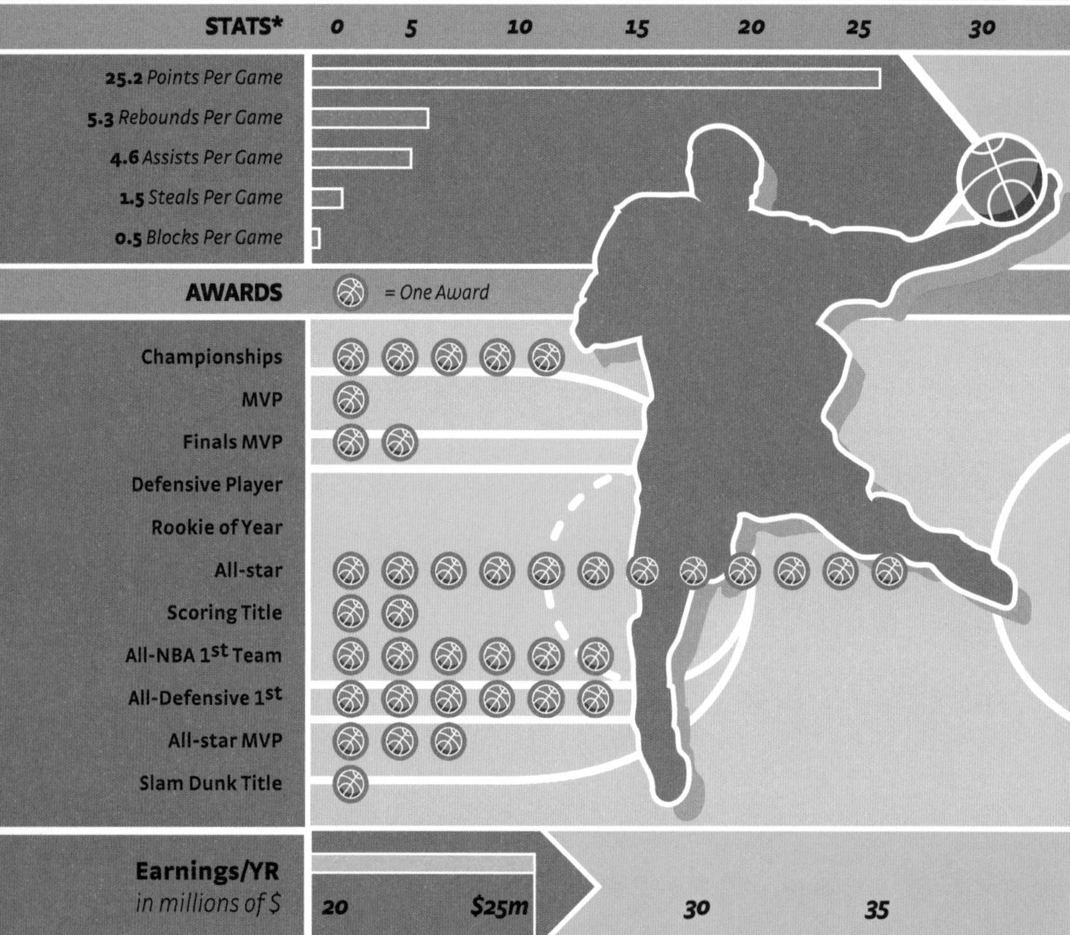

STATS*
0
5
10
15
20
25
30
25.2 Points Per Game
5.3 Rebounds Per Game
4.6 Assists Per Game
1.5 Steals Per Game
0.5 Blocks Per Game
AWARDS
= One Award
Championships
MVP
Finals MVP
Defensive Player
Rookie of Year
All-star
Scoring Title
All-NBA 1st Team
All-Defensive 1st
All-star MVP
Slam Dunk Title
Earnings/YR
in millions of $
20
$25m
30
35

THE **GREATEST** OF ALL TIME

Kobe Bryant is still playing professional basketball, but he's 31 and Michael Jordan first retired at the age of 30, so perhaps it's a good time to compare the careers of the two men that most basketball fans consider to be the greatest, ever.

JERSEY #23 45 9

MICHAEL JORDAN

WEIGHT: **215lbs / 97.5kg** *HEIGHT:* **6ft 6in / 1.98m** *AGE:* **47**

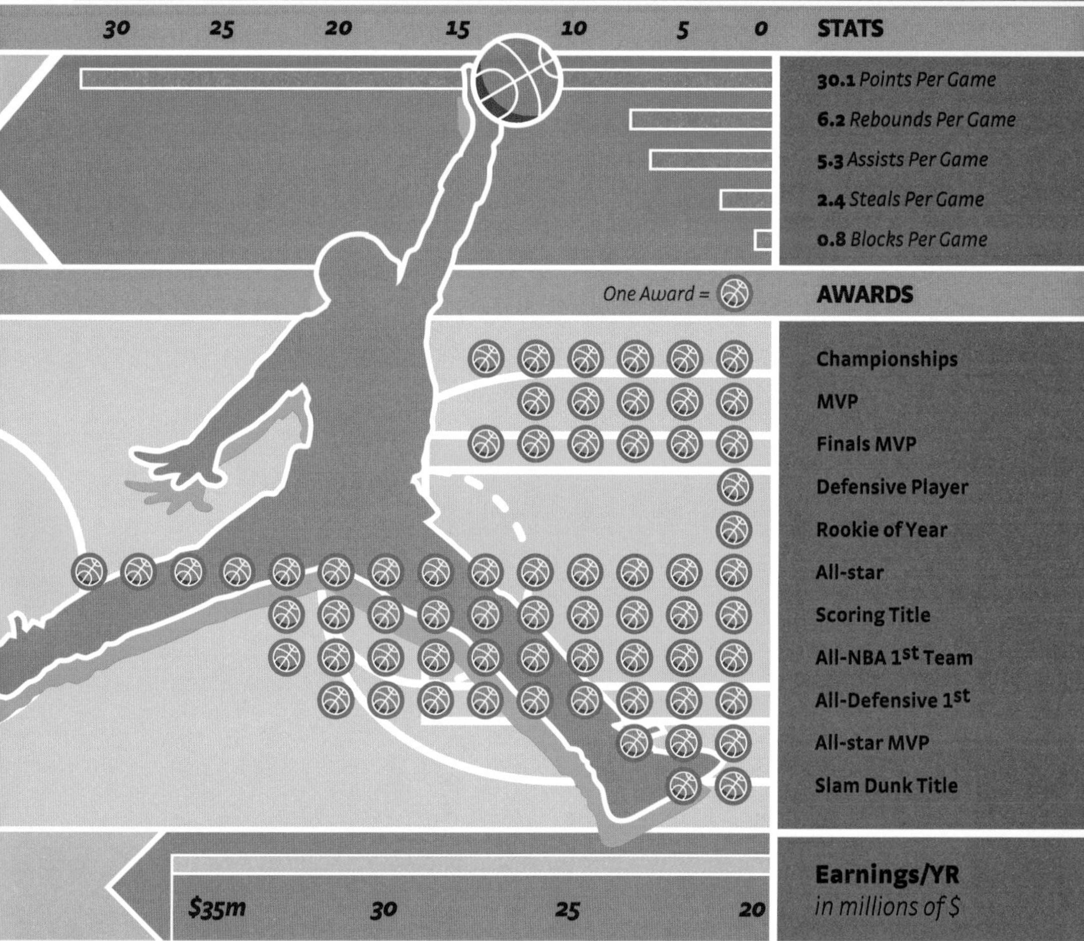
30
25
20
15
10
5
0
STATS
30.1 Points Per Game
6.2 Rebounds Per Game
5.3 Assists Per Game
2.4 Steals Per Game
0.8 Blocks Per Game
One Award =
AWARDS
Championships
MVP
Finals MVP
Defensive Player
Rookie of Year
All-star
Scoring Title
All-NBA 1st Team
All-Defensive 1st
All-star MVP
Slam Dunk Title
$35m
30
25
20
Earnings/YR
in millions of $

THE DRUGS **DON'T WORK**

Professional sport is rife with competitors using banned drugs to gain an edge or at least parity. Cyclists and weightlifters, it seems, will take anything to help their performance, especially these eight most regularly tested banned substances.

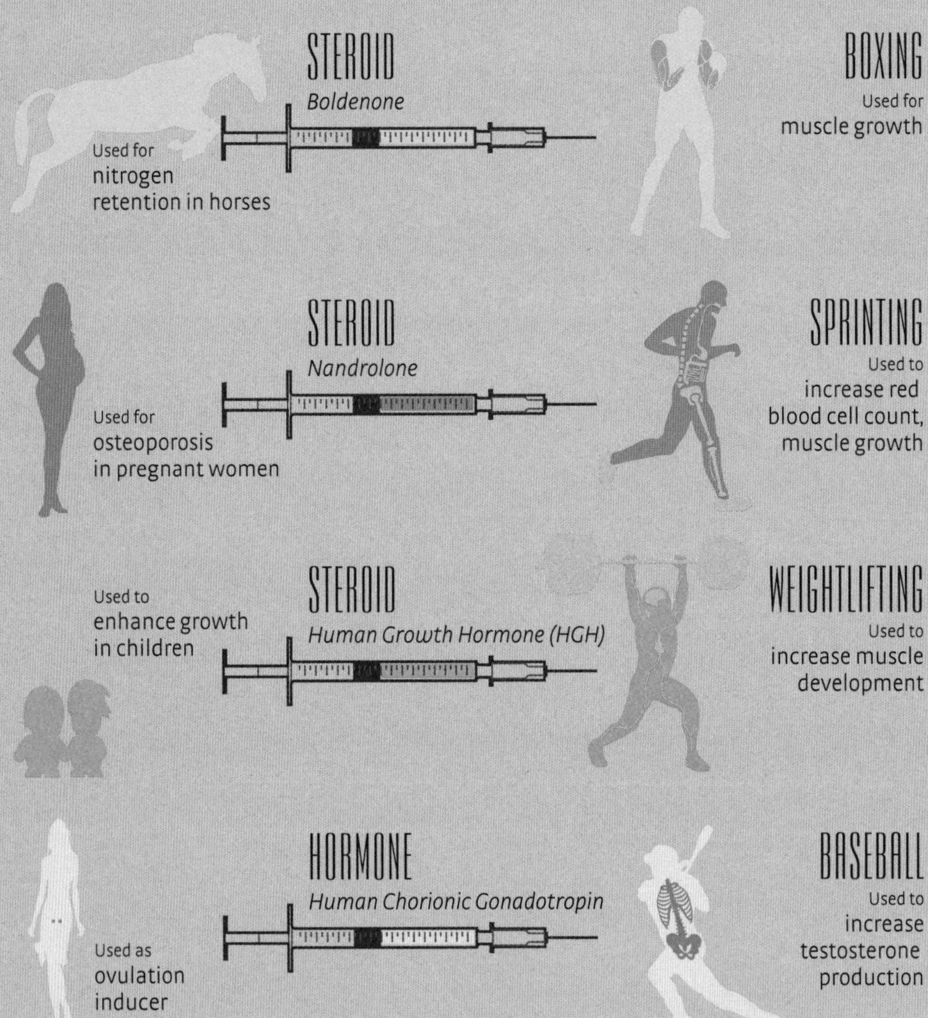

STEROID
Boldenone
Used for
nitrogen
retention in horses
BOXING
Used for
muscle growth
STEROID
Nandrolone
Used for
osteoporosis
in pregnant women
SPRINTING
Used to
increase red
blood cell count,
muscle growth
STEROID
Human Growth Hormone (HGH)
Used to
enhance growth
in children
WEIGHTLIFTING
Used to
increase muscle
development
HORMONE
Human Chorionic Gonadotropin
Used as
ovulation
inducer
BASEBALL
Used to
increase
testosterone
production

STIMULANT
Pseudoephedrine
Used as
nasal
decongestant
ICE HOCKEY
Used to
increase mental
and physical
function
BETA BLOCKER
Propranolol
Used for
hypertension
and
tachycardia
SPORT SHOOTING
Used to
reduce anxiety,
slow heart rate
MASKING AGENT
Bromatane
Used as
stimulant
for Russian
cosmonauts
SOCCER
Used to
reduce pain,
stimulate
blood flow
PEPTIDE
Erythopoietin (EPO)
Used for
kidney disease
CYCLING
Used to
increase red
blood cell
count

wikipedia.org

HOW DID WE GET TO **EXTREME IRONING?**

HELI-SKIING

1958, Alaska, USA
(Bengt "Binks" Sandahl, USA)

EQUIPMENT REQUIRED
A helicopter, skiing gear, snow-covered mountain slopes

WHAT TO DO
Jump from the helicopter at the top of a snow slope, ski to the bottom of the mountain or helicopter landing point

BASE JUMPING

1981, Houston, TX, USA, (Phil Smith, Phil Mayfield, Carl Boenish, Jean Boenish, USA)

EQUIPMENT REQUIRED
Two parachutes, four different tall structures to jump from; buildings, antennas, span (i.e. bridge) and earth (i.e. cliffs)

WHAT TO DO
Jump and glide to the ground using parachute from building, antenna, span and earth high points

ACTIVE VOLCANO HANG GLIDING

1991, Cotopaxi, Ecuador
(Judy Leden, UK)

EQUIPMENT REQUIRED
Hang glider, active volcano, helicopter or climbing gear

WHAT TO DO
Get to top of an active volcano with a hang glider and jump

Surfing, snowboarding, skiing and all forms of water-skiing might be dangerous sports, but they're not extreme. To be classified as such an extreme sport has to involve threat to life and take place in dangerous, remote or improbable terrain – or at high altitudes. Here's how we got from helicopters to ironing boards in extreme sports.

EXTREME IRONING

1997, Leicester, England
(Phil Shaw AKA Steam, UK)

EQUIPMENT REQUIRED

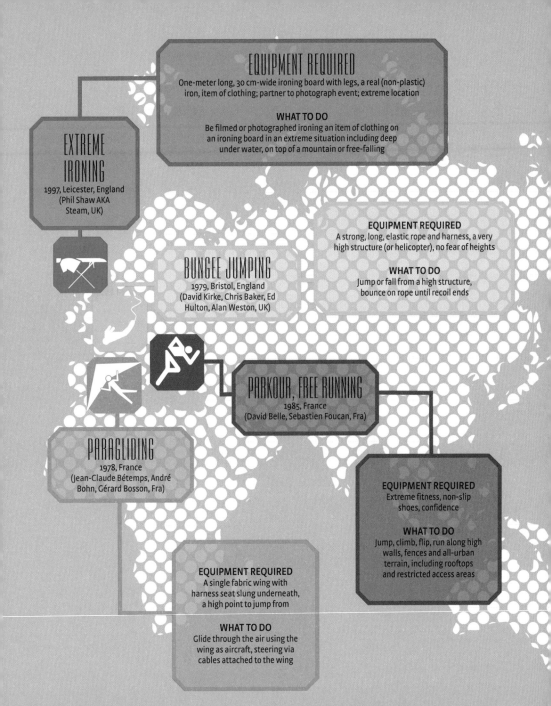

One-meter long, 30 cm-wide ironing board with legs, a real (non-plastic) iron, item of clothing; partner to photograph event; extreme location

WHAT TO DO

Be filmed or photographed ironing an item of clothing on an ironing board in an extreme situation including deep under water, on top of a mountain or free-falling

BUNGEE JUMPING

1979, Bristol, England
(David Kirke, Chris Baker, Ed Hulton, Alan Weston, UK)

EQUIPMENT REQUIRED

A strong, long, elastic rope and harness, a very high structure (or helicopter), no fear of heights

WHAT TO DO

Jump or fall from a high structure, bounce on rope until recoil ends

PARKOUR, FREE RUNNING

1985, France
(David Belle, Sebastien Foucan, Fra)

EQUIPMENT REQUIRED

Extreme fitness, non-slip shoes, confidence

WHAT TO DO

Jump, climb, flip, run along high walls, fences and all-urban terrain, including rooftops and restricted access areas

PARAGLIDING

1978, France
(Jean-Claude Bétemps, André Bohn, Gérard Bosson, Fra)

EQUIPMENT REQUIRED

A single fabric wing with harness seat slung underneath, a high point to jump from

WHAT TO DO

Glide through the air using the wing as aircraft, steering via cables attached to the wing

wikipedia.org, xtremeironing.com

ARE YOU **TOUGH ENOUGH?**

If you want to really test your strength, endurance and guts, try a Tough Mudder course, "probably the toughest event on the planet." More than 1 million people in seven countries have tried their 10–12 mile obstacle courses – with a 78% completion average. And this is why.

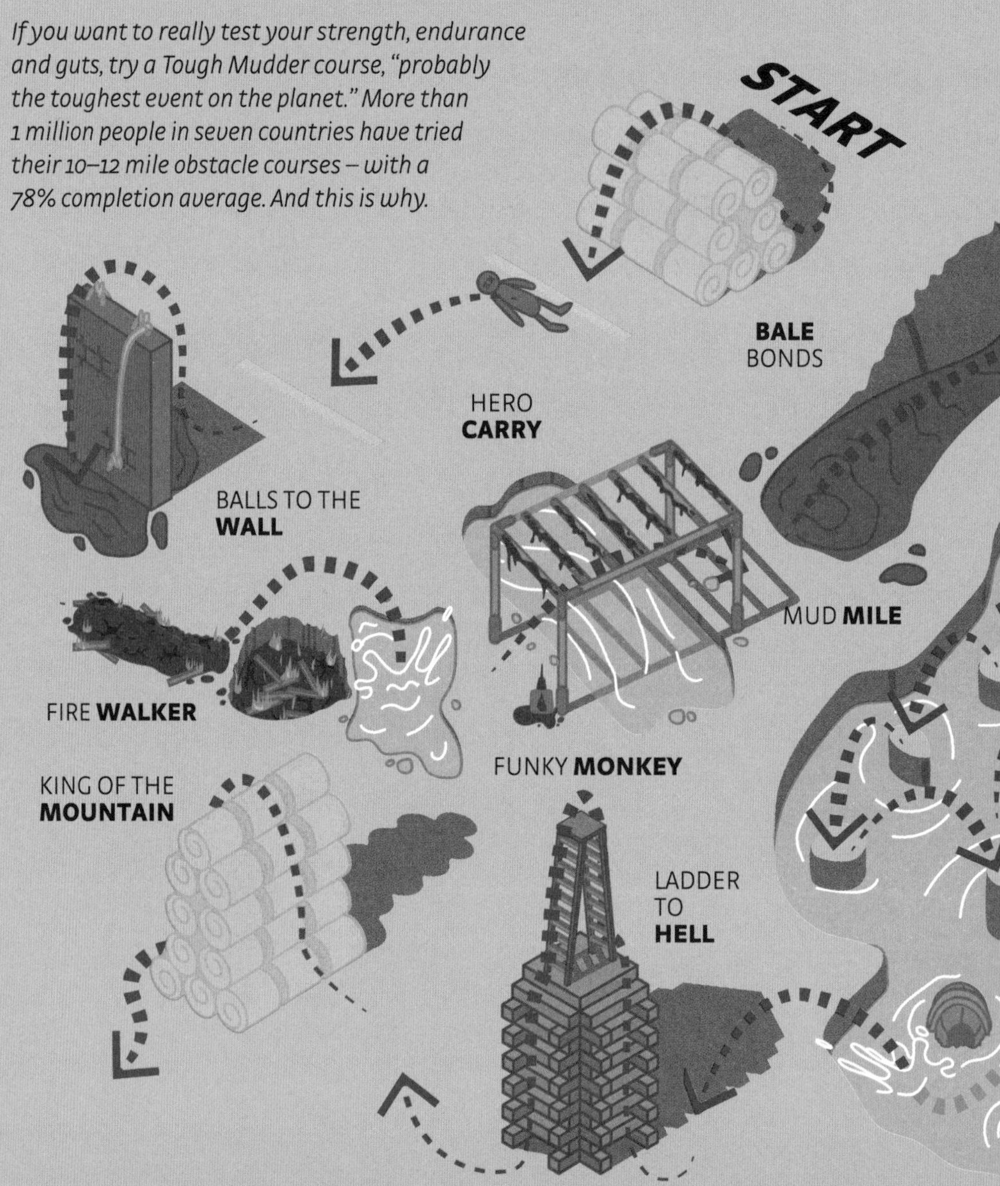
START
BALE BONDS
HERO CARRY
BALLS TO THE WALL
MUD MILE
FIRE WALKER
FUNKY MONKEY
KING OF THE MOUNTAIN
LADDER TO HELL

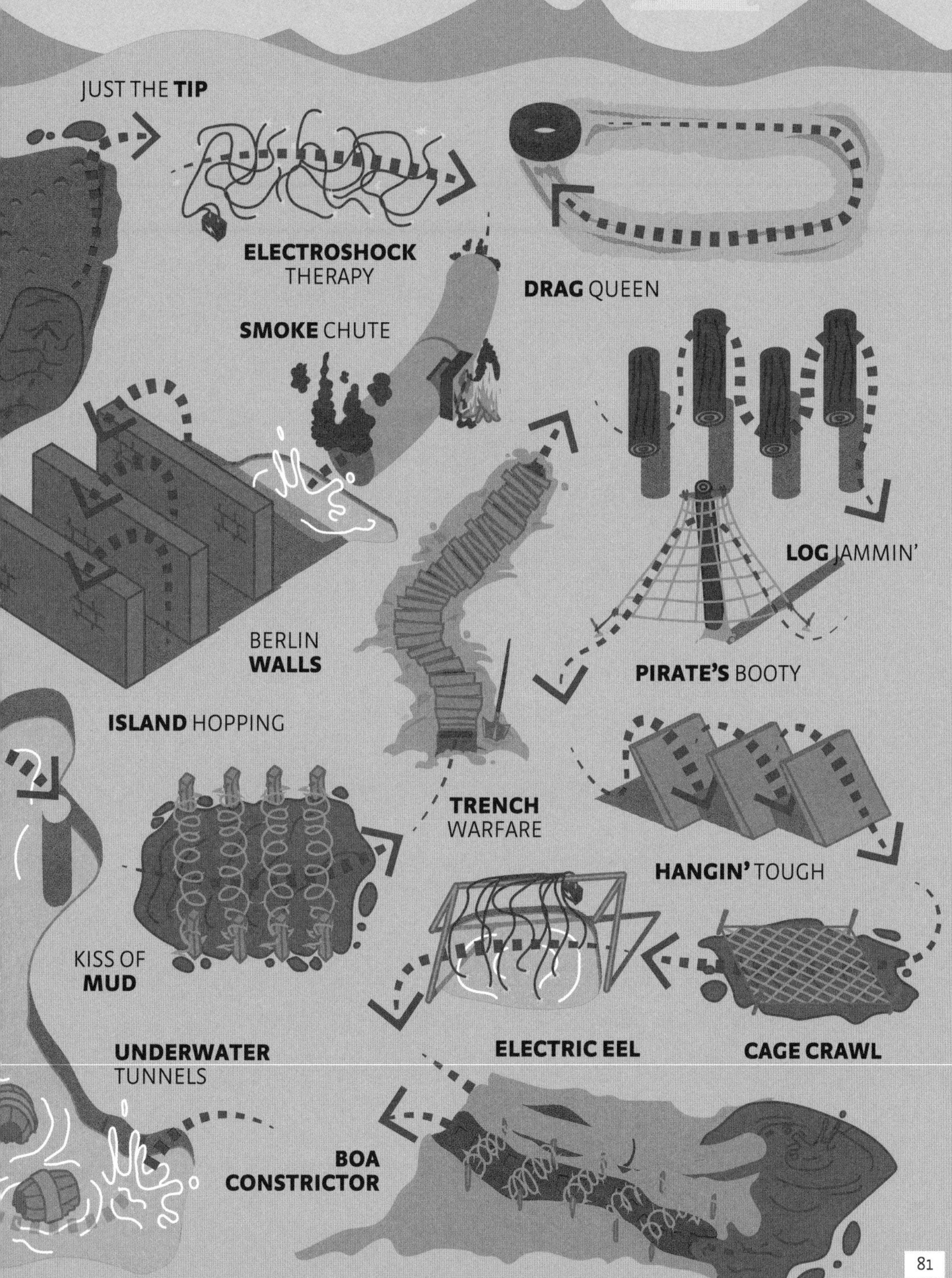
JUST THE **TIP**
ELECTROSHOCK THERAPY
DRAG QUEEN
SMOKE CHUTE
LOG JAMMIN'
BERLIN **WALLS**
PIRATE'S BOOTY
ISLAND HOPPING
TRENCH WARFARE
HANGIN' TOUGH
KISS OF **MUD**
UNDERWATER TUNNELS
ELECTRIC EEL
CAGE CRAWL
BOA CONSTRICTOR

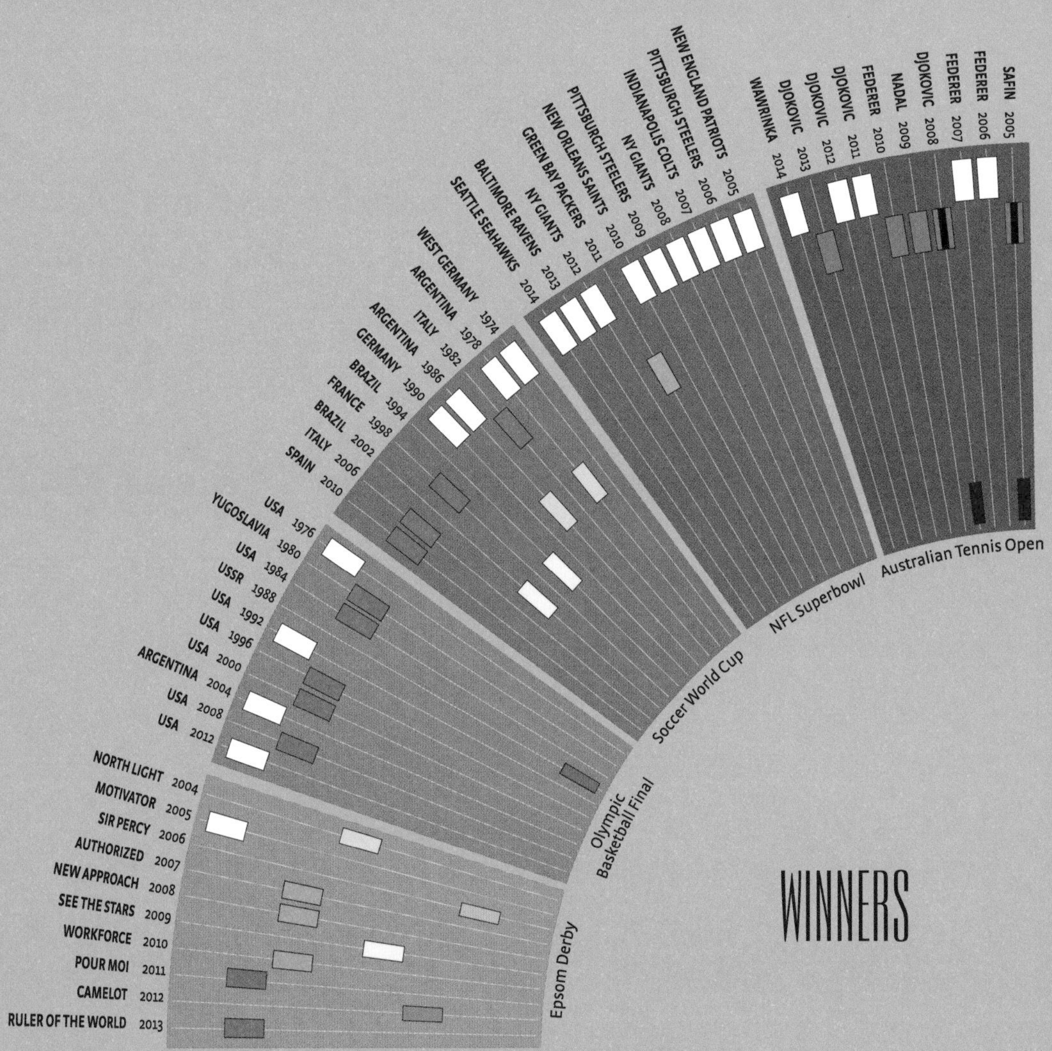

WINNERS
Epsom Derby
NORTH LIGHT 2004
MOTIVATOR 2005
SIR PERCY 2006
AUTHORIZED 2007
NEW APPROACH 2008
SEE THE STARS 2009
WORKFORCE 2010
POUR MOI 2011
CAMELOT 2012
RULER OF THE WORLD 2013
Olympic Basketball Final
USA 1976
YUGOSLAVIA 1980
USA 1984
USSR 1988
USA 1992
USA 1996
USA 2000
ARGENTINA 2004
USA 2008
USA 2012
Soccer World Cup
WEST GERMANY 1974
ARGENTINA 1978
ITALY 1982
ARGENTINA 1986
GERMANY 1990
BRAZIL 1994
FRANCE 1998
BRAZIL 2002
ITALY 2006
SPAIN 2010
NFL Superbowl
NEW ENGLAND PATRIOTS 2005
PITTSBURGH STEELERS 2006
INDIANAPOLIS COLTS 2007
NY GIANTS 2008
PITTSBURGH STEELERS 2009
NEW ORLEANS SAINTS 2010
GREEN BAY PACKERS 2011
NY GIANTS 2012
BALTIMORE RAVENS 2013
SEATTLE SEAHAWKS 2014
Australian Tennis Open
SAFIN 2005
FEDERER 2006
FEDERER 2007
DJOKOVIC 2008
NADAL 2009
FEDERER 2010
DJOKOVIC 2011
DJOKOVIC 2012
DJOKOVIC 2013
WAWRINKA 2014

2005 HEWITT
2006 BACHDATIS
2007 GONZALEZ
2008 TSONGA
2009 FEDERER
2010 MURRAY
2011 MURRAY
2012 NADAL
2013 MURRAY
2014 NADAL
Australian Tennis Open
2005 PHILADELPHIA EAGLES
2006 SEATTLE SEAHAWKS
2007 CHICAGO BEARS
2008 NEW ENGLAND PATRIOTS
2009 ARIZONA CARDINALS
2010 INDIANAPOLIS COLTS
2011 PITTSBURGH STEELERS
2012 NEW ENGLAND PATRIOTS
2013 SAN FRANCISCO 49ERS
2014 DENVER BRONCOS
NFL Superbowl
1974 NETHERLANDS
1978 NETHERLANDS
1982 GERMANY
1986 GERMANY
1990 ARGENTINA
1994 ITALY
1998 BRAZIL
2002 GERMANY
2006 FRANCE
2010 NETHERLANDS
Soccer World Cup
1976 YUGOSLAVIA
1980 ITALY
1984 SPAIN
1988 YUGOSLAVIA
1992 CROATIA
1996 YUGOSLAVIA
2000 FRANCE
2004 ITALY
2008 SPAIN
2012 SPAIN
Olympic Basketball Final
LOSERS

WEAR WHITE TO **WIN**

Is there such a thing as a lucky color in sport? Plenty of sports people think so, and using five different sports as a gauge, there appears to be something to the idea that wearing a certain color strip can help ensure success.

ALI'S **SHUFFLE**

Muhammad Ali began his career by dancing his way around opponents, flicking out punishment. As he grew older he took some punches, but always moved and hit. Here are 4 of Ali's most famous bouts and his movement in them.

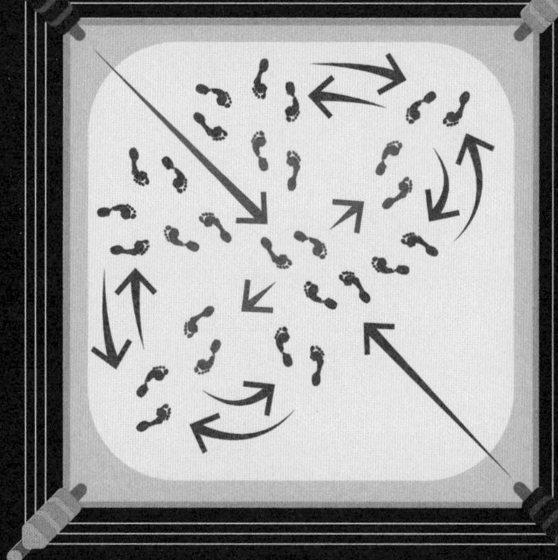

ALI VS SONNY LISTON

Miami Beach USA
25 February 1964
6 rounds, KO to Ali

Ali floated around Liston who stood in the center of the ring, stinging him like a bee.

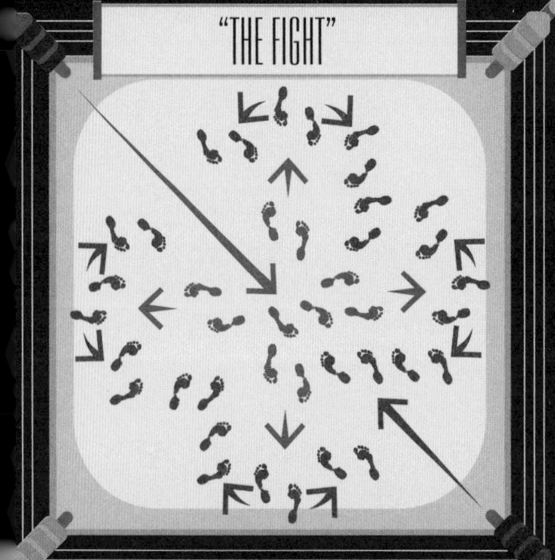
"THE FIGHT"

ALI VS JOE FRAZIER

"The Fight"
New York, USA
8 March 1971
15 rounds, points decision to Frazier

Ali floated but Frazier caught him at the end of round 3, and had him against the ropes for three rounds until Ali floated again.

"THE RUMBLE IN THE JUNGLE"

ALI VS GEORGE FOREMAN

"The Rumble In The Jungle"
Kinshasa, Zaire
30 October 1974
8 rounds, KO to Ali

Ali went to the ropes and stood there with Foreman hitting his arms for 5 rounds before advancing on him like a rolling stone.

ALI VS JOE FRAZIER III

"The Thrilla In Manila"
Quezon City, Philippines
1 October 1975
14 rounds, KO to Ali

Ali floated around Frazier for 3 rounds, then Joe caught him and knocked Ali onto the ropes in the 6th. After that they traded punches with Joe center of the ring, his face swelling.

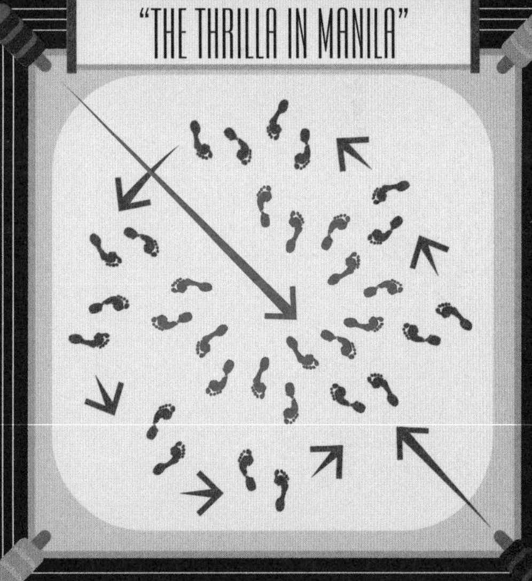
"THE THRILLA IN MANILA"

THE HARDER **THEY HIT**

Many sports involve hitting things with other things. Bats and clubs come in a variety of shapes and sizes and not surprisingly can impart a varying degree of force. But which is the most efficient?

GOLF

GOLF CLUB (IRONS)

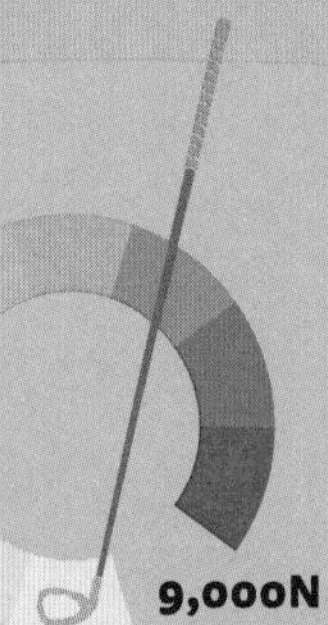
9,000N

Not regulated

Min 45.7cm/18in, max 121.9cm/48in

No limit

Distance from heel to toe and distance from front to back

CRICKET

CRICKET BAT

Single piece smooth wood

96.5 cm/38in, 10.8cm/4 1/4in

No limit

Handle up to 45.72

3,400N

PING PONG

PING PONG RACKET

85% wood, non-wooded adhesive layer up to 7.5% of total thickness (or 0.35mm/ 9/64in max)

25cm/10in, 15cm/6in

No limit

No limit, surface may have pimpled rubber. If pimples face out, the max thickness is 2mm/ 5/64in, if they face inwards max thickness is 4mm/5/32in.

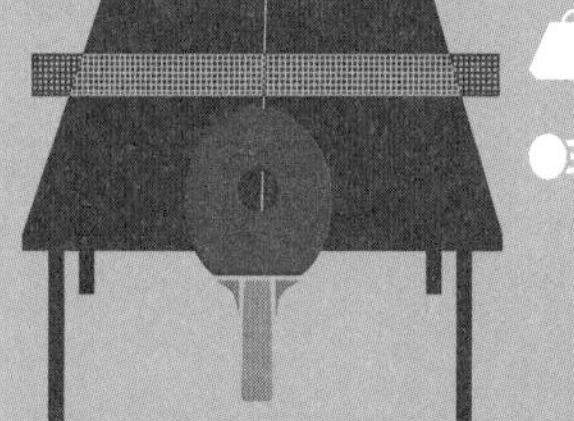

livestrong.com, hypertextbook.com/facts, physics.usyd.edu.au, squashplayer.co.uk, badmintoncentral.com, itftennis.com, mlb.mlb.com, lords.org, etta.co.uk, randa.org, worldsquash.org, bwfbadminton.org

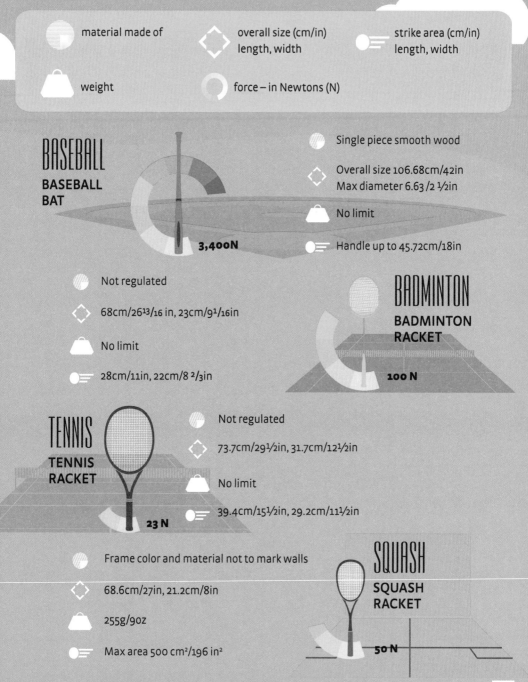

material made of

overall size (cm/in) length, width

strike area (cm/in) length, width

weight

force – in Newtons (N)

BASEBALL

BASEBALL BAT

3,400N

Single piece smooth wood

Overall size 106.68cm/42in
Max diameter 6.63 /2 1/2in

No limit

Handle up to 45.72cm/18in

BADMINTON

BADMINTON RACKET

100 N

Not regulated

68cm/26 13/16 in, 23cm/9 1/16in

No limit

28cm/11in, 22cm/8 2/3in

TENNIS

TENNIS RACKET

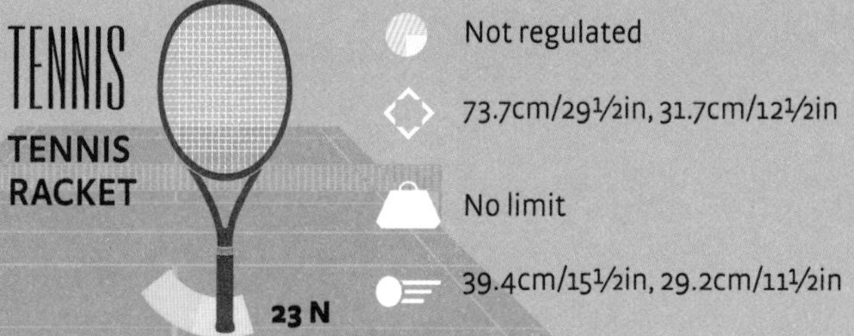

23 N

Not regulated

73.7cm/29 1/2in, 31.7cm/12 1/2in

No limit

39.4cm/15 1/2in, 29.2cm/11 1/2in

SQUASH

SQUASH RACKET

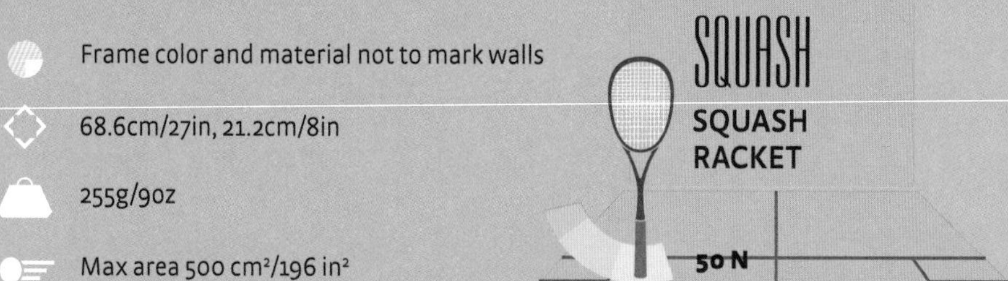

50 N

Frame color and material not to mark walls

68.6cm/27in, 21.2cm/8in

255g/9oz

Max area 500 cm^2/196 in^2

VORSPRUNG DURCH **TECHNIK**

Since the World Rally Championships were inaugurated in 1973 the winning car has been sold in a road-going equivalent. Here's how the rally winner compares with the people's version in engine size and power.

RALLY CAR — Engine cc — COUNTRY YEAR — BHP — STREET CAR

max BHP

max Engine CC

Rally Engine cc	Rally car	Rally BHP	Country / Year	Street Engine cc	Street car	Street BHP
1605	ALPINE RENAULT A110	138	France 1973	1605	RENAULT 17TS 8V	107
2419	LANCIA FULVIA HF / STRATOS HF	187	Italy 1974	2419	LANCIA STRATOS	187
2419	LANCIA STRATOS HF	187	Italy 1975	2419	LANCIA STRATOS	187
2419	LANCIA STRATOS HF	187	Italy 1976	2419	LANCIA STRATOS	187
1995	FIAT 131 ABARTH	212	Italy 1977	1995	FIAT 131 ABARTH	137
1995	FIAT 131 ABARTH	212	Italy 1978	1995	FIAT 131 ABARTH	137
1993	FORD ESCORT RS1800	250	US/UK 1979	1993	FORD ESCORT RS1800	113
1995	FIAT 131 ABARTH	212	Italy 1980	1995	FIAT 131 ABARTH	137
2172	TALBOT SUNBEAM LOTUS	250	Italy 1981	2172	TALBOT SUNBEAM LOTUS	150
2144	AUDI QUATTRO	350	Germany 1982	2144	AUDI QUATTRO	197
2111	LANCIA 037	331	Italy 1983	1995	LANCIA 037 RALLYE	205
2109	AUDI QUATTRO A1 / A2	370	Germany 1984	2133	AUDI QUATTRO S1	302
1775	PEUGEOT 205 TURBO 16 / 16E2	350	France 1985	1775	PEUGEOT 205 T16	197
1775	PEUGEOT 205 TURBO 16 E2	430	France 1986	1775	PEUGEOT 205 T16	197
1995	LANCIA DELTA HF 4WD	250	Italy 1987	1995	LANCIA DELTA HF 4WD TURBO	165
1995	LANCIA DELTA HF 4WD / INTEGRALE 8V	250	Italy 1988	1995	LANCIA DELTA HF 4WD INTEGRALE 8V	185
1995	LANCIA DELTA INTEGRALE 16V	345	Italy 1989	1995	LANCIA DELTA INTEGRALE 16V	197
1995	LANCIA DELTA INTEGRALE 16V	345	Italy 1990	1995	LANCIA DELTA INTEGRALE 16V	197
1995	LANCIA DELTA INTEGRALE 16V	345	Italy 1991	1995	LANCIA DELTA INTEGRALE 16V	197
1998	LANCIA DELTA HF INTEGRALE	215	Italy 1992	1998	LANCIA DELTA HF INTEGRALE	178

1

1998	TOYOTA CELICA GT-FOUR ST185	299	Japan 1993	1998	TOYOTA CELICA GT-4	201
1998	TOYOTA CELICA GT-FOUR ST185	299	Japan 1994	1998	TOYOTA CELICA GT-4	201
1994	SUBARU IMPREZA WRC555	295	Japan 1995	1998	SUBARU IMPREZA 22B STI	276
1994	SUBARU IMPREZA WRC555	295	Japan 1996	1998	SUBARU IMPREZA S201 STI	296
1994	SUBARU IMPREZA WRC 97	300	Japan 1997	1998	SUBARU IMPREZA WRX STI TYPE RA	276
1997	MITSUBISHI LANCER EVOLUTION IV/V	280	Japan 1998	1997	MITSUBISHI LANCER EVO V GSR GF-CP9A	276
1972	TOYOTA COROLLA WRC	299	Japan 1999	1587	TOYOTA COROLLA RXI	154
1997	PEUGEOT 206 WRC	300	France 2000	1997	PEUGEOT 206 RC	174
1997	PEUGEOT 206 WRC	300	France 2001	1997	PEUGEOT 206 RC	174
1997	PEUGEOT 206 WRC	300	France 2002	1997	PEUGEOT 206 RC	174
1998	CITROEN XSARA WRC	315	France 2003	1998	CITROEN XSARA VTS / FWD	161
1998	CITROEN XSARA WRC	315	France 2004	1998	CITROEN XSARA VTS / FWD	161
1998	CITROEN XSARA WRC	315	France 2005	1998	CITROEN XSARA VTS / FWD	161
1998	FORD FOCUS RS WRC 06	300	US/UK 2006	1998	FORD FOCUS RS	301
1998	FORD FOCUS RS WRC 06/07	300	US/UK 2007	1998	FORD FOCUS RS	301
1998	CITROEN C4 WRC	315	France 2008	1998	CITROEN C4 COUPE 2.0i16V	178
1998	CITROEN C4 WRC	315	France 2009	1998	CITROEN C4 COUPE 2.0i16V	178
1998	CITROEN C4 WRC	315	France 2010	1998	CITROEN C4 COUPE 2.0i16V	178
1598	CITROEN DS3 WRC	300	France 2011	1598	CITROEN DS3 RACING	200
1598	CITROEN DS3 WRC	300	France 2012	1598	CITROEN DS3 RACING	200
1600	VOLKSWAGEN POLO R WRC	315	Germany 2013	1600	VOLKSWAGEN POLO R WRC	217

wikipedia.org, carfolio.com

THE BIG **MONEY**

Does size matter in sport? You can (mostly) bet it does. As this graphic shows, having a few extra inches in height can make a big difference to sporting success.

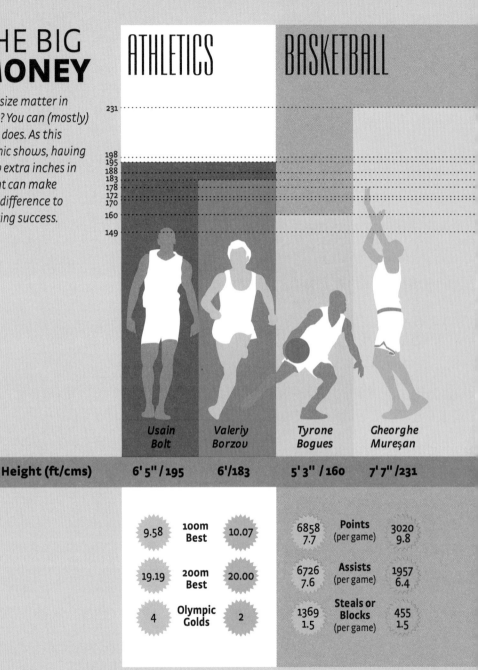

ATHLETICS

BASKETBALL

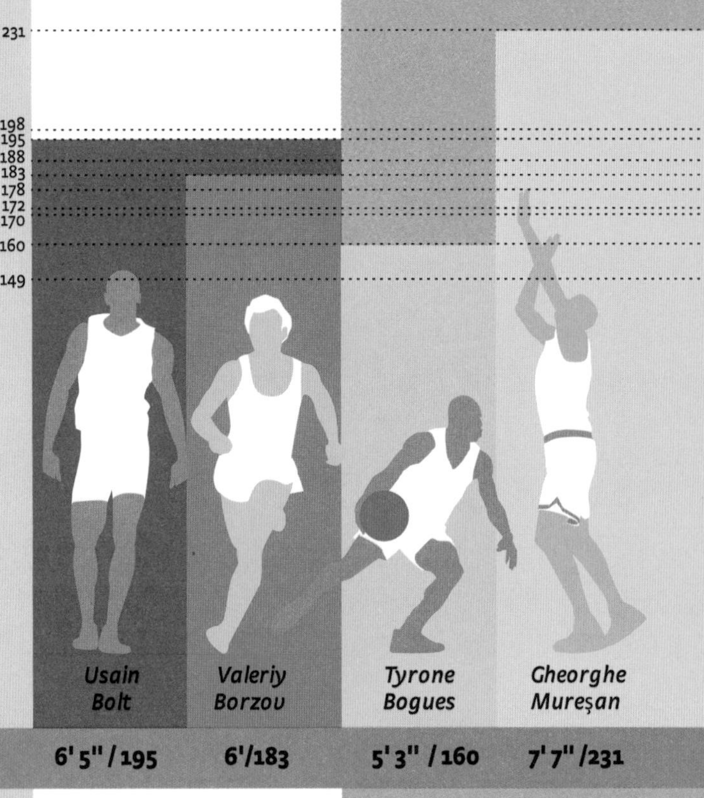
231
198
195
188
183
178
172
170
160
149
Usain Bolt
Valeriy Borzov
Tyrone Bogues
Gheorghe Mureşan

Height (ft/cms)	6' 5" / 195	6'/183	5' 3" / 160	7' 7" /231

Usain Bolt		Valeriy Borzov
9.58	100m Best	10.07
19.19	200m Best	20.00
4	Olympic Golds	2

Tyrone Bogues		Gheorghe Mureşan
6858 7.7	Points (per game)	3020 9.8
6726 7.6	Assists (per game)	1957 6.4
1369 1.5	Steals or Blocks (per game)	455 1.5

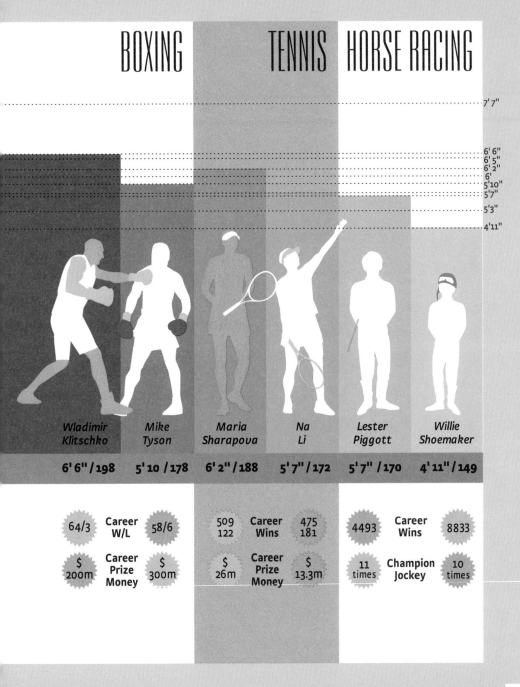

BOXING

TENNIS

HORSE RACING

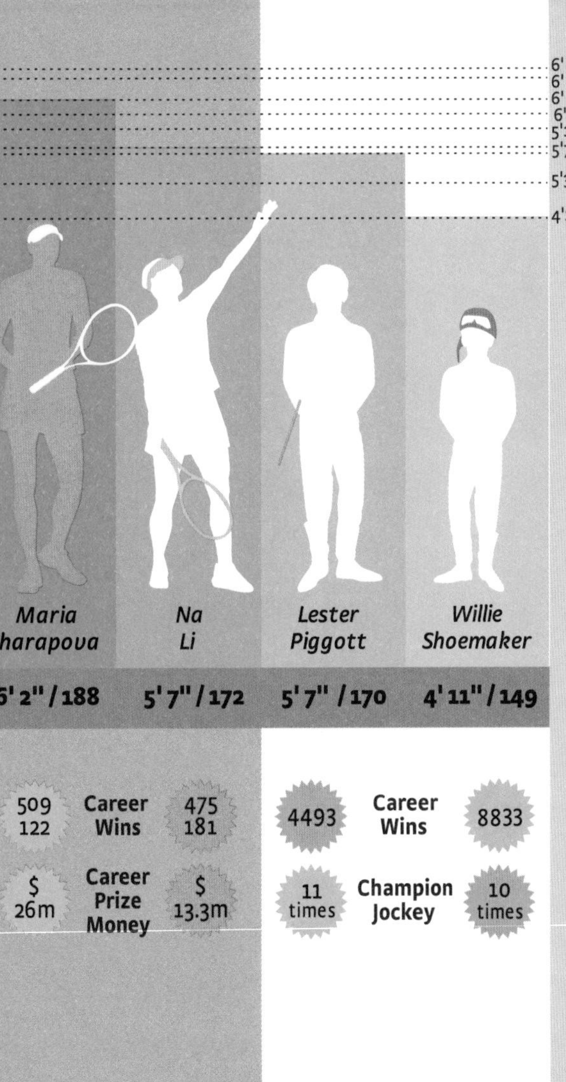
7'7"
6'6"
6'5"
6'2"
6'
5'10"
5'7"
5'3"
4'11"
Wladimir Klitschko
Mike Tyson
Maria Sharapova
Na Li
Lester Piggott
Willie Shoemaker
6'6"/198
5'10 /178
6'2"/188
5'7"/172
5'7" /170
4'11"/149
64/3 Career W/L 58/6
$ 200m Career Prize Money $ 300m
509 122 Career Wins 475 181
$ 26m Career Prize Money $ 13.3m
4493 Career Wins 8833
11 times Champion Jockey 10 times

BREAKING **ADAM'S RIB**

If sports are gender specific then perhaps there's something in the way that each are rewarded for success. Women are gaining parity in some areas, but still have a long way to cycle in others.

SPORTS THAT PAY MALE AND FEMALE WINNERS EQUAL PRIZE MONEY

- ATP and WTA Tennis Grand Slams
- Major city marathons
- FINA International Swimming competitions
- International Weightlifting Federation and Commonwealth WF Championships
- Badminton World Federation World Superseries
- International Aerobics Foundation World Cup 2014
- International Race Walking

Percent distribution by sex of people aged 15 years and older who engage in sports or exercise on an average day, by activity

Activity	percentage of men	percentage of women
Basketball	86	14
Golfing	82	18
Soccer	80	20
Baseball, softball	72	28
Racket sports	69	31
Cycling	66	34
Weightlifting	64	36
Running	58	42
Hiking	56	44
Bowling	54	46
Dancing	44	56
Walking	43	57
Yoga	20	80
Aerobics	17	83
Swimming, surfing, water-skiing	47	53
Using cardiovascular equipment	44	56

SPORTS THAT PAY GENDER-DEFINING AMOUNTS

(2013 figures)

US Open Golf male winner prize money — $7.5m

US Open Golf female winner prize money — $3.25m

Average wage for NBA basketball male professional — $5.2m

Average wage for NBA basketball female professional — $72,000

Average wage for Major Soccer League male player — $70,000

Average wage for National Women's Soccer League female player — $15,000

Average wage in UK football league lowest division for men — $107,000

Average wage in UK football league for women — $30,000

Average wage for Major League Baseball male player — $3.27m

Average wage for National Pro Fastpitch female softball player — $7,500

Male winner of Giro Italia cycle race — $123,000

Female winner of Giro Rosa cycle race (Italy) — $608

N.B. there is no women's Tour De France

Men's International Squash Open Tournament prize money — $45,600

Women's International Squash Open Tournament prize money — $17,850

Men's Association of Surfing Professionals World Tour prize money — $450,000

Women's Association of Surfing Professionals World Tour prize money — $120,000

bls.gov, wikipedia.org, fina.org, usatoday.com, iwf.net, active.com, equalizersoccer.com

PERFECT **PITCH**

The golf swing is probably the most over-analyzed sporting movement in the history of analyzing sporting movements. It should be simple, the golf ball is stationary after all. Move the club head back as far as you can then bring it forward at pace and send the ball as far as possible in a straight line. If only.

ADDRESS

1 Feet shoulder-width apart, arms straight, wrists strong, ball should be nearer the front foot but not too far from the middle of your stance.

THE BACK SWING

2 Initial back swing – first couple of feet – club head goes back in a straight line, top half of body pivoting about your waist.

3 Club is now vertical and still in line with where you want the ball to go, arms should be as straight as possible and parallel with each other and the ground.

4 Back swing continues to club horizontal – should be pointing straight back.

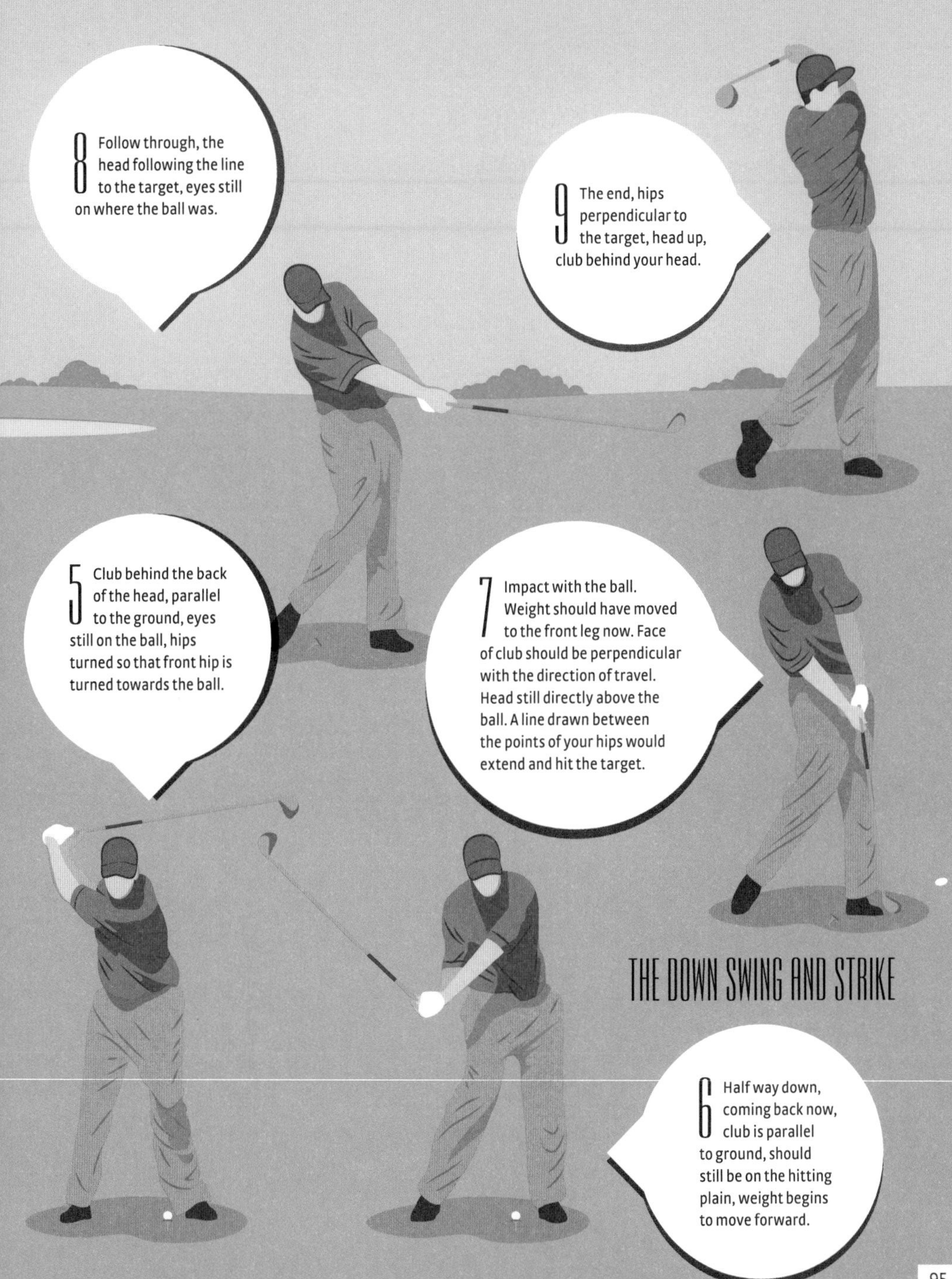
8 Follow through, the head following the line to the target, eyes still on where the ball was.
9 The end, hips perpendicular to the target, head up, club behind your head.
5 Club behind the back of the head, parallel to the ground, eyes still on the ball, hips turned so that front hip is turned towards the ball.
7 Impact with the ball. Weight should have moved to the front leg now. Face of club should be perpendicular with the direction of travel. Head still directly above the ball. A line drawn between the points of your hips would extend and hit the target.
THE DOWN SWING AND STRIKE
6 Half way down, coming back now, club is parallel to ground, should still be on the hitting plain, weight begins to move forward.

NATIONAL **SPORTS DAY**

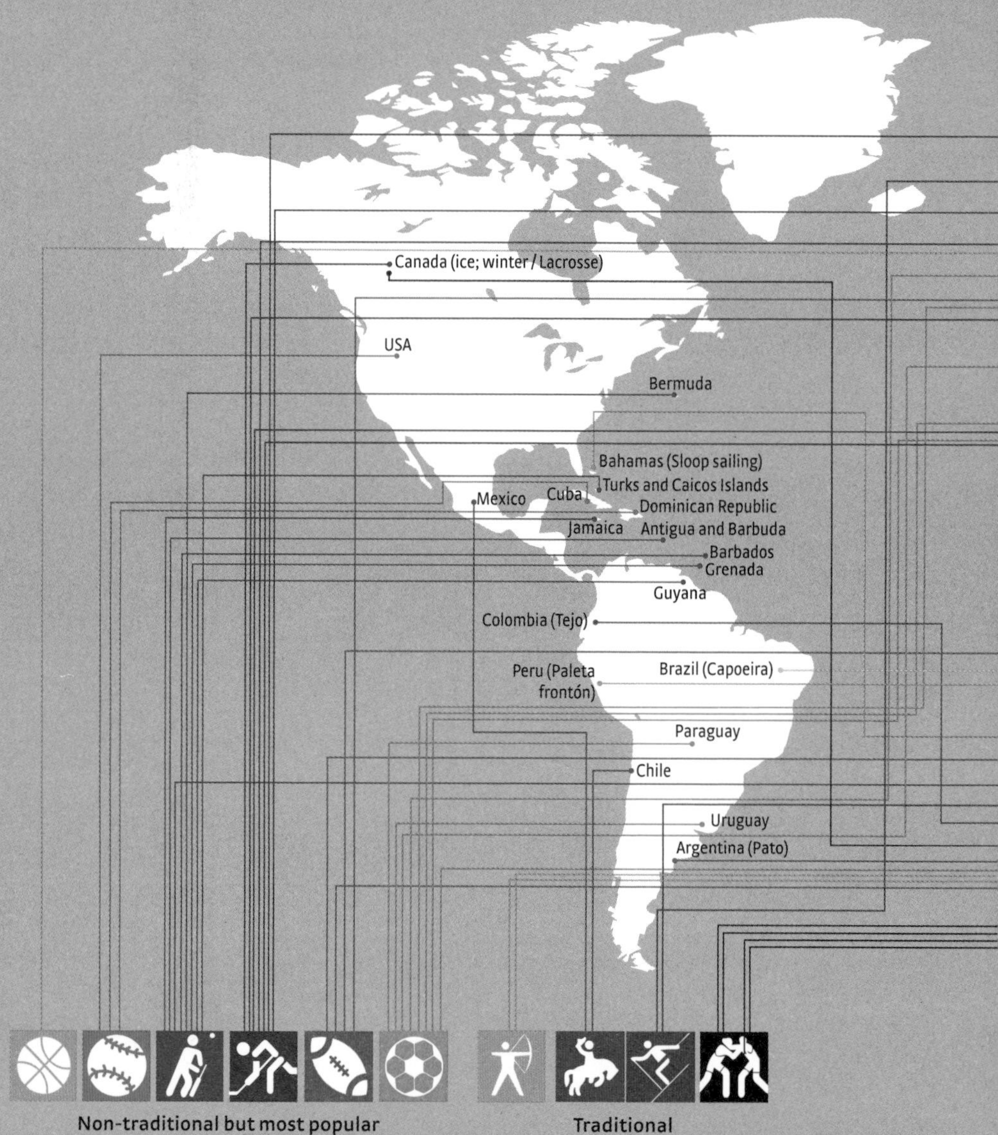

Canada (ice; winter / Lacrosse)
USA
Bermuda
Bahamas (Sloop sailing)
Turks and Caicos Islands
Mexico
Cuba
Dominican Republic
Jamaica
Antigua and Barbuda
Barbados
Grenada
Guyana
Colombia (Tejo)
Peru (Paleta frontón)
Brazil (Capoeira)
Paraguay
Chile
Uruguay
Argentina (Pato)
Non-traditional but most popular
Traditional

Soccer has become a de facto "national" game for many countries, but there are still significant numbers of people who play much older sports developed and played solely in their country. These are the most popular traditional and adopted sports around the world.

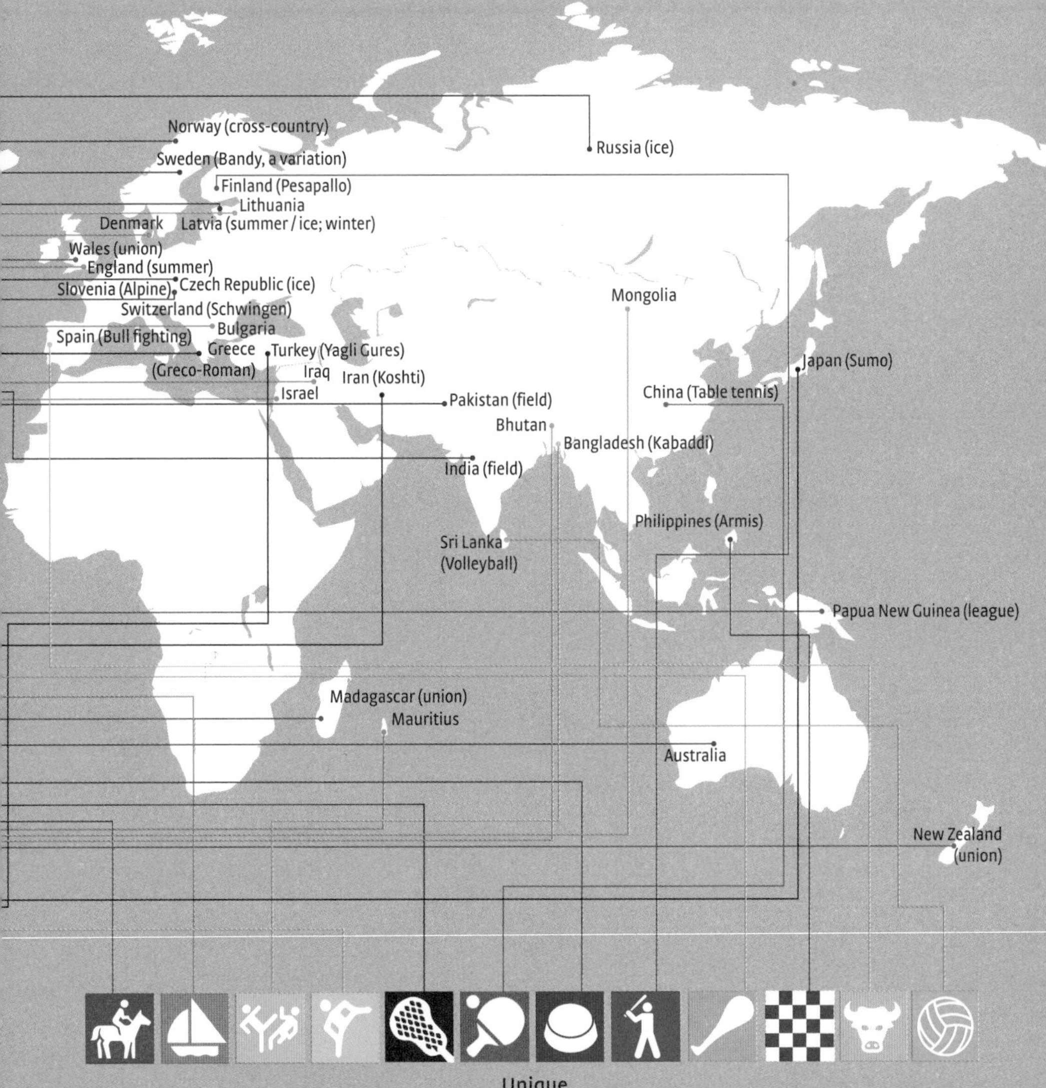

Norway (cross-country)
Russia (ice)
Sweden (Bandy, a variation)
Finland (Pesapallo)
Lithuania
Denmark
Latvia (summer / ice; winter)
Wales (union)
England (summer)
Slovenia (Alpine)
Czech Republic (ice)
Switzerland (Schwingen)
Bulgaria
Spain (Bull fighting)
Greece
(Greco-Roman)
Turkey (Yagli Gures)
Iraq
Iran (Koshti)
Israel
Pakistan (field)
Mongolia
Japan (Sumo)
China (Table tennis)
Bhutan
Bangladesh (Kabaddi)
India (field)
Philippines (Armis)
Sri Lanka
(Volleyball)
Papua New Guinea (league)
Madagascar (union)
Mauritius
Australia
New Zealand
(union)
Unique

PLAYER A – THE FAVORITE

VS

PLAYER B – THE OUTSIDER

ONE MUST WIN, NO TIES ACCEPTED

4/6 (1.67) **A**

$$\text{Margin} = \frac{1}{1.67} + \frac{1}{1.67} = 1.075$$

The .075 is bookmaker's buffer. It doesn't guarantee a profit but it does give them the edge.

WHAT ARE THE **ODDS?**

In gambling, even when punters win, the bookies still win. But how do they do it? The common denominator in all betting markets from two-horse races (a tennis match), via three-horse races (when a tie can count) to forty-horse races (races with 40 horses in them) is that the market setter (the bookmaker) builds in a margin. This is how they do it.

B 11/10 (2.1)

You can see this best illustrated when the "real odds" of a two-horse race are evens but the odds offered still give a margin. For the toss of a coin it should be:

Heads 1/1 (2) V Tails 1/1 (2) Margin = $\frac{1}{2} + \frac{1}{2} = 1.00$

But would be given as:

Heads 5/6 (1.83) v Tails 5/6 (1.83)

Margin = $\frac{1}{1.83} + \frac{1}{1.83} = 1.09$

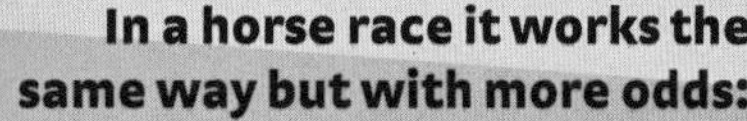

In a horse race it works the same way but with more odds:

Horse A	11/10	2.1
Horse B	13/8	2.62
Horse C	7/1	8
Horse D	12/1	13
Horse E	20/1	21
Horse F	25/1	26
Horse G	25/1	26
Horse H	50/1	51

In this case the margin = 1.2

Obviously if everyone bet on Player A or Horse A the bookie would lose but this is the art of market making. The odds change as the money is bet so that, with the help of the buffer or margin, the bookies will win, whoever wins.

WORLD ARMCHAIR **SPORTS CHAMPS**

Some live events unify the world like no other – the funeral of Princess Diana in 1997 had 2.5 billion viewers around the globe – and some unite fans of a sport in front of the TV in numbers that far exceed the crowds present in the venue (the 2010 FI race in Bahrain, pop. 1.3m, drew 54m). Here are the most viewed sports events for the world's major sporting nations.

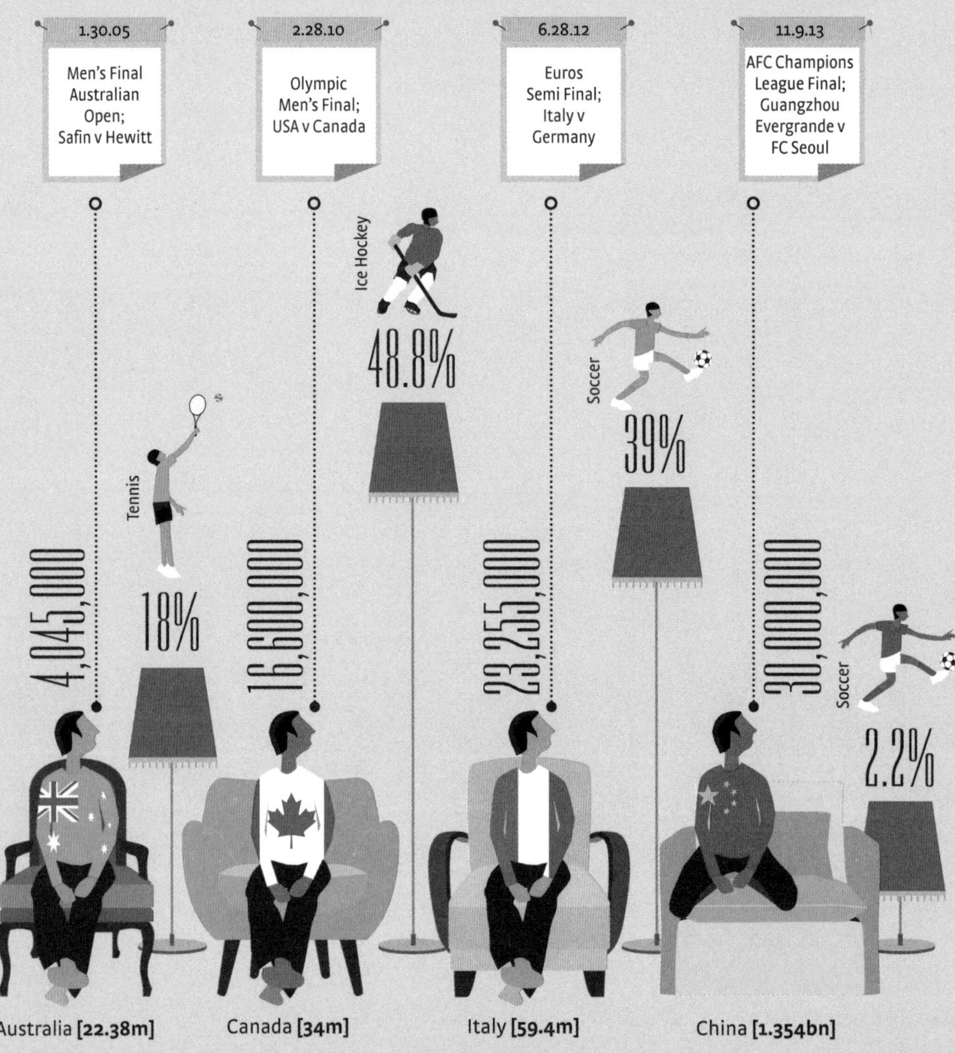
1.30.05
Men's Final Australian Open; Safin v Hewitt
2.28.10
Olympic Men's Final; USA v Canada
6.28.12
Euros Semi Final; Italy v Germany
11.9.13
AFC Champions League Final; Guangzhou Evergrande v FC Seoul
4,045,000
Tennis
18%
16,600,000
Ice Hockey
48.8%
23,255,000
Soccer
39%
30,000,000
Soccer
2.2%
Australia [22.38m]
Canada [34m]
Italy [59.4m]
China [1.354bn]

[ ] Population
Event
Date
Viewing Figures
% pop'

7.7.10
World Cup Semi Final; Germany v Spain
31,100,000
Soccer
38%
Germany [82m]

7.30.66
World Cup Final; England v West Germany
32,300,000
Soccer
59%
Great Britain [54.6m]

2.5.12
Super Bowl; New York Giants v New England
111,300,000
Football
35.6%
USA [312.8m]

4.2.11
World Cup Final; India v Sri Lanka
135,000,000
Cricket
11%
India [1.2bn]

NAMED FOR **SUCCESS**

Since ancient times people have named their children after gods and goddesses, heroes and heroines. In modern times with gods mostly gone, sporting stars have, it appears, inspired parents to take the name of a successful athlete and give it to their offspring. Here we track the appearance of sports stars' names in the top 1000 baby names over several decades.

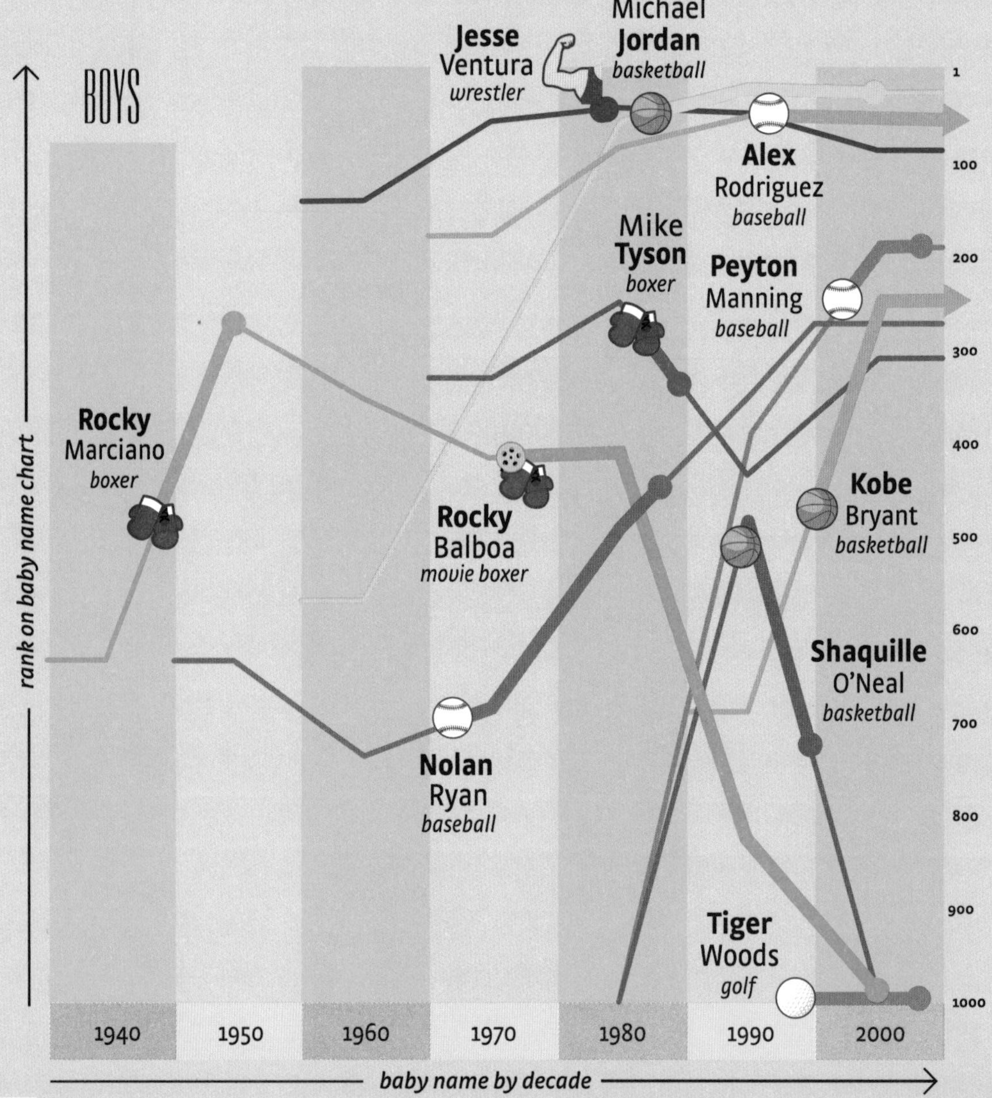

BOYS
rank on baby name chart
baby name by decade
1940
1950
1960
1970
1980
1990
2000
1
100
200
300
400
500
600
700
800
900
1000
Jesse Ventura wrestler
Michael Jordan basketball
Alex Rodriguez baseball
Mike Tyson boxer
Peyton Manning baseball
Rocky Marciano boxer
Rocky Balboa movie boxer
Kobe Bryant basketball
Shaquille O'Neal basketball
Nolan Ryan baseball
Tiger Woods golf

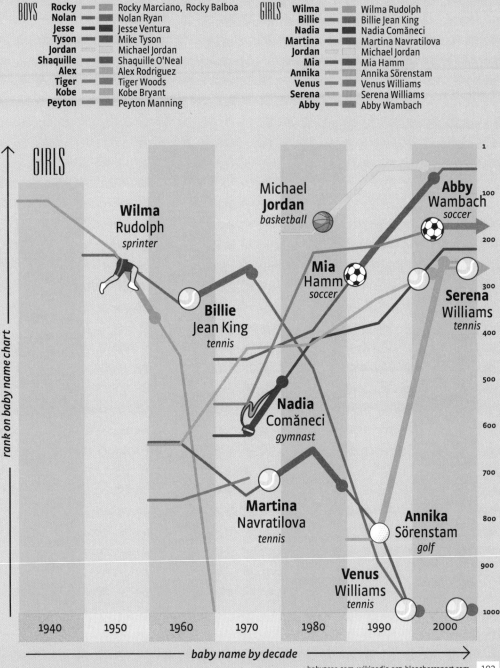

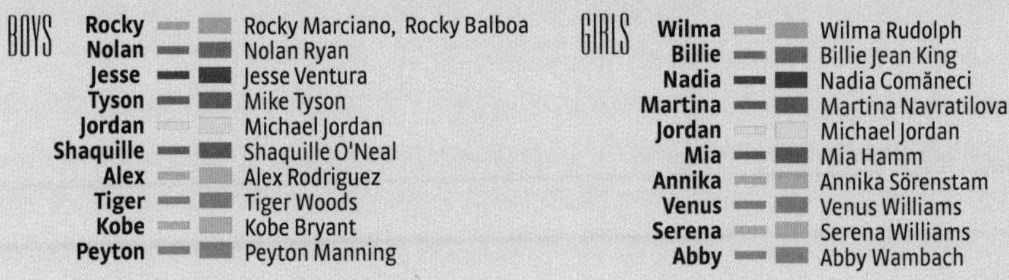
BOYS
Rocky — Rocky Marciano, Rocky Balboa
Nolan — Nolan Ryan
Jesse — Jesse Ventura
Tyson — Mike Tyson
Jordan — Michael Jordan
Shaquille — Shaquille O'Neal
Alex — Alex Rodriguez
Tiger — Tiger Woods
Kobe — Kobe Bryant
Peyton — Peyton Manning
GIRLS
Wilma — Wilma Rudolph
Billie — Billie Jean King
Nadia — Nadia Comăneci
Martina — Martina Navratilova
Jordan — Michael Jordan
Mia — Mia Hamm
Annika — Annika Sörenstam
Venus — Venus Williams
Serena — Serena Williams
Abby — Abby Wambach

GIRLS

Wilma Rudolph *sprinter*

Billie Jean King *tennis*

Michael **Jordan** *basketball*

Mia Hamm *soccer*

Nadia Comăneci *gymnast*

Martina Navratilova *tennis*

Abby Wambach *soccer*

Serena Williams *tennis*

Annika Sörenstam *golf*

Venus Williams *tennis*

1
100
200
300
400
500
600
700
800
900
1000

1940 1950 1960 1970 1980 1990 2000

rank on baby name chart

baby name by decade

baby2see.com, wikipedia.org, bleacherreport.com

BUY **ANY** TICKETS

The cost of attending one-off sporting events varies enormously from sport to sport, and day to day. Secondary ticket sales, whether via official means or by tout, raise prices enormously. However, standard ticket prices at big and small events around the world are often higher, and lower, than you might think, as this comparison shows.

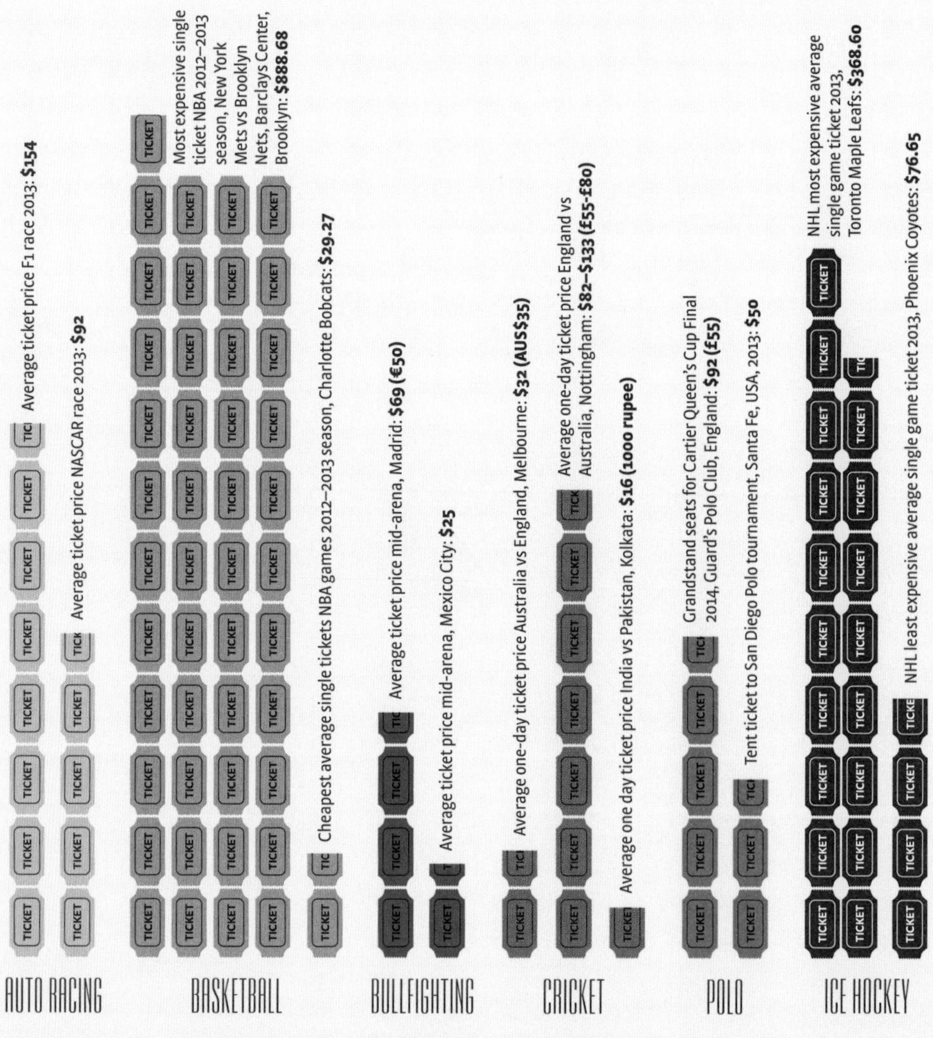
AUTO RACING
Average ticket price F1 race 2013: **$154**
Average ticket price NASCAR race 2013: **$92**
BASKETBALL
Most expensive single ticket NBA 2012–2013 season, New York Mets vs Brooklyn Nets, Barclays Center, Brooklyn: **$888.68**
Cheapest average single tickets NBA games 2012–2013 season, Charlotte Bobcats: **$29.27**
BULLFIGHTING
Average ticket price mid-arena, Madrid: **$69 (€50)**
Average ticket price mid-arena, Mexico City: **$25**
CRICKET
Average one-day ticket price Australia vs England, Melbourne: **$32 (AUS$35)**
Average one-day ticket price England vs Australia, Nottingham: **$82–$133 (£55-£80)**
Average one day ticket price India vs Pakistan, Kolkata: **$16 (1000 rupee)**
POLO
Grandstand seats for Cartier Queen's Cup Final 2014, Guard's Polo Club, England: **$92 (£55)**
Tent ticket to San Diego Polo tournament, Santa Fe, USA, 2013: **$50**
ICE HOCKEY
NHL most expensive average single game ticket 2013, Toronto Maple Leafs: **$368.60**
NHL least expensive average single game ticket 2013, Phoenix Coyotes: **$76.65**

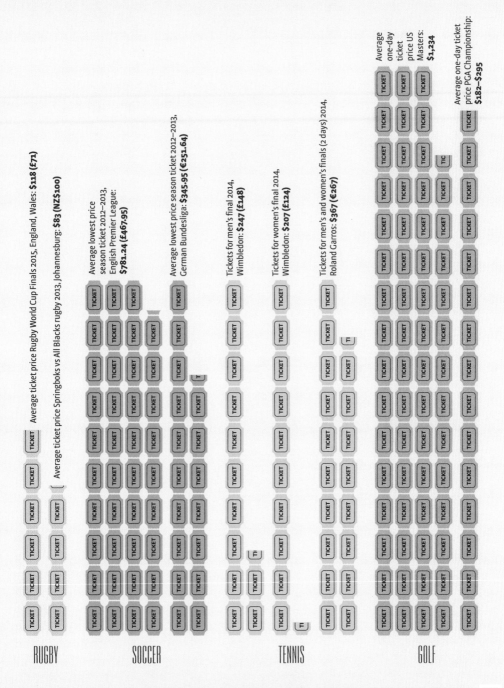

RUGBY

Average ticket price Rugby World Cup Finals 2015, England, Wales: **$118 (£71)**

Average ticket price Springboks vs All Blacks rugby 2013, Johannesburg: **$83 (NZ$100)**

SOCCER

Average lowest price season ticket 2012–2013, English Premier League: **$781.24 (£467.95)**

Average lowest price season ticket 2012–2013, German Bundesliga: **$345.95 (€251.64)**

TENNIS

Tickets for men's final 2014, Wimbledon: **$247 (£148)**

Tickets for women's final 2014, Wimbledon: **$207 (£124)**

Tickets for men's and women's finals (2 days) 2014, Roland Garros: **$367 (€267)**

GOLF

Average one-day ticket price US Masters: **$1,234**

Average one-day ticket price PGA Championship: **$182–$295**

tickets.formula1.com, wimbledon.com/tickets, rolandgarros.fft, nhl.com, nba.com, wikipedia.org

THE SPRINT
SWIMMER
ROUTINE

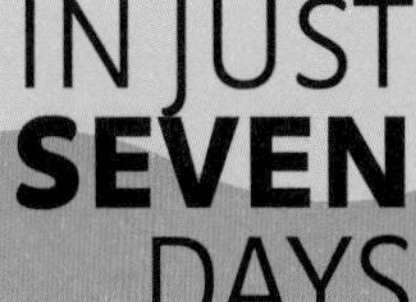
IN JUST
SEVEN
DAYS

Whatever the sport, serious athletes have to train hard and intensely all week. Here's exactly how hard and in what ways sprint swimmers and sprint runners train before an event.

MONDAY

 **7.30–10am**

Swim 3,000m – 7,000m in Olympic-sized pool

 **3–5pm**

30-minute warm-up swim, then 3,000m at a good pace. Warm-down using pull-buoys and floats

 **5.30–7pm**

Strength training

TUESDAY

 **6–8am**

High-intensity 3,000m

 **5–7pm**

Aerobic session – 8,000m steady endurance training

WEDNESDAY

 **am**

Rest

 **3–5pm**

3,000m swim, 30-minute warm-up and warm-down swims before and after

 **5.30–7pm**

Weights training

THE SPRINT
RUNNER
ROUTINE

MONDAY

(high intensity)

 **7–9am**

Warm-up (600m jog, stretches, 200m sprints), 5 times 20m, 30m, 40m ladder runs at 90–100% speed, walk return rest, 3 min between

Jump circuit

2 sets of 10 hurdle hops

Weight lifting

Cool down

TUESDAY

(low intensity)

 **9–11am**

Warm-up

General strengthening exercises (inc sit ups, pushups, squats etc) 2 sets of 20.

Throwing ball or weights 2 sets of 10

Hurdle stretches 2 sets of 10

Weight lifting

Cool down

WEDNESDAY

(high intensity)

 **7–9am**

Warm-up

3 × 4 100m runs with 3-min rests between and 5-min rests between sets

Throw ball or weight

Weight training

Cool down

6–8am

Swim 3,000m plus warm-up and warm-down swims

5–7pm

Aerobic session – up to 8,000m endurance training

6–8am

Swim 3,000m plus warm-up and warm-down swims

5–7pm

Aerobic session – up to 8,000m steady swimming endurance training

7–9am

Pool session 3,000m with 30-minute warm-up and warm-down using floats and pull-buoys

pm

Rest

Rest day

THURSDAY

(low intensity)

9–11am

Warm-up

General strengthening, 2 circuits of 25 exercises

Throw ball or weights set of 10

Hurdle stretches 2 sets of 10

Weight training

Cool down

FRIDAY

(moderate intensity)

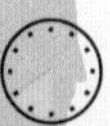

7–9am

Warm-up

Running up hill at pace, 3 times 8 sets of 450m, walk back rest 3 min between sets

Eight sets of 5 hurdle hops

Weight training

Cool down

SATURDAY

(high intensity)

7–9am

Warm-up

Run 2 lots of 2 sets of 250m at 85-90% capacity, rest 3-5 mins between

Hurdle stepovers with alternating legs and standing jumps

Weight training

Cool down

SUNDAY

(easy cycling etc)

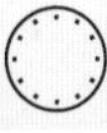

Active rest day

sportsmedecineabout.com, guardian.co.uk, wikihow.com, edb.utexas.edu

EAT TO **WIN**

The dietary requirements of athletes who excel in different sports are constantly monitored by trainers. There are 'special' diets set out in numerous training regimes for different activities, but are they really all that different? Here are six different sports and a typical day's diet for each.

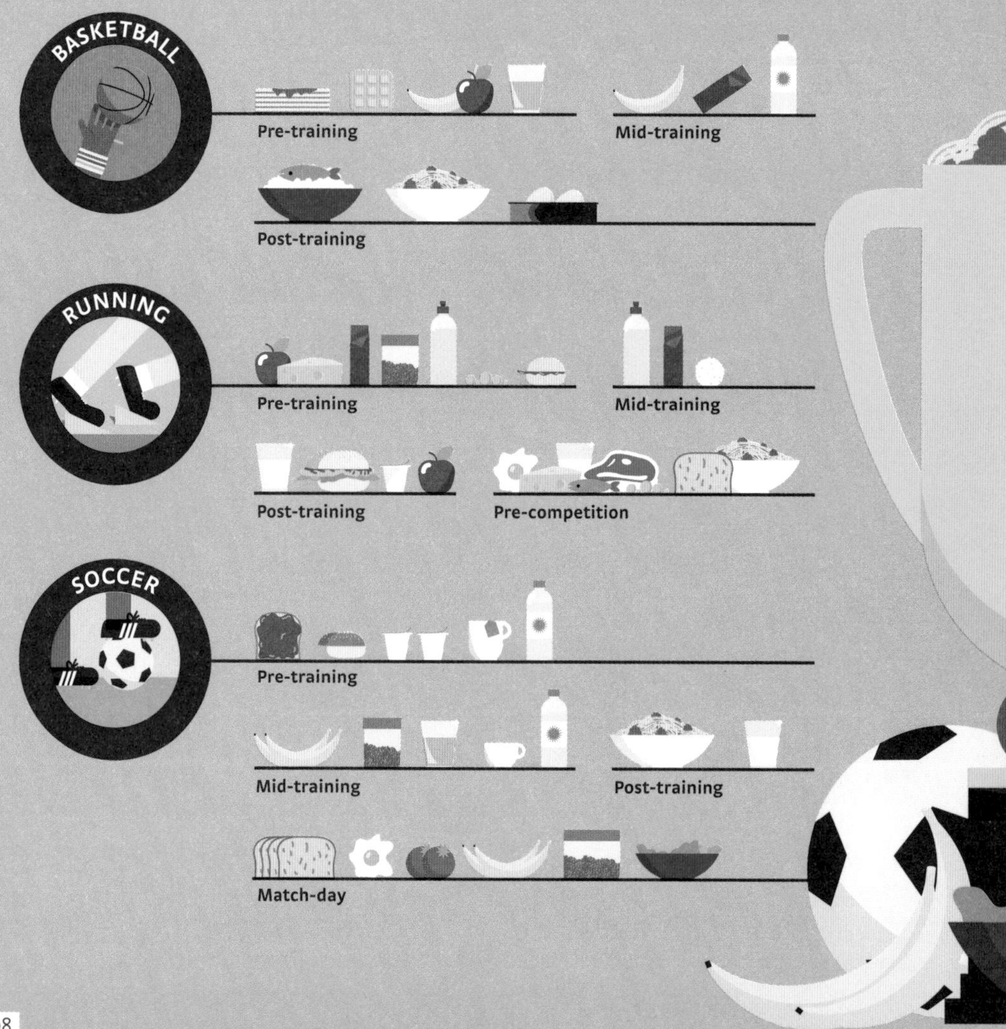

BASKETBALL
Pre-training
Mid-training
Post-training
RUNNING
Pre-training
Mid-training
Post-training
Pre-competition
SOCCER
Pre-training
Mid-training
Post-training
Match-day

GOLF
Pre-round
Mid-round
Post-round
TENNIS
Pre-training
Mid-training
Post-training
SWIMMING
Pre-training
Post-training
Competition day breakfast
Competition
between heats

eatright.org, sportsnutritionhealth.org, ext.colostate.edu, wikipedia.org

WHY DADDY WANTED ME **TO BE A SPORTS STAR**

Truly successful sports stars of today begin their trek to the top at a very young age, and they never have to get a day job. More often than not parents, particularly fathers, did mundane jobs and hoped their children wouldn't have to follow in their footsteps. Here's the contrast between what top stars have earned in their sport, and what they would earn at their father's jobs.

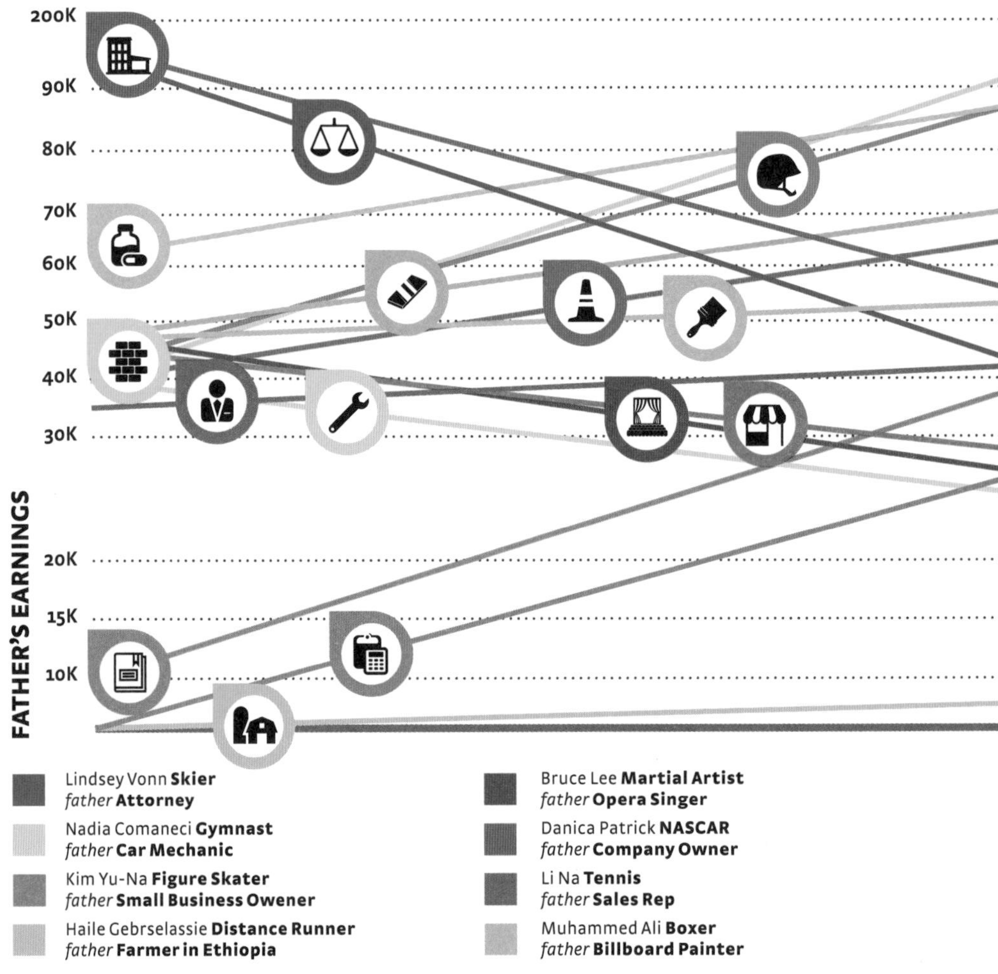

200K
90K
80K
70K
60K
50K
40K
30K
20K
15K
10K
FATHER'S EARNINGS
Lindsey Vonn **Skier**
father **Attorney**
Nadia Comaneci **Gymnast**
father **Car Mechanic**
Kim Yu-Na **Figure Skater**
father **Small Business Owener**
Haile Gebrselassie **Distance Runner**
father **Farmer in Ethiopia**
Bruce Lee **Martial Artist**
father **Opera Singer**
Danica Patrick **NASCAR**
father **Company Owner**
Li Na **Tennis**
father **Sales Rep**
Muhammed Ali **Boxer**
father **Billboard Painter**

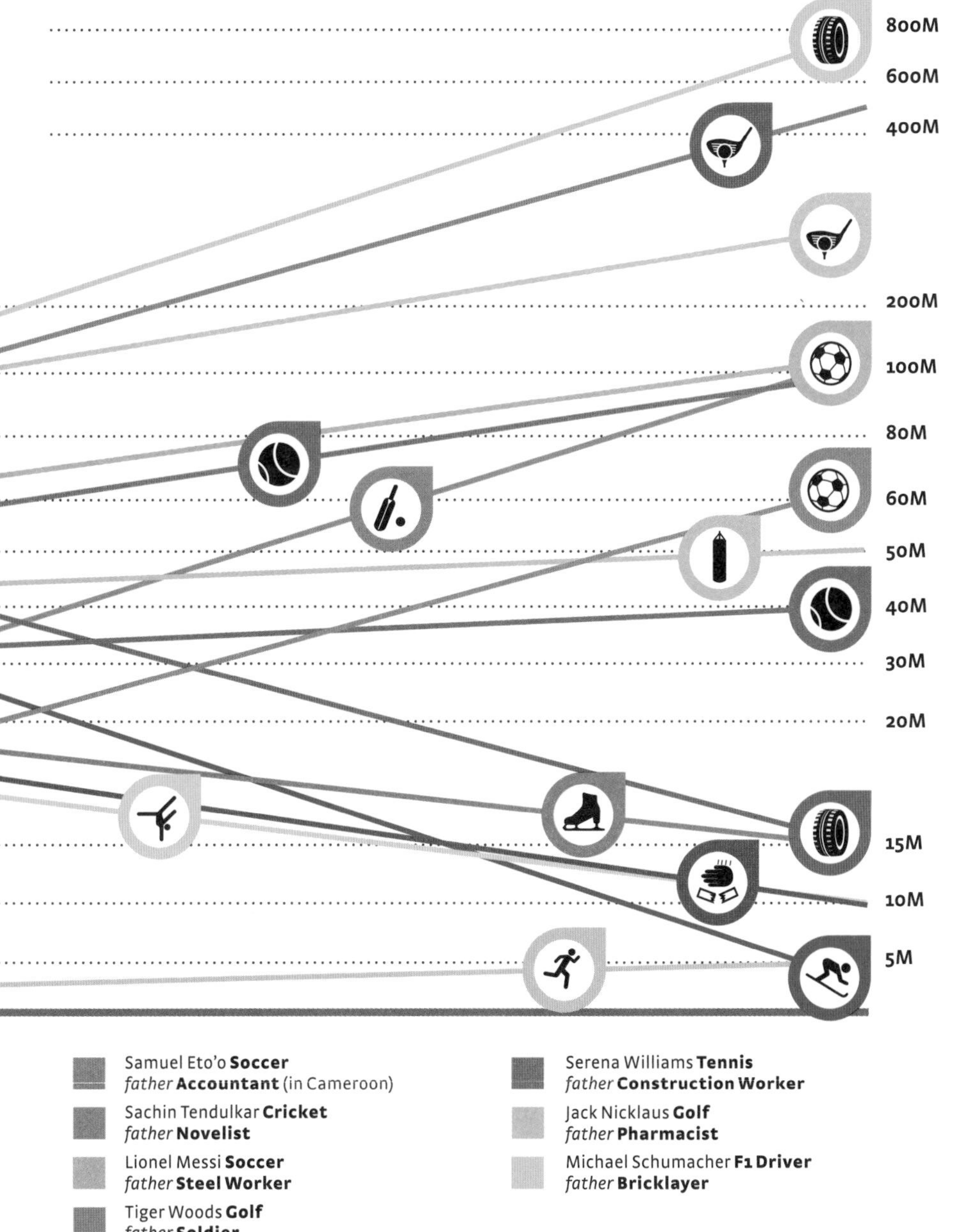
ATHLETE'S EARNINGS
800M
600M
400M
200M
100M
80M
60M
50M
40M
30M
20M
15M
10M
5M
Samuel Eto'o **Soccer**
father **Accountant** (in Cameroon)
Sachin Tendulkar **Cricket**
father **Novelist**
Lionel Messi **Soccer**
father **Steel Worker**
Tiger Woods **Golf**
father **Soldier**
Serena Williams **Tennis**
father **Construction Worker**
Jack Nicklaus **Golf**
father **Pharmacist**
Michael Schumacher **F1 Driver**
father **Bricklayer**

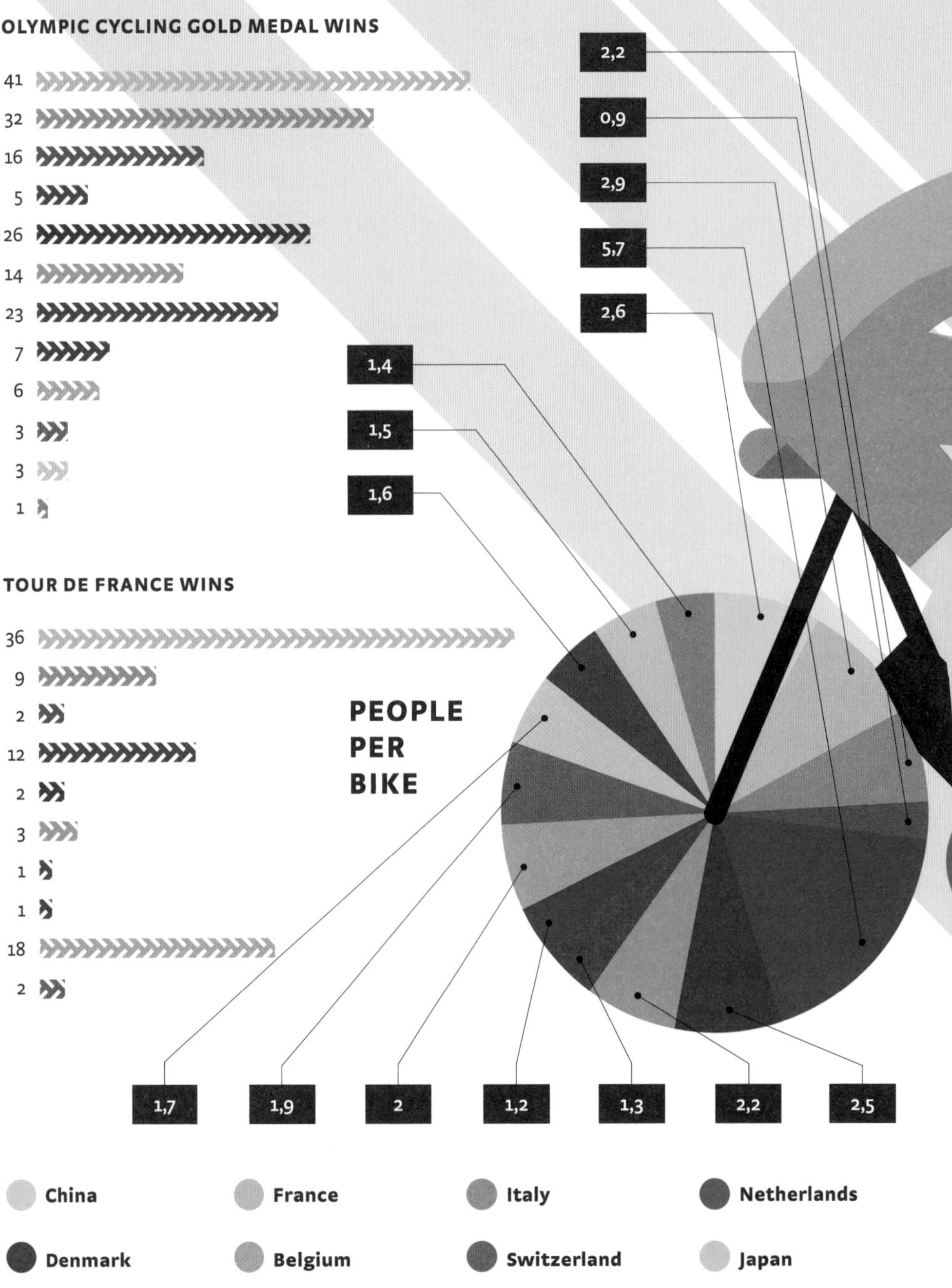
OLYMPIC CYCLING GOLD MEDAL WINS
41
32
16
5
26
14
23
7
6
3
3
1
TOUR DE FRANCE WINS
36
9
2
12
2
3
1
1
18
2
PEOPLE PER BIKE
2,2
0,9
2,9
5,7
2,6
1,4
1,5
1,6
1,7
1,9
2
1,2
1,3
2,2
2,5
China
France
Italy
Netherlands
Denmark
Belgium
Switzerland
Japan

CHAIN REACTION

Common sense would say that a country with a very high proportion of the population who partake in a sport stands a very good chance of being the best in competition at that sport. Statistics tell us that isn't the case when it comes to cycling, though. Here are the countries with the highest per capita bike ownership and their relative successes in the Olympics, Tour de France and Giro d'Italia cycle races.

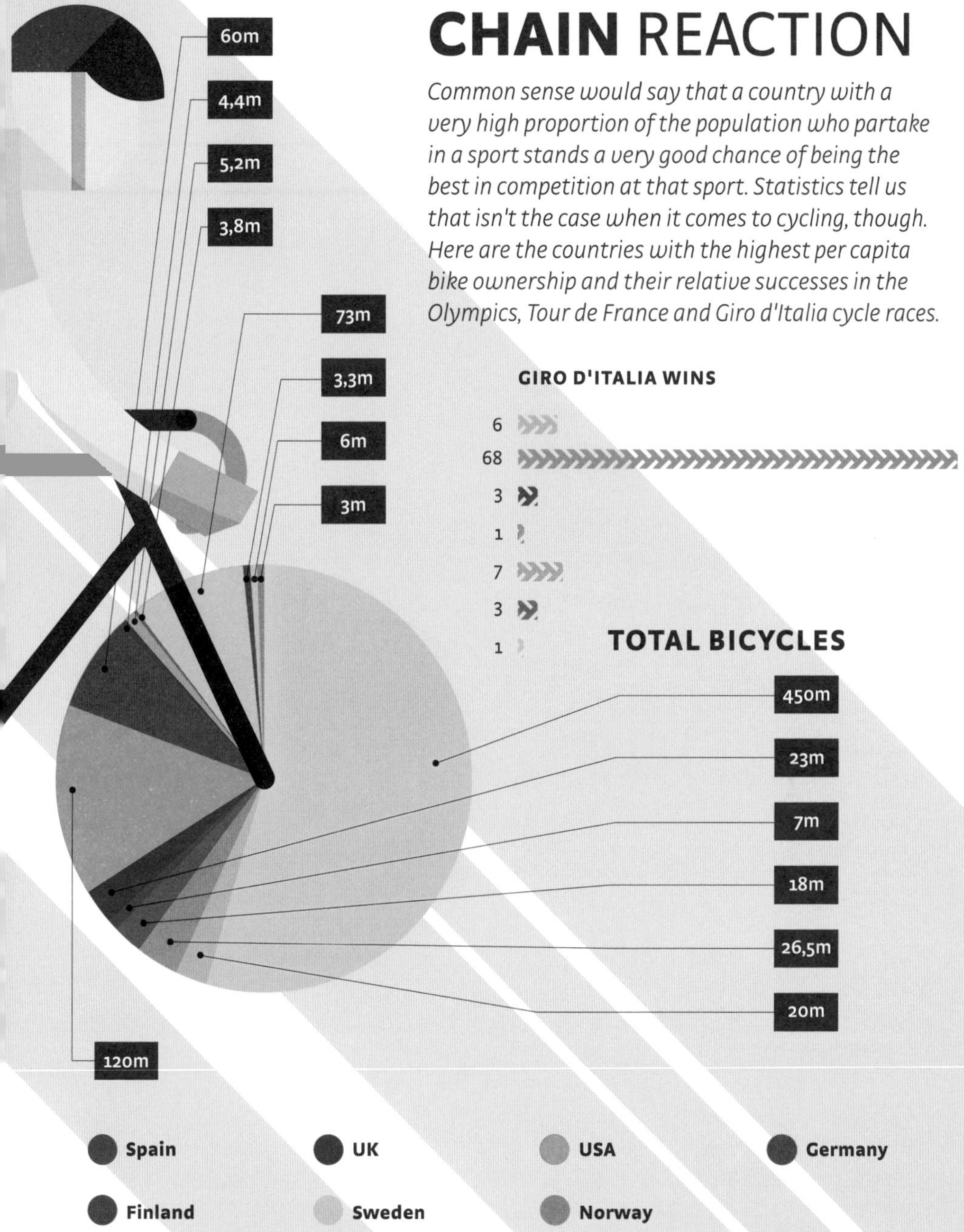

60m
4,4m
5,2m
3,8m
73m
3,3m
6m
3m

GIRO D'ITALIA WINS

6
68
3
1
7
3
1

TOTAL BICYCLES

450m
23m
7m
18m
26,5m
20m
120m

Spain
UK
USA
Germany
Finland
Sweden
Norway

bovagrai.info, wikipedia.org

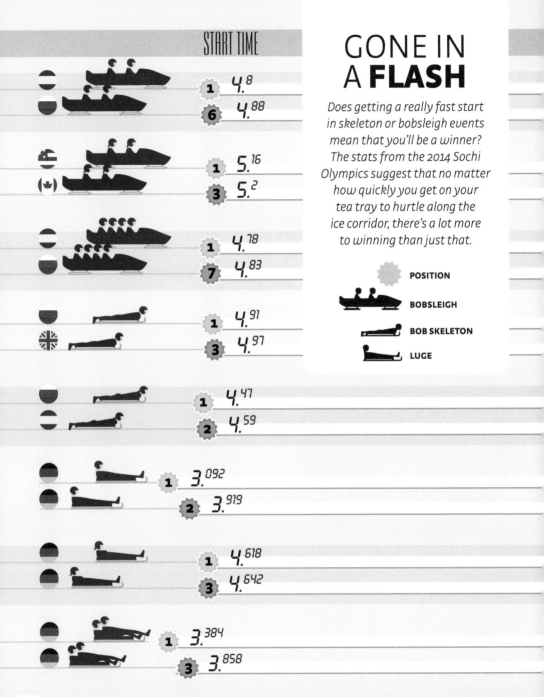

GONE IN A **FLASH**

Does getting a really fast start in skeleton or bobsleigh events mean that you'll be a winner? The stats from the 2014 Sochi Olympics suggest that no matter how quickly you get on your tea tray to hurtle along the ice corridor, there's a lot more to winning than just that.

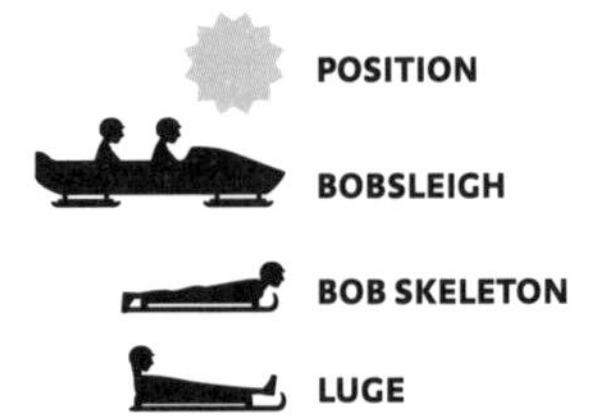
POSITION
BOBSLEIGH
BOB SKELETON
LUGE

START TIME

Position	Start time
1	4.8
6	4.88
1	5.16
3	5.2
1	4.78
7	4.83
1	4.91
3	4.97
1	4.47
2	4.59
1	3.092
2	3.919
1	4.618
3	4.642
1	3.384
3	3.858

ATHLETES		FINISH TIME
OSKARS MELBARDIS, DAUMANTS DREISKINS	8	249.7
ALEXEY VOEVODA, ALEXANDER ZUBKOV	1	248.556
ELANA MEYERS, LAURYN WILLIAMS	2	255.772
KAILLIE HUMPHRIES, HEATHER MOYSE	1	254.848
JANIS STRENGA, ARVIS VILKASTE, OSKARS MELBARDIS, DAUMANTS DREISKINS	3	243.364
ALEXEY NEGODAYLO, DMITRY TRUNENKOV, ALEXEY VOEVODA, ALEXANDER ZUBKOV	1	242.924
ELENA NIKITINA	6	256.652
LIZZIE YARNOLD	1	255.596
ALEXANDER TRETIAKOV	1	246.488
MARTINS DUKURS	2	247.676
TATJANA HUEFNER	2	221.2276
NATALIE GEISENBERGER	1	220.8316
ANDI LANGENHAM	4	229.218
FELIX LOCH	1	227.7616
TONI EGGERT, SASCHA BENECKEN	4	219.9736
TOBIAS WENDEL, TOBIAS ARLT	1	218.064

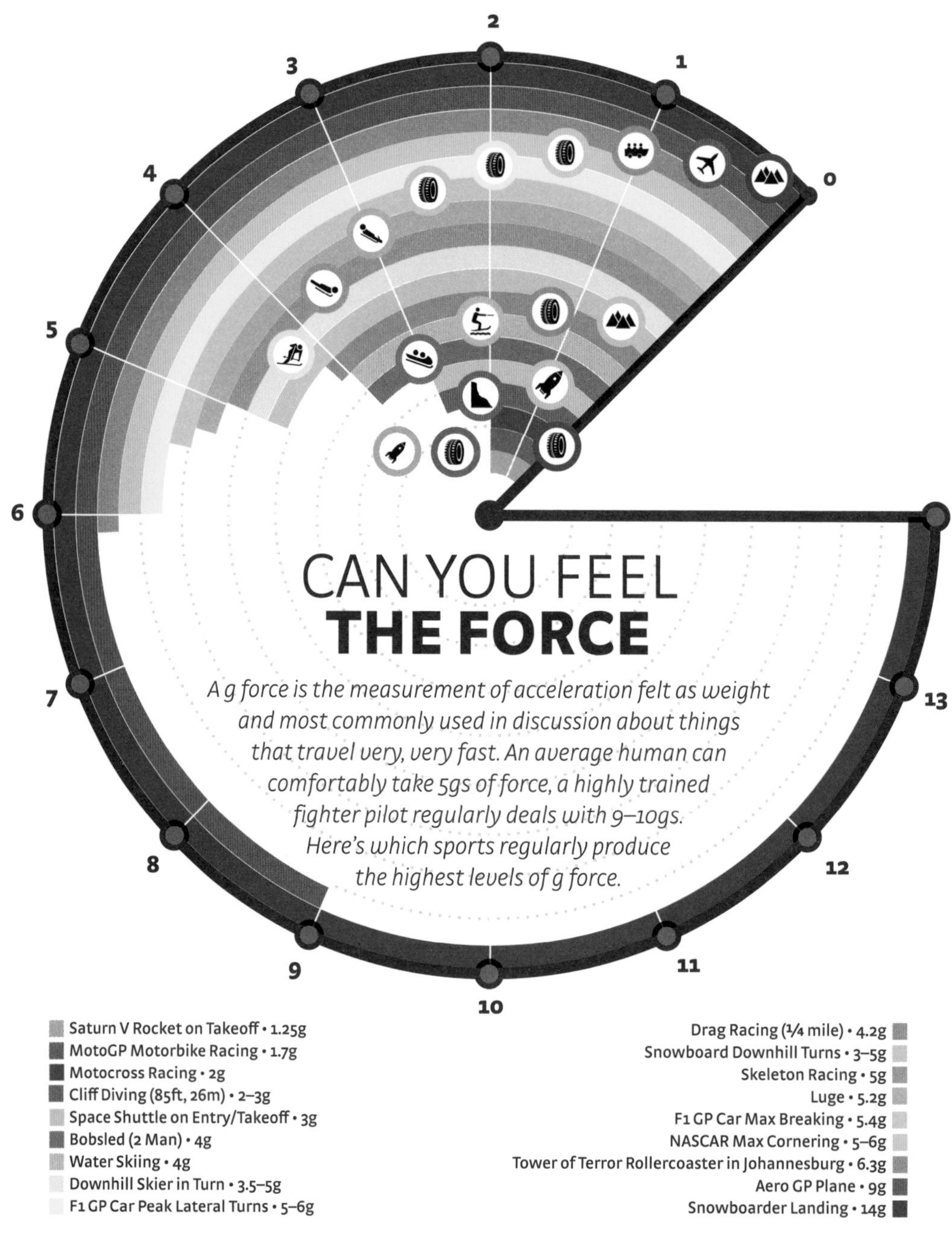
0
1
2
3
4
5
6
7
8
9
10
11
12
13
14
CAN YOU FEEL
THE FORCE
A g force is the measurement of acceleration felt as weight and most commonly used in discussion about things that travel very, very fast. An average human can comfortably take 5gs of force, a highly trained fighter pilot regularly deals with 9–10gs. Here's which sports regularly produce the highest levels of g force.
Saturn V Rocket on Takeoff • 1.25g
MotoGP Motorbike Racing • 1.7g
Motocross Racing • 2g
Cliff Diving (85ft, 26m) • 2–3g
Space Shuttle on Entry/Takeoff • 3g
Bobsled (2 Man) • 4g
Water Skiing • 4g
Downhill Skier in Turn • 3.5–5g
F1 GP Car Peak Lateral Turns • 5–6g
Drag Racing (1/4 mile) • 4.2g
Snowboard Downhill Turns • 3–5g
Skeleton Racing • 5g
Luge • 5.2g
F1 GP Car Max Breaking • 5.4g
NASCAR Max Cornering • 5–6g
Tower of Terror Rollercoaster in Johannesburg • 6.3g
Aero GP Plane • 9g
Snowboarder Landing • 14g

 usatoday.com, faqs.org, blog.alpinereplay.com, howstuffworks.com, aero-gp.com, journals.humankinetics.com

All medals are 3mm thick and 60mm in diameter

Most medals handed out at a single Olympics:
Summer*: 962 **Winter****: 295

WORTH (2014) $600
TOTAL WEIGHT 531g/18.7oz
7.5% gold plate
weight: 6g/0.2oz
92.5% silver (0.925 grade) **weight:** 525g/18.5oz

GOLD MEDAL

Total Gold used in making Winter 2014 Medals:
5kg/13lbs

Most valuable Gold medal:
$1.5m at auction 2014
(Jesse Owens' Gold from the 1936 Berlin Olympics)

WORTH (2014) $300
TOTAL WEIGHT 525g/18.5oz
All silver (0.925 grade)

SILVER MEDAL

Total Silver used in making Winter 2014 medals:
1814kg/4000lbs

WORTH (2014) $3
TOTAL WEIGHT 460g/16.2oz
97% copper **weight:** 446.1g/15.714 oz
2.5% zinc
weight: 11.5g / 0.405 oz
0.5% tin
weight: 2.4g / 0.081 oz

BRONZE MEDAL

Total Bronze used in making Winter 2014 medals:
698kg/1540lbs

WHAT **MEDALS** ARE MADE FROM

Gold, silver and bronze medals for finishing first, second and third in an Olympic event were first introduced in 1904, and they were made of each precious metal. However, since 1912 the gold medals have mostly been made of silver. Here's the worth, weight, and composition of all three medals.

* 2012 London Summer Olympics
** 2014 Sochi Winter Olympics
chemistry.about.com, en.wikipedia.org, sochi2014.com, kgw.com

WINNING **WHEELS**

The individual who carries home the Tour de France's yellow jersey as overall winner, as well as the team that helps carry him home, get all the publicity in the cycling world. But less is written or said about the bikes. Here are the component parts manufacturers of past Tour de France winners from 1995 to 2013.

1995 **Miguel Indurain** (ESP)
Selle Italia
Pinarello Espada Oria tubed steel frame
Compagnolo
Compagnolo
Used plastic pedals
1996 **Bjarne Riis** (DEN)
Selle Italia Flite
Pinarello Keral Lite steel frame
Campagnolo
Campagnolo
Look
1997 **Jan Ullrich** (GER)
Selle Italia
Pinarello Paris steel frame
Lightweight carbon fiber
Campagnolo
Time
1998 **Marco Pantani** (ITA)
Selle Italia Flite signature ed
Mercatone Uno Bianchi Mega Pro XL
Campagnolo
Campagnolo
Time Equipe Pro
1999–2004 **Lance Armstrong** (USA)
Selle Italia Flite
Trek 5500 CCLV carbon fiber frame
Rolf
Shimano Dura Ace
Look
2005 **Lance Armstrong** (USA)
Selle Italia Flite
Trek Madone SSLx
Bontrager
Shimano Dura-Ace
Shimano

2006 **Óscar Pereiro** (ESP)

Selle Italia Flite

Pinarello Prince

Campagnolo Carbon

Campagnolo Record

Look Keo

2007 **Alberto Contador** (ESP)

San Marco Concor Light

Trek Madone Pro 5.2

Bontrager Race XXX Lite

Shimano Dura Ace 7800

Shimano Dura Ace

2008 **Carlos Sastre** (ESP)

Prologo Scratch

Cervélo R3-SL

Zipp 202

Shimano Dura Ace 7800

Speedway Zero

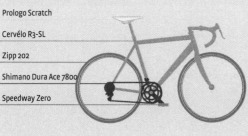

2009 **Alberto Contador** (ESP)

Selle Italia SLR

Trek Madone 6

Bontrager Race XXX Lite

SRAM Red

Look Keo 2 Max Carbon

2010 **Andy Schlek** (LUX)

Prologo Scratch

Specialized S-Works Tarmac SL3

Zipp carbon

SRAM Red

Speedway Zero

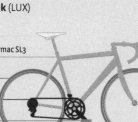

2011 **Cadel Evans** (AUS)

Fizik Antares

BMC TeamMachine SLR01

Easton EC90

Shimano Dura Ace Di2

Speedway Zero

2012 **Bradley Wiggins** (UK)

Fizik Arione

Pinarello Dogma 2

Shimano C50

Shimano Dura Ace Di2

Speedplay Zero Nanogram

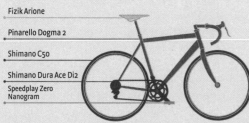

2013 **Chris Froome** (UK)

Fizik Antare

Pinarello Dogma 65.1

Shimano C24

Shimano Dura Ace Di2

Dura Ace PD-9000

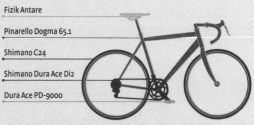

bikeradar.com, cyclingnews.com, velonews.com. wikipedia.org

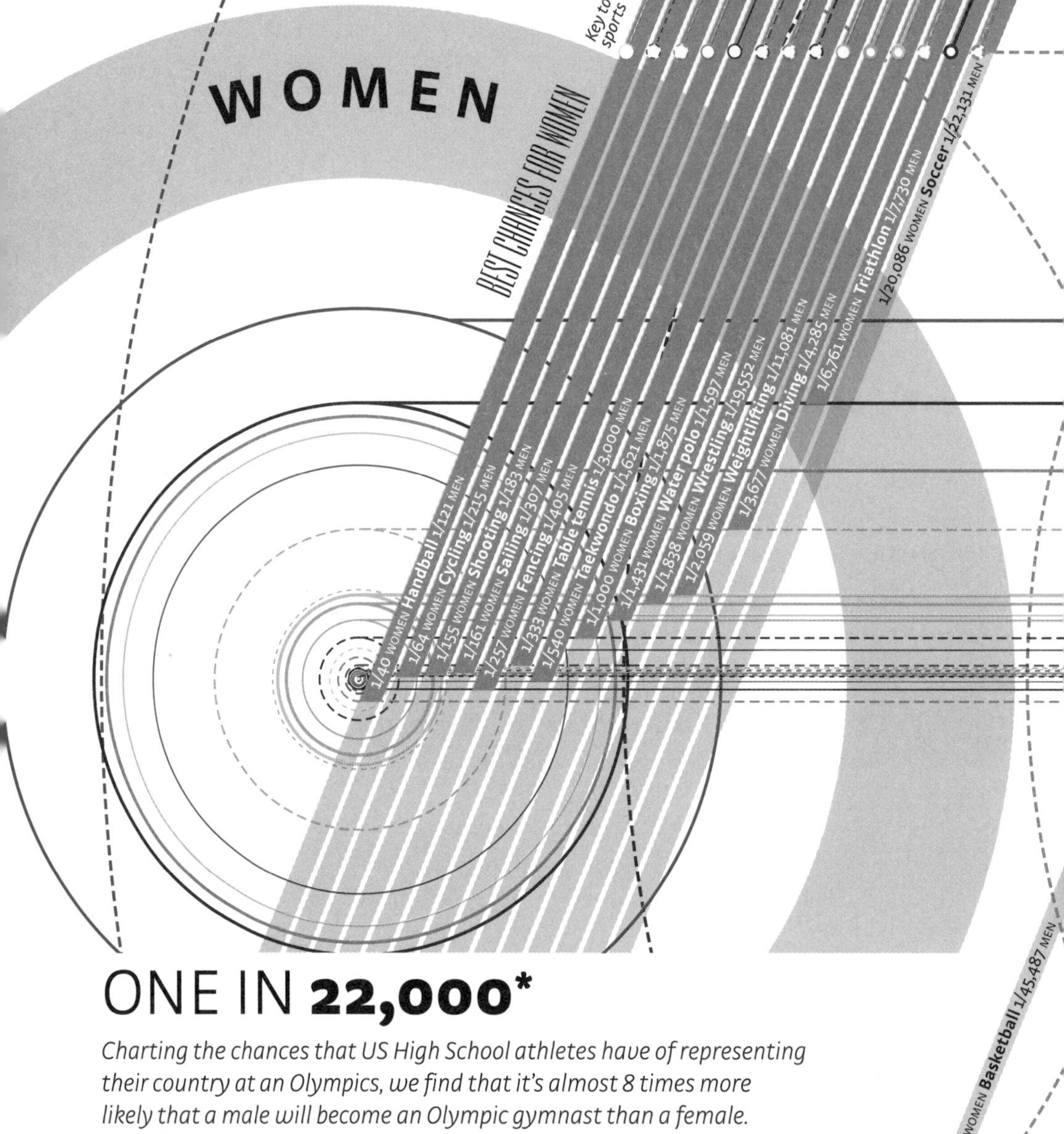
WOMEN
BEST CHANCES FOR WOMEN
Key to sports
1/40 WOMEN Handball 1/121 MEN
1/64 WOMEN Cycling 1/215 MEN
1/155 WOMEN Shooting 1/183 MEN
1/161 WOMEN Sailing 1/307 MEN
1/257 WOMEN Fencing 1/405 MEN
1/333 WOMEN Table tennis 1/3,000 MEN
1/540 WOMEN Taekwondo 1/1,621 MEN
1/1,000 WOMEN Boxing 1/1,875 MEN
1/1,431 WOMEN Water polo 1/1,597 MEN
1/1,838 WOMEN Wrestling 1/19,552 MEN
1/2,059 WOMEN Weightlifting 1/11,081 MEN
1/3,677 WOMEN Diving 1/4,285 MEN
1/6,761 WOMEN Triathlon 1/7,730 MEN
1/20,086 WOMEN Soccer 1/22,131 MEN
1/45,487 WOMEN Basketball 1/45,487 MEN

ONE IN **22,000***

Charting the chances that US High School athletes have of representing their country at an Olympics, we find that it's almost 8 times more likely that a male will become an Olympic gymnast than a female. But a female wrestler has almost a 10 and a half times better chance than a male. Here are the odds on all the major sports by gender.

* the chances of a male soccer player reaching an Olympics squad

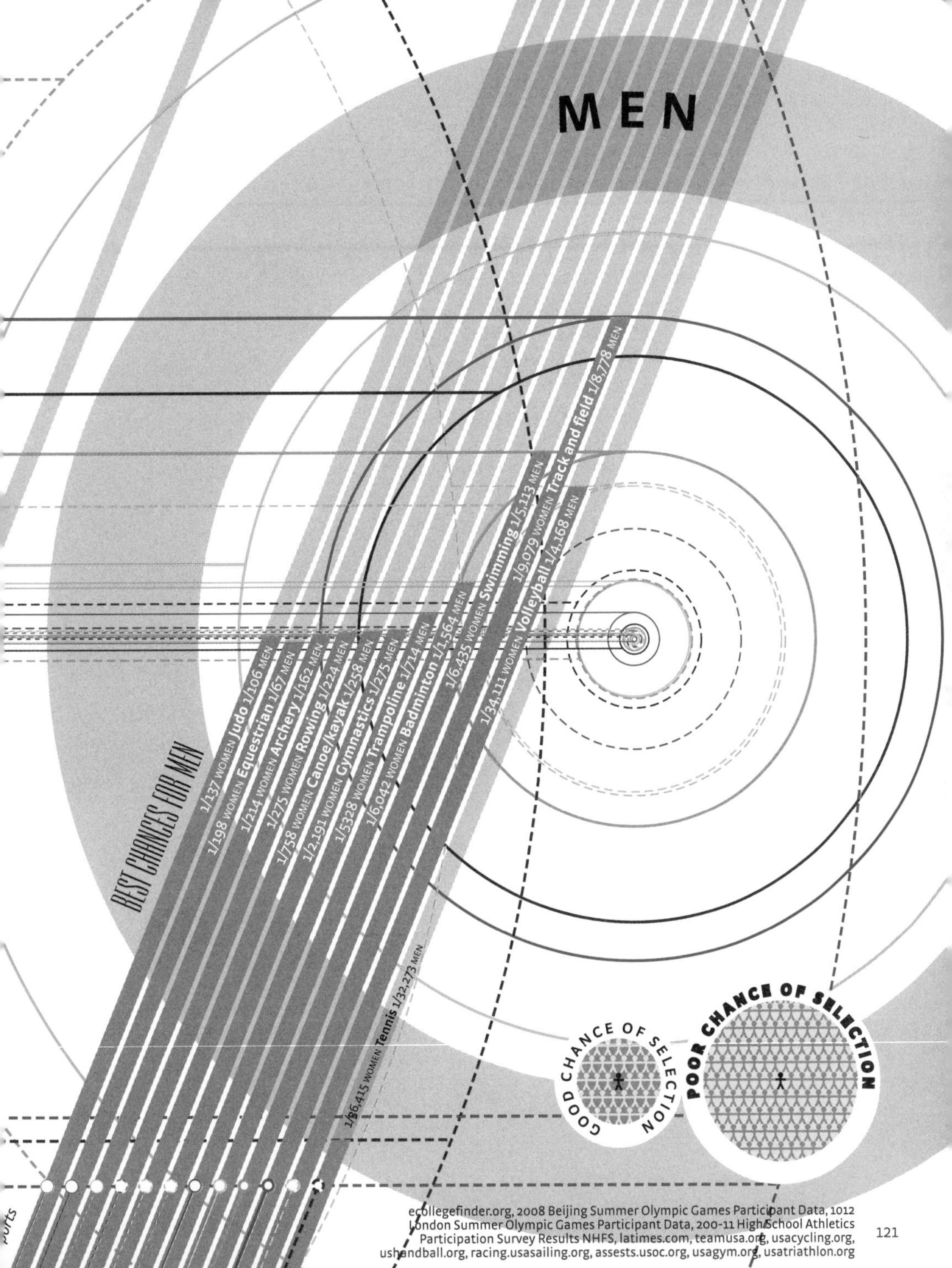
MEN
BEST CHANCES FOR MEN
1/137 WOMEN Judo 1/106 MEN
1/198 WOMEN Equestrian 1/67 MEN
1/214 WOMEN Archery 1/162 MEN
1/275 WOMEN Rowing 1/224 MEN
1/758 WOMEN Canoe/kayak 1/258 MEN
1/2,191 WOMEN Gymnastics 1/275 MEN
1/5328 WOMEN Trampoline 1/714 MEN
1/6,042 WOMEN Badminton 1/1,564 MEN
1/6,435 WOMEN Swimming 1/5,113 MEN
1/34,111 WOMEN Volleyball 1/4,168 MEN
1/9,079 WOMEN Track and field 1/8,778 MEN
1/36,415 WOMEN Tennis 1/32,273 MEN
GOOD CHANCE OF SELECTION
POOR CHANCE OF SELECTION
ecollegefinder.org, 2008 Beijing Summer Olympic Games Participant Data, 1012 London Summer Olympic Games Participant Data, 200-11 High School Athletics Participation Survey Results NHFS, latimes.com, teamusa.org, usacycling.org, ushandball.org, racing.usasailing.org, assests.usoc.org, usagym.org, usatriathlon.org

THEY **DIED** TRYING

Excluding truly dangerous sports that require engines and weapons, the roll of honor for professional competitors who have died while in action is depressingly long. High among the causes of death for these fifteen most popular sports are heart attacks, closely followed by head injuries.

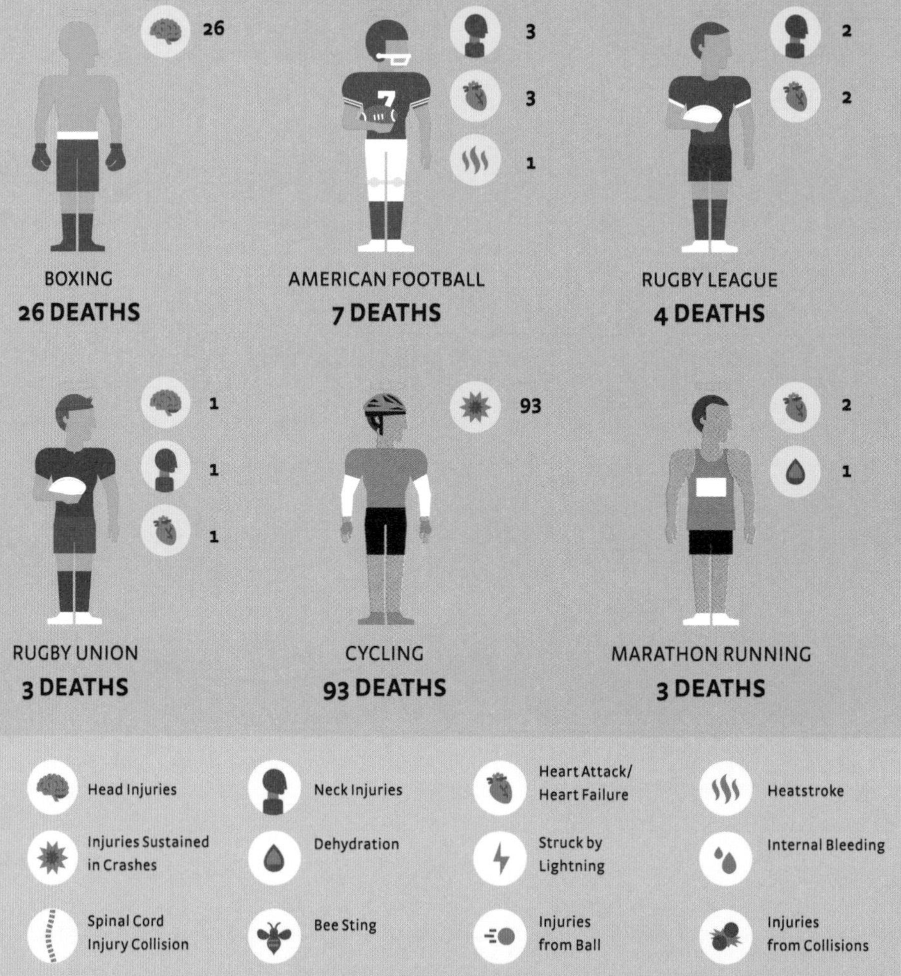

26
3
3
1
2
2
BOXING
26 DEATHS
AMERICAN FOOTBALL
7 DEATHS
RUGBY LEAGUE
4 DEATHS
1
1
1
93
2
1
RUGBY UNION
3 DEATHS
CYCLING
93 DEATHS
MARATHON RUNNING
3 DEATHS
Head Injuries
Neck Injuries
Heart Attack/ Heart Failure
Heatstroke
Injuries Sustained in Crashes
Dehydration
Struck by Lightning
Internal Bleeding
Spinal Cord Injury Collision
Bee Sting
Injuries from Ball
Injuries from Collisions

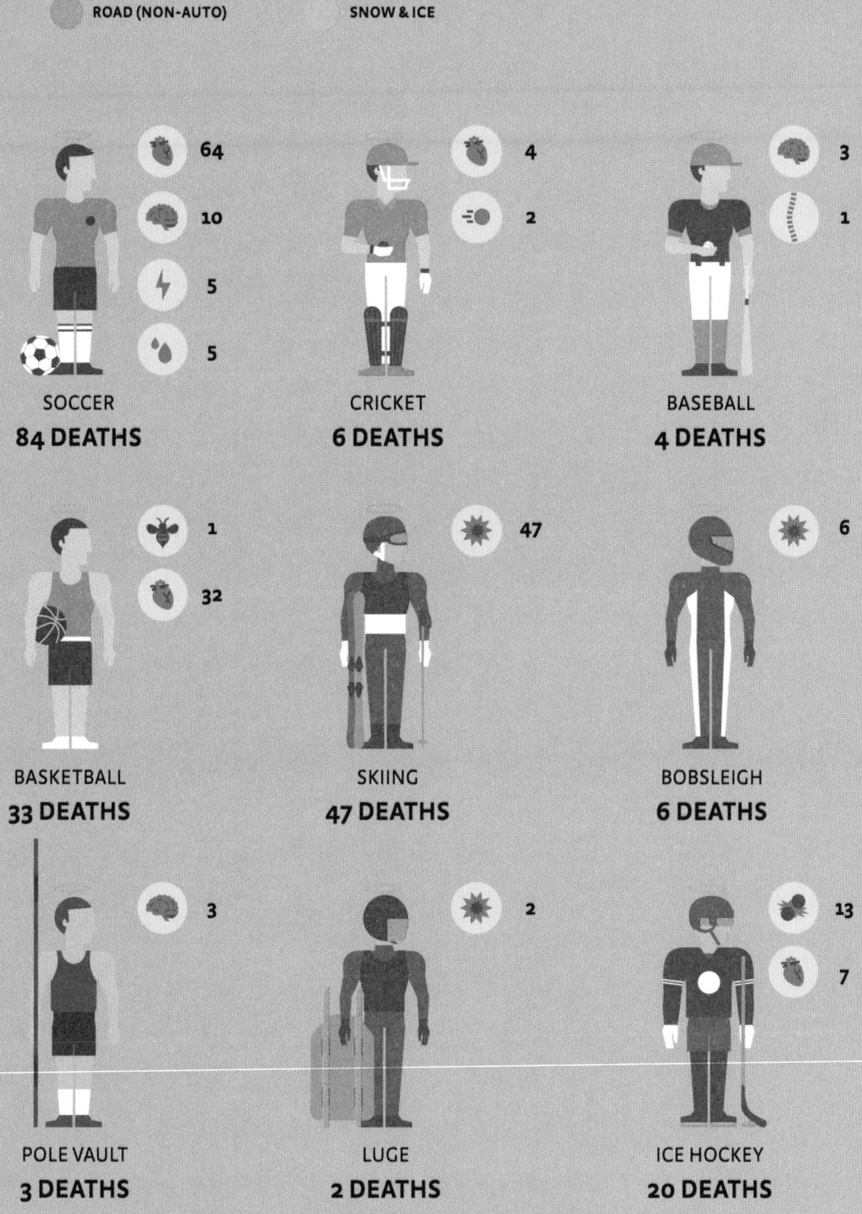

CONTACT SPORTS
BALL GAMES
TRACK AND FIELD
ROAD (NON-AUTO)
SNOW & ICE
64
10
5
5
SOCCER
84 DEATHS
4
2
CRICKET
6 DEATHS
3
1
BASEBALL
4 DEATHS
1
32
BASKETBALL
33 DEATHS
47
SKIING
47 DEATHS
6
BOBSLEIGH
6 DEATHS
3
POLE VAULT
3 DEATHS
2
LUGE
2 DEATHS
13
7
ICE HOCKEY
20 DEATHS

LOCATION

Frozen Head State Park, TN, USA
Death Valley CA, USA
France, Italy, Switzerland
Honolulu, Hawaii, USA
Sahara Desert, Morocco, Africa

Badwater Ultramarathon
120°F/49°C

48hrs

Marathon des Sables
100°F/37.7°C
6 days

Hawaiian Iron Man Triathlon
82–95°F/27.7–35°C
17hrs

Ultra-Trail du Mont Blanc
32.3–84°F/-0.2–29°C

46hrs

Dachhiri Dawa Sherpa (Nepal)
***20hr 5min,** 2003*

Barkley Marathons
25-68°F/-3–20°C

60hrs

Brett Maune (US)
***52:03:08,** 2012*

TEMPERATURE

DISTANCE

3.8 km *2.4 miles*	**160 km** *100 miles*	**166 km** *103 miles*

MADE OF **IRON**

Forget the mere marathon, these are the hardest, longest, toughest and most testing events in any runner's life – Iron Man and Ultra events can break the hardest athlete. These five have proven too extreme for all but the strongest and most persistent to complete. But those who finish, do it in incredible times.

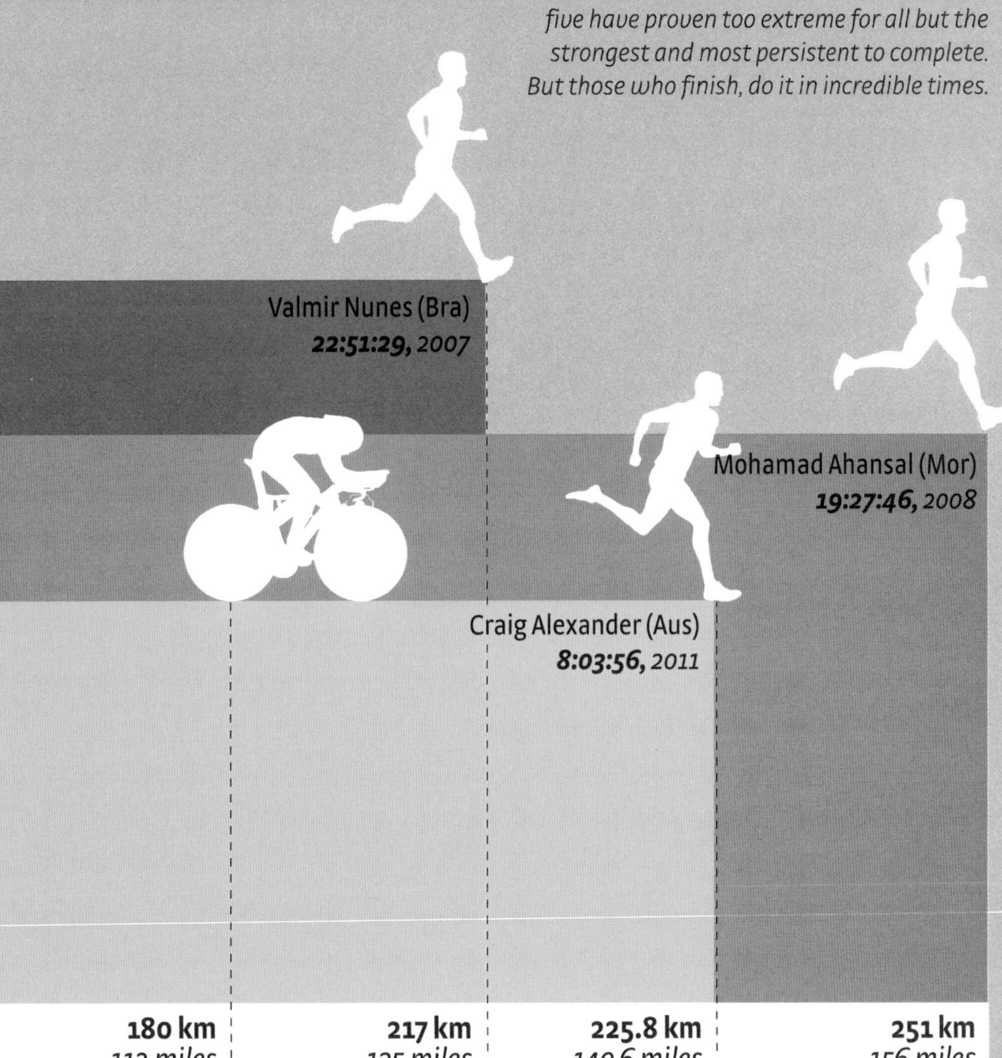

Valmir Nunes (Bra)
22:51:29, 2007
Mohamad Ahansal (Mor)
19:27:46, 2008
Craig Alexander (Aus)
8:03:56, 2011
180 km
112 miles
217 km
135 miles
225.8 km
140.6 miles
251 km
156 miles

news.discovery.com, wikipedia.org, darabound.com, badwater.com, mattmahoney.net, ultratrailmb.com, ironman.com

FISHING FOR **FINGERS**

Here we calculate the winning catches at the World Freshwater Fishing Championships from 1994 to 2013 as fish fingers caught per hour (ffph). The quantity of fish fingers is based on 28g/1oz fingers, with 58 %, i.e. 6.24g/0.570z of fish per finger. The World Championship format is for two 4-hour sessions on consecutive days.

YEAR	CHAMPION ANGLER	COUNTRY
1994	Bob Nudd	England
1995	Jean	France
1996	Alan Scotthorne	England
1997	Alan Scotthorne	England
1998	Alan Scotthorne	England
1999	Bob Nudd	England
2000	Iocopo Falsini	Italy
2001	Umberto Ballabeni	Italy
2002	Juan Blaso	Spain
2003	Alan Scotthorne	England
2004	Tamas Walter	Hungary
2005	Guido Nullens	Belgium
2006	Tamas Walter	Hungary
2007	Alan Scotthorne	England
2008	Will Raison	England
2009	Igor Potapov	Russia
2010	Frank Meis	Luxembourg
2011	Andrea Fini	Italy
2012	Sean Ashby	England
2013	Didier Delannoy	France

ANGLERS WITH THE MOST WINS

ALAN SCOTTHORNE (ENGLAND)
Most wins: 5
Years : 1996, 97, 98, 2003, 07
Average catch ffph: 87

BOB NUDD (ENGLAND)
Most wins: 2
Years : 1994, 99
Average catch ffph: 238

TAMAS WALTER (HUNGARY)
Most wins: 2
Years : 2004, 06
Average catch ffph: 75.5

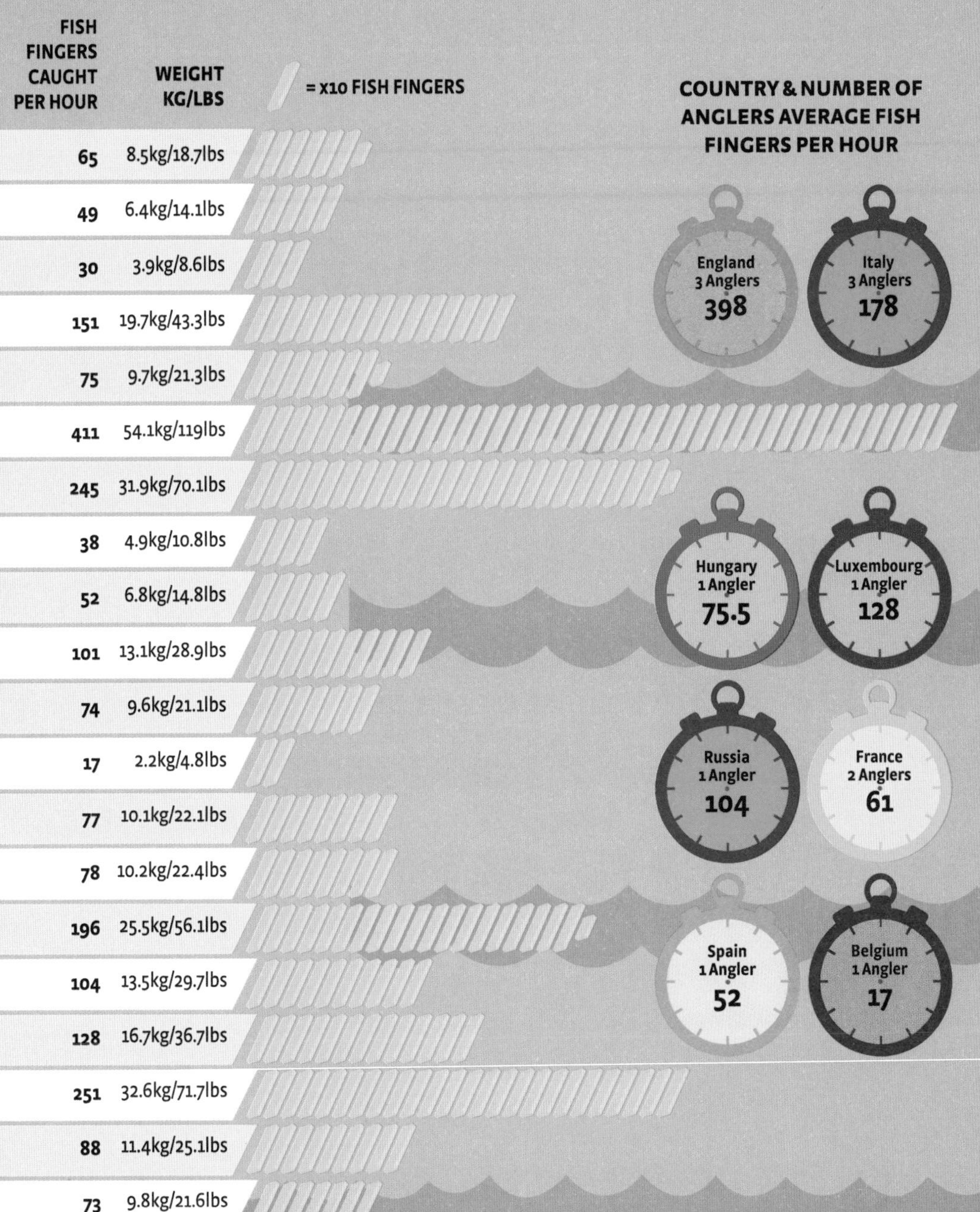

FISH FINGERS CAUGHT PER HOUR
WEIGHT KG/LBS
= x10 FISH FINGERS
65 8.5kg/18.7lbs
49 6.4kg/14.1lbs
30 3.9kg/8.6lbs
151 19.7kg/43.3lbs
75 9.7kg/21.3lbs
411 54.1kg/119lbs
245 31.9kg/70.1lbs
38 4.9kg/10.8lbs
52 6.8kg/14.8lbs
101 13.1kg/28.9lbs
74 9.6kg/21.1lbs
17 2.2kg/4.8lbs
77 10.1kg/22.1lbs
78 10.2kg/22.4lbs
196 25.5kg/56.1lbs
104 13.5kg/29.7lbs
128 16.7kg/36.7lbs
251 32.6kg/71.7lbs
88 11.4kg/25.1lbs
73 9.8kg/21.6lbs
COUNTRY & NUMBER OF ANGLERS AVERAGE FISH FINGERS PER HOUR
England 3 Anglers 398
Italy 3 Anglers 178
Hungary 1 Angler 75.5
Luxembourg 1 Angler 128
Russia 1 Angler 104
France 2 Anglers 61
Spain 1 Angler 52
Belgium 1 Angler 17

wikipedia.org, angling-news.co.uk, worldfishing2013.org

GUNS AND **ARROWS**

Comparing the world champion in archery (who is legally blind and has 10% vision), the world champion darts player and the two champion riflemen, we get a percentage view of who's more eagle-eyed.

6cm/2.3in
(the Bullseye)

70m/229ft

2.59cm²/1in²
(treble-20)

20
1
18
4
13
6
10
15
2
17
3
19
7
16
8
11
14
9
12
5

2.369m/7ft 7in

PHIL TAYLOR
2002 World Championship

IM DONG-HYUN
2012 Olympics

Only four shooters, the different targets are a dart board, an archery target, a gun target and clay pigeons.

Avg score as % of max

Darts	*62*
Archery	*97*
Shooting	*98*
Clay Pigeon shoot	*94*

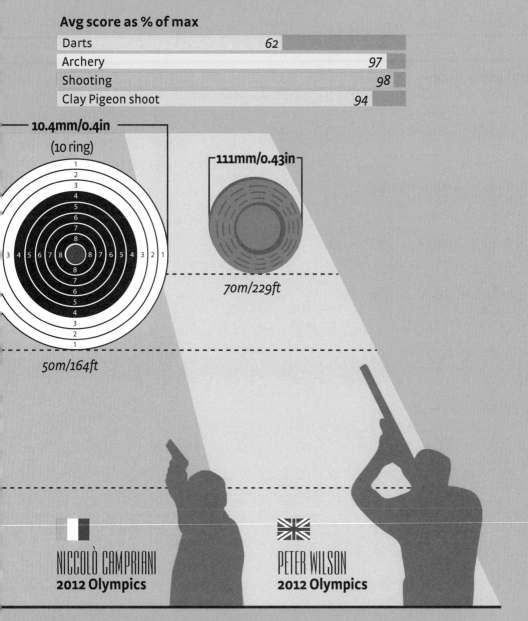

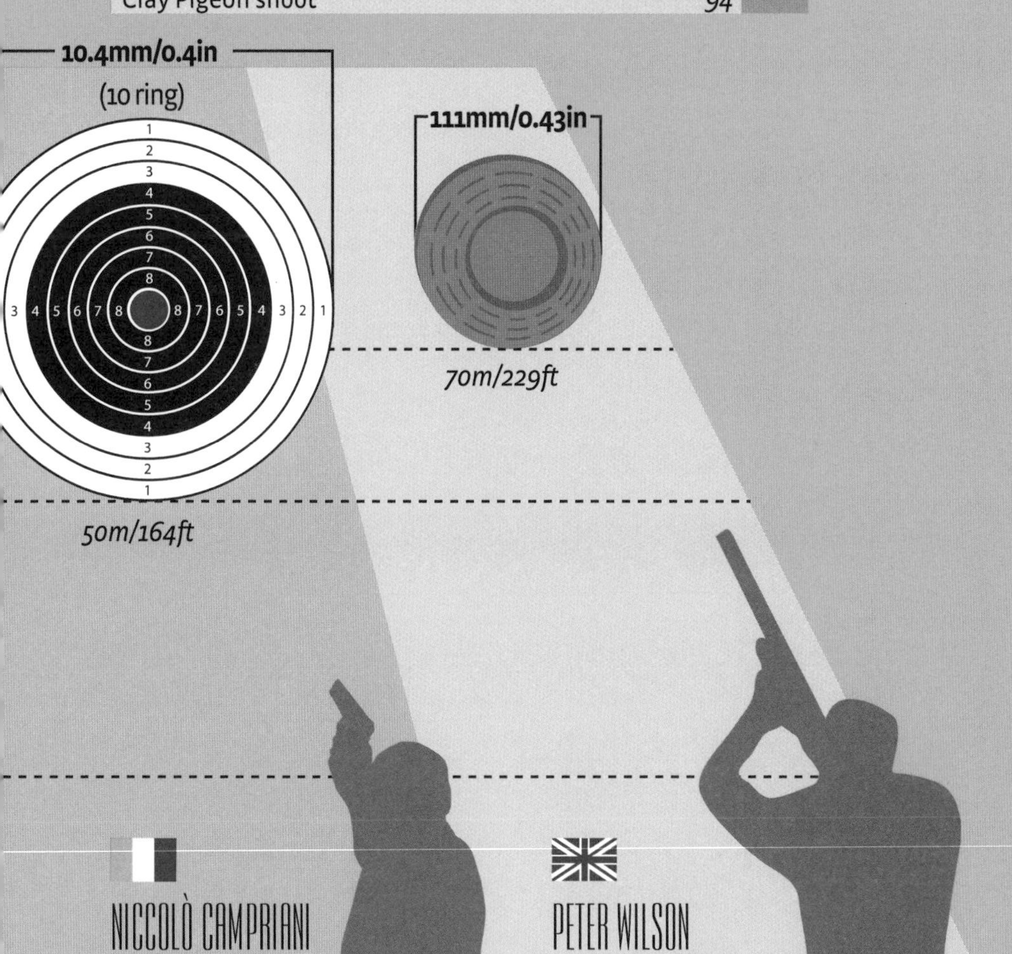

10.4mm/0.4in
(10 ring)
111mm/0.43in
70m/229ft
50m/164ft
NICCOLÒ CAMPRIANI
2012 Olympics
PETER WILSON
2012 Olympics

wikipedia.org, darting.com, sizes.com

WELL **BELOW PAR**

All golfers aspire to play as well as Tiger, Nicklaus or Mickelson because of their consistently excellent play. Few golfers would expect for seasoned pros to play as badly as the average amateur putter. But occasionally, even the greats get the game very wrong, as these stats show.

HIGHEST OVER PAR SHOT FOR A SINGLE HOLE

PLAYER	PAR		SHOTS OVER	HOLE
TOMMY ARMOUR	5	*Shawnee US Open 1927*	23	
RAY AINSLEY	4	*Cherry Hills US Open 1938*	19	
HANS MERRELL	3	*Bing Crosby Pro-Am Cypress Point 1959*	19	16
MITSUHIRO TATEYAMA	3	*Acom International, Ishioka 2006*	19	8
JOHN DALY	5	*Bay Hills Invitational 1998*	18	6
GARY MCCORD	5	*FedEx St. Jude Classic, Memphis 1986*	16	16
KEVIN NA	4	*TPC San Antonio 2011*	16	9
PORKY OLIVER	3	*Bing Crosby Pro-Am, Cypress Point 1953*	16	16
ED DOUGHERTY	4	*AT&T Pebble Beach National Pro-Am 1990*	14	17
JOHN DALY	5	*US Open, Pebble Beach 2000*	14	18
TOM WEISKOPF	3	*Augusta National 1980*	13	12
TOMMY NAKAJIMA	5	*Masters, Augusta 1978*	13	13

WORST ROUND OF GOLF PLAYED BY A PROFESSIONAL

PLAYER	WORST ROUND		SHOTS OVER
MIKE REASOR	237	**FOUR QUALIFYING ROUNDS** *Tallahassee Open, FL, USA 1974*	93
MAURICE FLITCROFT	121	*Royal Birkdale, Southport, England 1976*	51
DIANA LUNA	95	*Royal Lytham & St Annes, England 2003*	23
TIGER WOODS	298	**FULL TOURNAMENT SCORE** *Bridgestone Invitational, Akron, OH, USA 2010*	18
JACK NICKLAUS	83	*Sandwich, Kent, England 1981*	13
JACK NICKLAUS	85	*Augusta, USA 2003*	13
JOHN DALY	85	*Bay Hill, USA 1998*	13
KARRIE WEBB	83	*Pine Needles, USA 2007*	12
NANCY LOPEZ	83	*Blackwolf Run, USA 1998*	12
MICHELLE WIE	83	*Locust Hill 2012*	10
TIGER WOODS	81	*Muirfield, Scotland 2002*	10
PHIL MICKELSON	78	*Oak Hill, USA 2013*	8
MICKEY WRIGHT	80	*Baltusrol, USA 1961*	8
RORY MCILROY	79	*Muirfield, Scotland 2013*	7

golf.about.com, edition.cnn.com, wikipedia.org, espn.go.com, golf.com

EAT, PRAY, **EXERCISE**

In America, the land of choice, there are so many things to occupy time that could otherwise be spent keeping fit. Which might be why more than 313,000 Americans had liposuction in one year. Here's what Americans do instead of going to the gym.

	attendance 1 or more times a week	% US population	# practitioners in USA
Gym/healthclub	32.8m	10.5	personal trainers 231,500
Church	118m	37	pastors 600,000
Shopping mall	46.7m (shop to ease stress)	18	life coaches 15,800
McDonald's restaurant	136.8m	44	McDonald's branches 14,000
Cinema	27m	8	screens 39,918
Psychotherapist	22m	7	psychologists 85,000
TV room (NCIS)	21m	6.75	TV sets 114.7m
The outdoors	35.5m	11.5	state park sites 6,600

lhrsa.org, ptdirect.com, apa.org, mpaa.org, wikipedia.org

FULL HOUSE

If sport was played in stadiums without a crowd the results would still stand, but something would be missing. It appears that some sports bodies planned on getting enormous numbers at events, but rarely are they filled to capacity.

under capacity

over capacity

MARACANA

Built **1950**
Where **Brazil**
Sport **Soccer**

Record **199,854**
When **07/16/50**
World Cup Final

Capacity **200,000**
Capacity in 2014 **78,838**

HOLMENKOLLBAKKEN

Built **1892** Where **Norway** Sport **Ski-jumping**

Record **143,000**
When **1952, Olympic Games**

Capacity **150,000**

INDIANAPOLIS MOTOR SPEEDWAY

Built **1909**
Where **USA**
Sport **Speedway**
Capacity **250,000**

Record **350,000**
When **2007, US Grand Prix**

TOKYO RACECOURSE

Built **1933**
Where **Japan**
Sport **Horse racing**

Record **196,517**
When **05/27/90**

BADMINTON HOUSE PARK

Capacity **223,000**

Built **1612**
Where **England**
Sport **Eventing**

Record **175,000**
When **05/01/13**

Capacity **200,000**

indianapolismotorspeedway.com, tokyoracecourse.com, badminton-horse.co.uk, stadiumguide.com/maracana, holmenkollen.com, avstadiums.com

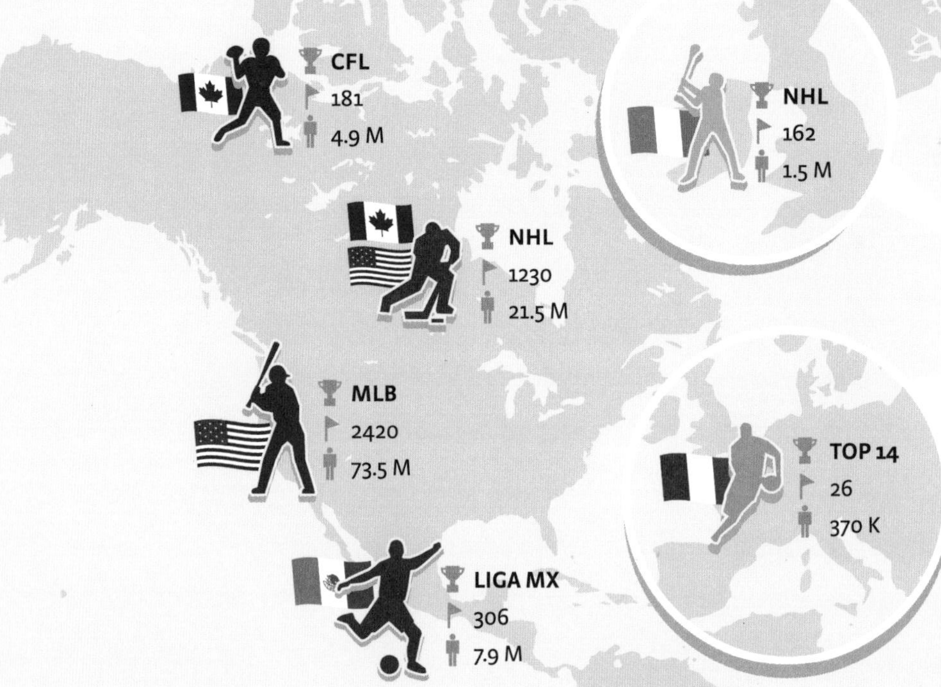
CFL
181
4.9 M
NHL
162
1.5 M
NHL
1230
21.5 M
MLB
2420
73.5 M
TOP 14
26
370 K
LIGA MX
306
7.9 M

TAKE ME OUT TO **THE BALLGAME**

Soccer is the most popular attendance sport in many countries around the world, but there are also impressive numbers of people who go to watch other games. Comparing the top five soccer leagues by attendance with other sporting competitions.

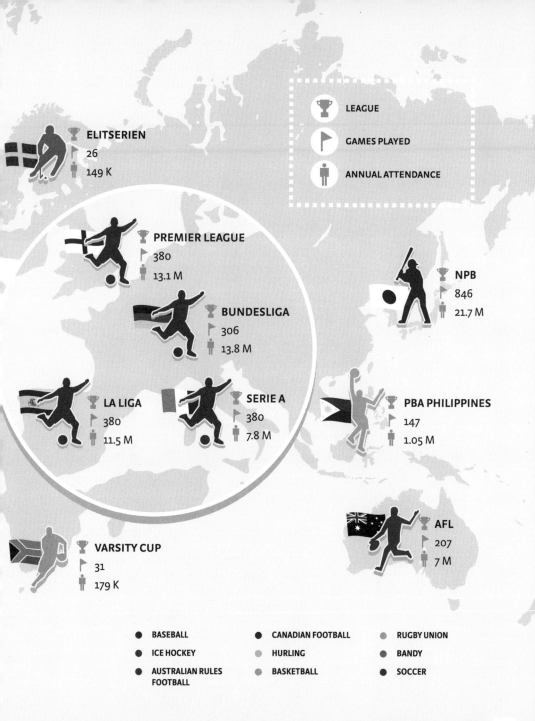

LEAGUE

GAMES PLAYED

ANNUAL ATTENDANCE

ELITSERIEN
26
149 K

PREMIER LEAGUE
380
13.1 M

BUNDESLIGA
306
13.8 M

NPB
846
21.7 M

LA LIGA
380
11.5 M

SERIE A
380
7.8 M

PBA PHILIPPINES
147
1.05 M

AFL
207
7 M

VARSITY CUP
31
179 K

- BASEBALL
- ICE HOCKEY
- AUSTRALIAN RULES FOOTBALL
- CANADIAN FOOTBALL
- HURLING
- BASKETBALL
- RUGBY UNION
- BANDY
- SOCCER

wikipedia.org, gaa.ie, stats.cfldb.ca

FORMULA FOR **WINNING F1**

The first Formula 1 autosport championship of the modern era was won by a 44-year-old Italian. Since then more than 30 drivers from 13 nations have won the title at different ages. Here's what the law of averages says about the optimum winners over the period 1950–2013.

3
Italy
2
USA
12
Germany
4
Austria
2
Spain
5
Australia
1
South Africa
8
Brazil
4
France
4
Finland
1
Canada
5
Argentina
14
UK
NUMBER OF DRIVERS
1
2
3
10
DRIVER'S COUNTRY
OF CHAMPIONSHIPS

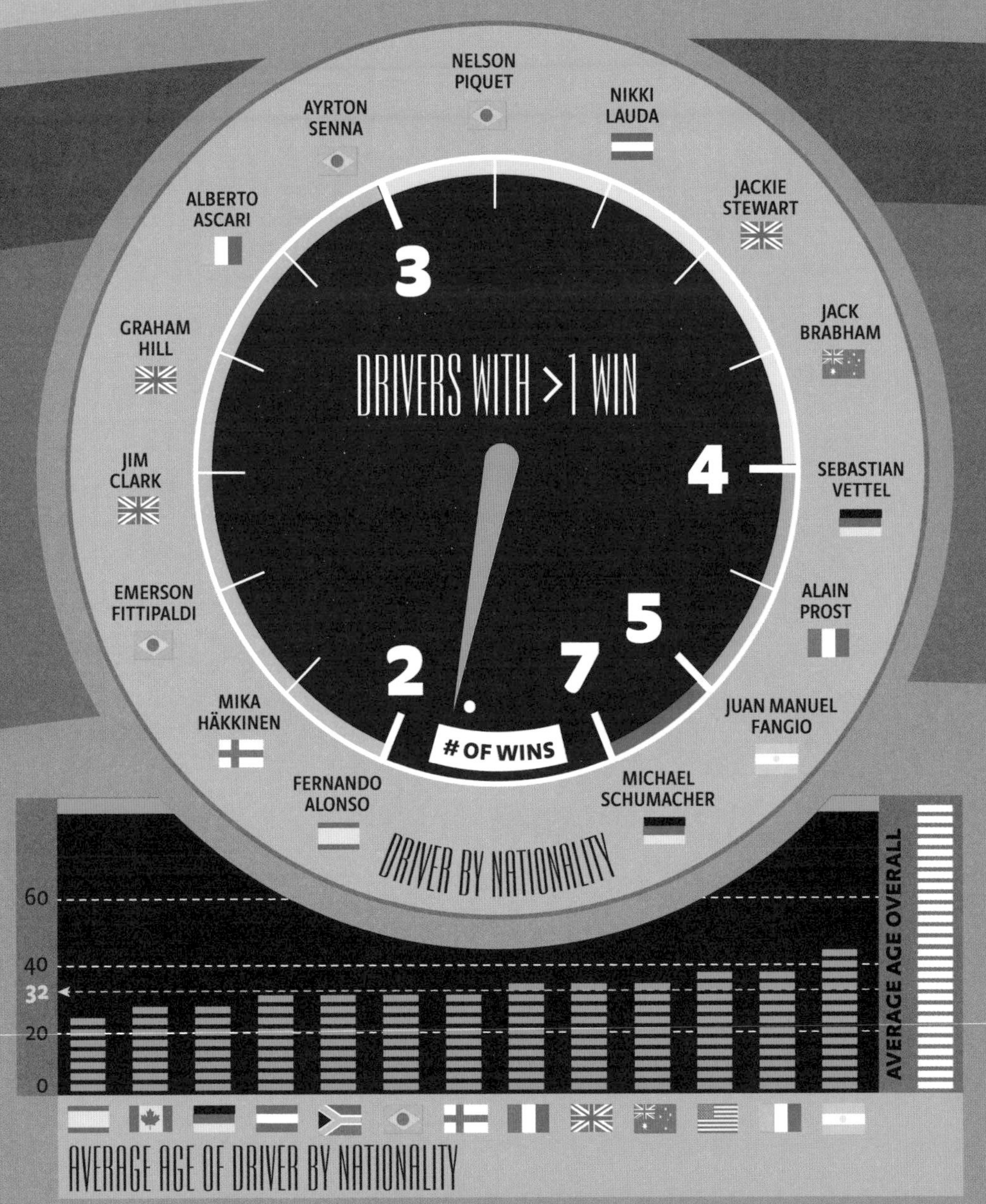

DRIVERS WITH >1 WIN
3
4
5
7
2
OF WINS
NELSON PIQUET
AYRTON SENNA
NIKKI LAUDA
ALBERTO ASCARI
JACKIE STEWART
GRAHAM HILL
JACK BRABHAM
JIM CLARK
SEBASTIAN VETTEL
EMERSON FITTIPALDI
ALAIN PROST
MIKA HÄKKINEN
JUAN MANUEL FANGIO
FERNANDO ALONSO
MICHAEL SCHUMACHER
DRIVER BY NATIONALITY
60
40
32
20
0
AVERAGE AGE OVERALL
AVERAGE AGE OF DRIVER BY NATIONALITY

DRESSAGE IS DIFFERENT FOR GIRLS

The individual dressage event at the Olympics has been a constant since 1912, but women were not allowed to compete until 1952 – when Denmark's Lise Hartel won silver. She did the same the next year, too. From 1972 on women have dominated the event's medal board, as these statistics show.

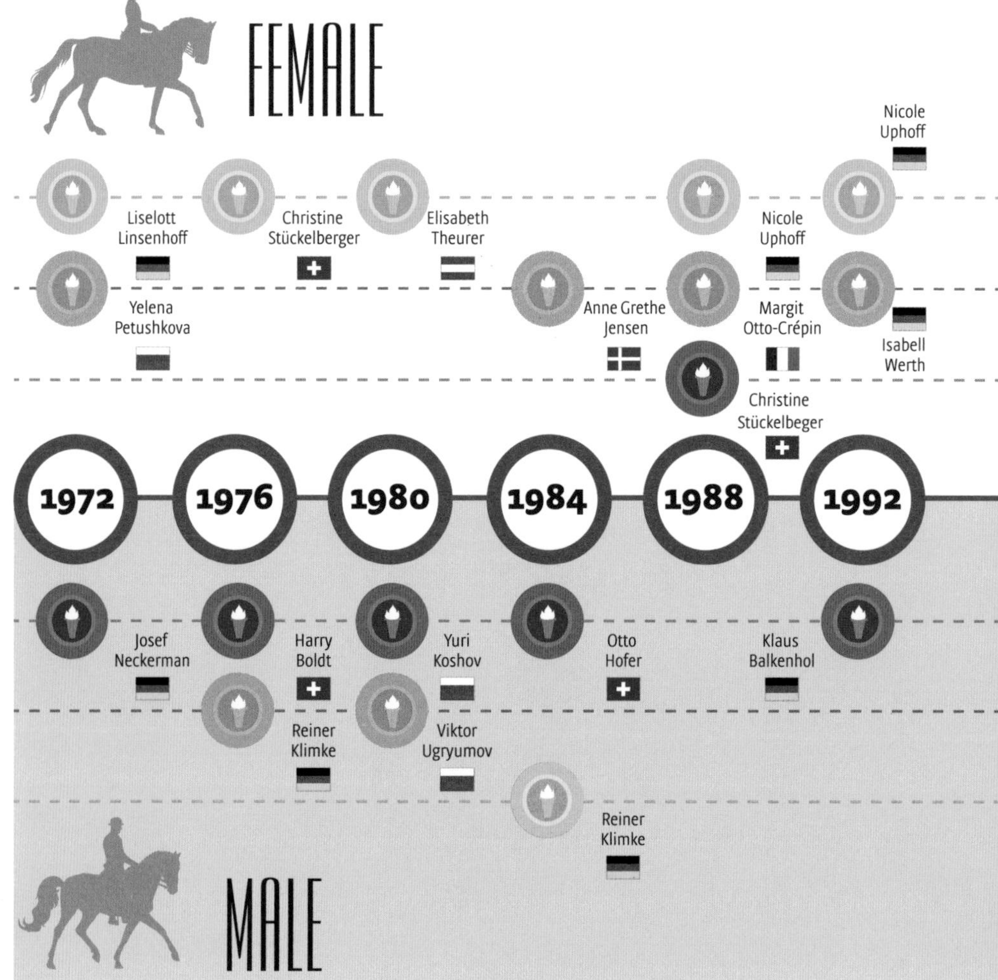

FEMALE
Liselott Linsenhoff
Yelena Petushkova
Christine Stückelberger
Elisabeth Theurer
Anne Grethe Jensen
Nicole Uphoff
Margit Otto-Crépin
Christine Stückelbeger
Nicole Uphoff
Isabell Werth
1972
1976
1980
1984
1988
1992
Josef Neckerman
Harry Boldt
Reiner Klimke
Yuri Koshov
Viktor Ugryumov
Otto Hofer
Reiner Klimke
Klaus Balkenhol
MALE

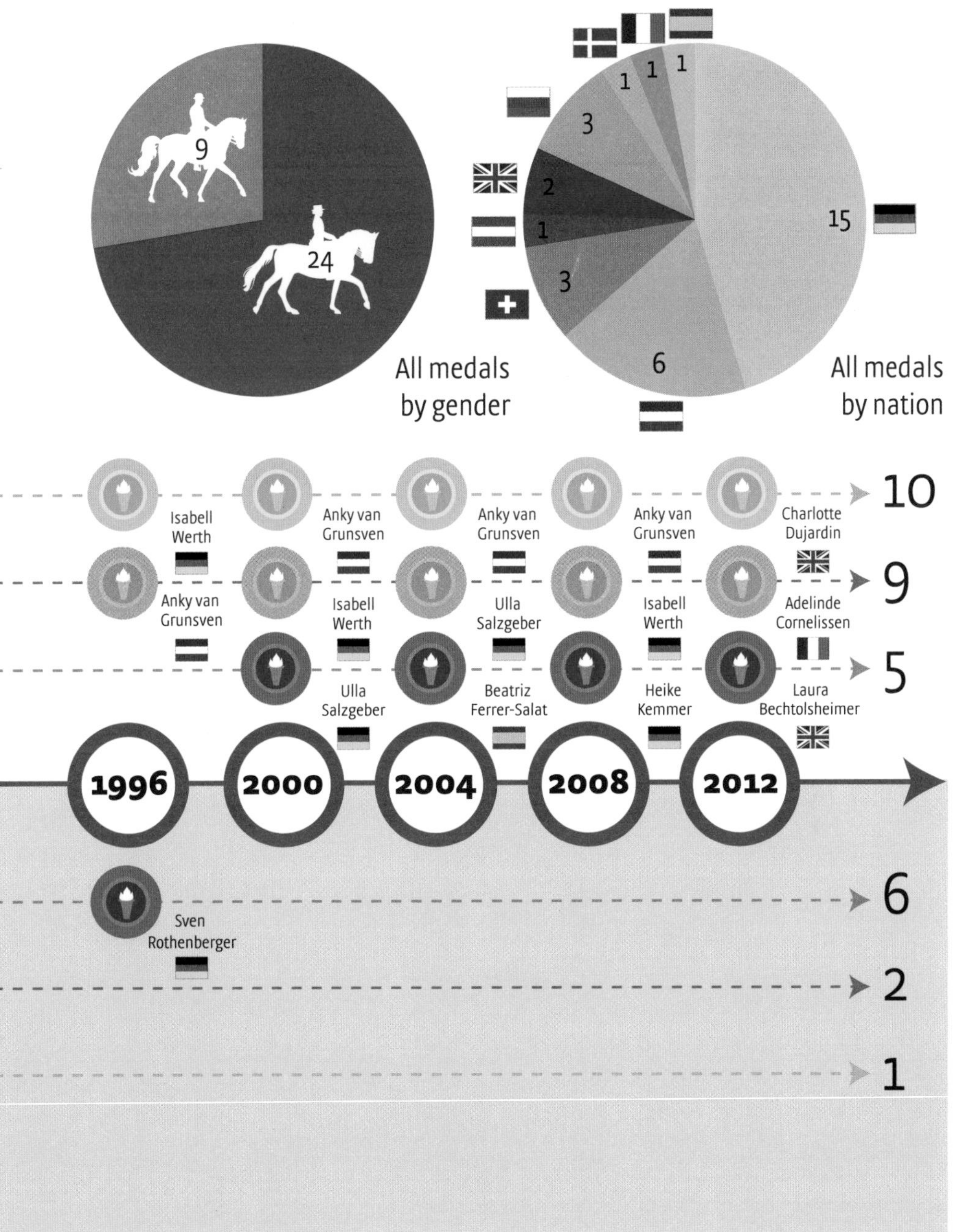

9
24
All medals
by gender
1
1
1
3
2
1
3
6
15
All medals
by nation
10
9
5
Isabell
Werth
Anky van
Grunsven
Anky van
Grunsven
Isabell
Werth
Ulla
Salzgeber
Anky van
Grunsven
Ulla
Salzgeber
Beatriz
Ferrer-Salat
Anky van
Grunsven
Isabell
Werth
Heike
Kemmer
Charlotte
Dujardin
Adelinde
Cornelissen
Laura
Bechtolsheimer
1996
2000
2004
2008
2012
6
Sven
Rothenberger
2
1

THE GOOD OLD, **BAD OLD DAYS**

There's a tendency among old-time sports fans to tut and claim that cheating along the lines of that so stupendously carried out by Lance Armstrong, enabling him to win 6 consecutive Tour De France, never happened in 'their day'. Oh really?

SOX

1904 — CYCLING

Tour De France Hipployte Aucouturier – towed by a car via wire to cork in mouth, won four stages.

1904 — MARATHON

The St Louis Olympics Marathon winner Fred Lorz – drove 11 of the 26 miles.

1919 — BASEBALL

Eight members of the Chicago White Sox team threw the World Series final.

1932 & 1936 — 100M SPRINT

Stella Walasiewicz: 2x gold women's 100m sprint 1932 Olympics, silver 1936, set 18 world records. Revealed to be male after death.

1936 — HIGH JUMP

German women's high jumper Dora Ratjen came 4th at 1936 Olympics. Her real name was Herman, and she was a he.

1951 — BASKETBALL

Over 30 players from seven different colleges (including City College of New York) found guilty of fixing basketball games for the Mafia.

FINISH

1968 — SAILING

Donald Crowhurst radioed fake progress reports during a round the world yacht race to show he was leading. Actual leader (Nigel Tetley) forced to retire. Crowhurst disappeared.

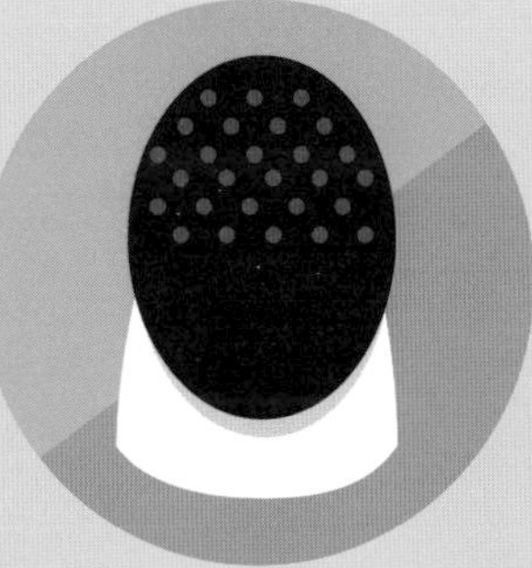

1976 — FENCING

At the Montreal Olympics Ukraine pentathlete Boris Onischenko wired his sword to show a hit when there had been none.

1980 — MARATHON

Rosie Ruiz, female winner of the Boston marathon in record time, spent most of it hiding in the crowd, emerging ahead of the pack near the finishing line.

1983 — BOXING

Boxing trainer Panama Lewis removed stuffing from his boxer's gloves, soaked his hand bandages in plaster of Paris and left the opponent almost blinded.

1985 — GOLF

Scottish golfer David Robertson fined £20,000 and banned for 20 years after repeatedly moving his ball closer to the green during the Open in Kent.

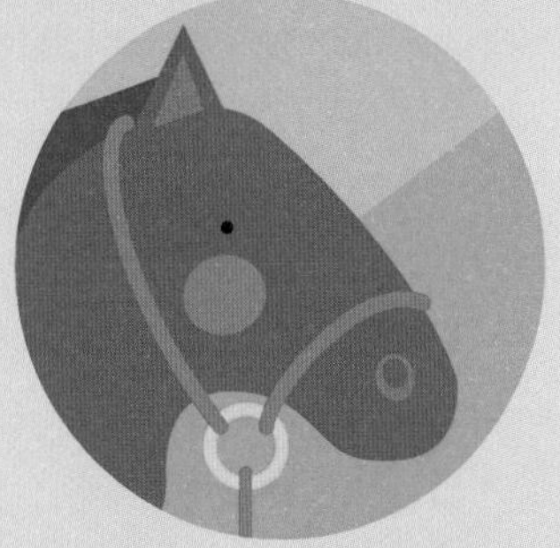

1990 — HORSE RACING

Jockey Sylvester Carmouche pulled his horse up when out of sight of the grandstand at the fog-bound Louisiana Delta Downs track, and re-started to break the course record and 'win'.

soccerlens.com, telegraph.co.uk, cracked.com

DEGREES OF SEPARATION: **MARIA SHARAPOVA**

Siberian-born tennis star Maria Sharapova is one of the world's most famous – and most Googled – sportswomen. Her four Grand Slam successes and 6 foot-two physique have earned her multiple endorsements and won her millions of fans. Her interests and contacts extend far beyond tennis, though, as this graphic demonstrates.

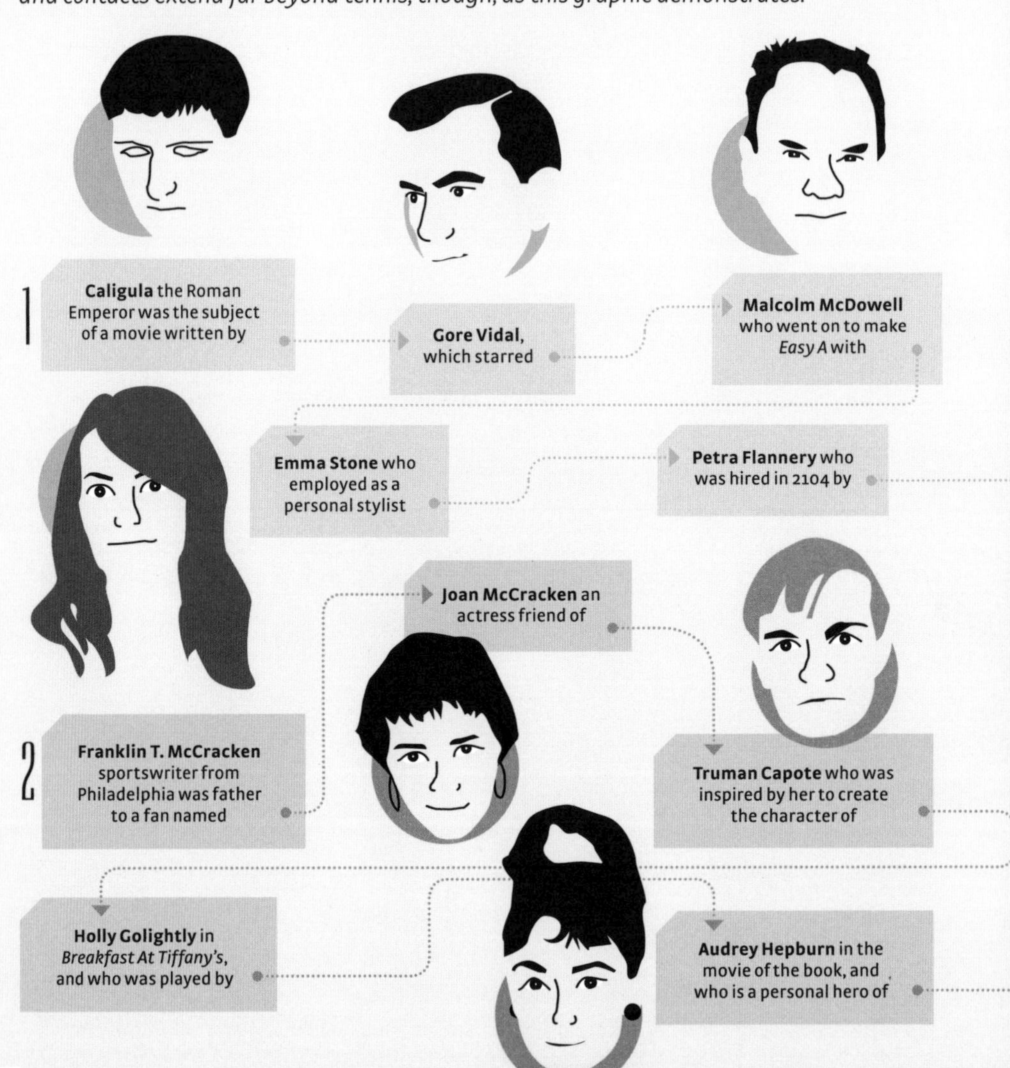

1
Caligula the Roman Emperor was the subject of a movie written by
Gore Vidal, which starred
Malcolm McDowell who went on to make *Easy A* with
Emma Stone who employed as a personal stylist
Petra Flannery who was hired in 2104 by
2
Franklin T. McCracken sportswriter from Philadelphia was father to a fan named
Joan McCracken an actress friend of
Truman Capote who was inspired by her to create the character of
Holly Golightly in *Breakfast At Tiffany's*, and who was played by
Audrey Hepburn in the movie of the book, and who is a personal hero of

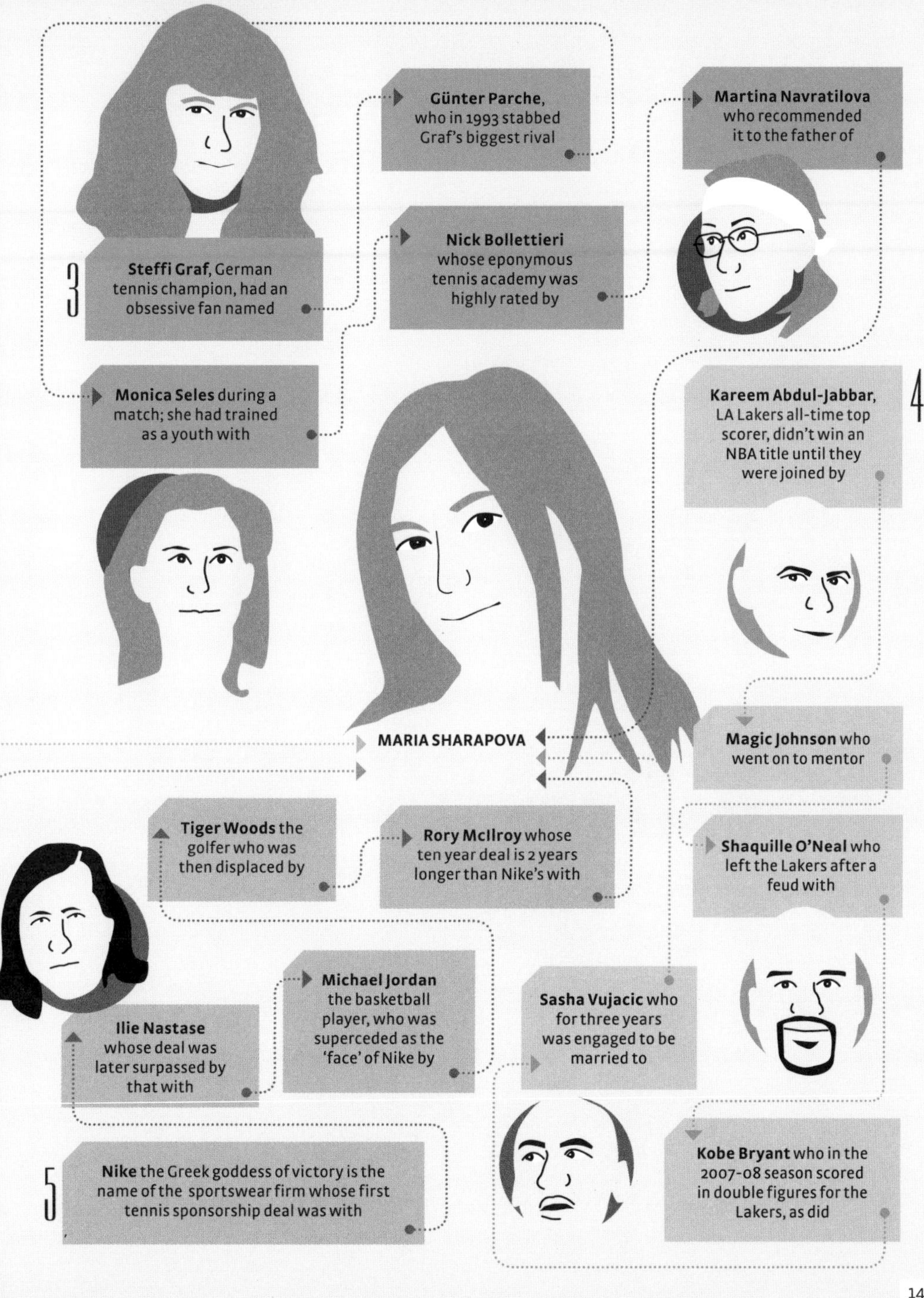

Günter Parche, who in 1993 stabbed Graf's biggest rival
Martina Navratilova who recommended it to the father of
Nick Bollettieri whose eponymous tennis academy was highly rated by
3 Steffi Graf, German tennis champion, had an obsessive fan named
Monica Seles during a match; she had trained as a youth with
4 Kareem Abdul-Jabbar, LA Lakers all-time top scorer, didn't win an NBA title until they were joined by
MARIA SHARAPOVA
Magic Johnson who went on to mentor
Tiger Woods the golfer who was then displaced by
Rory McIlroy whose ten year deal is 2 years longer than Nike's with
Shaquille O'Neal who left the Lakers after a feud with
Michael Jordan the basketball player, who was superceded as the 'face' of Nike by
Sasha Vujacic who for three years was engaged to be married to
Ilie Nastase whose deal was later surpassed by that with
5 Nike the Greek goddess of victory is the name of the sportswear firm whose first tennis sponsorship deal was with
Kobe Bryant who in the 2007-08 season scored in double figures for the Lakers, as did

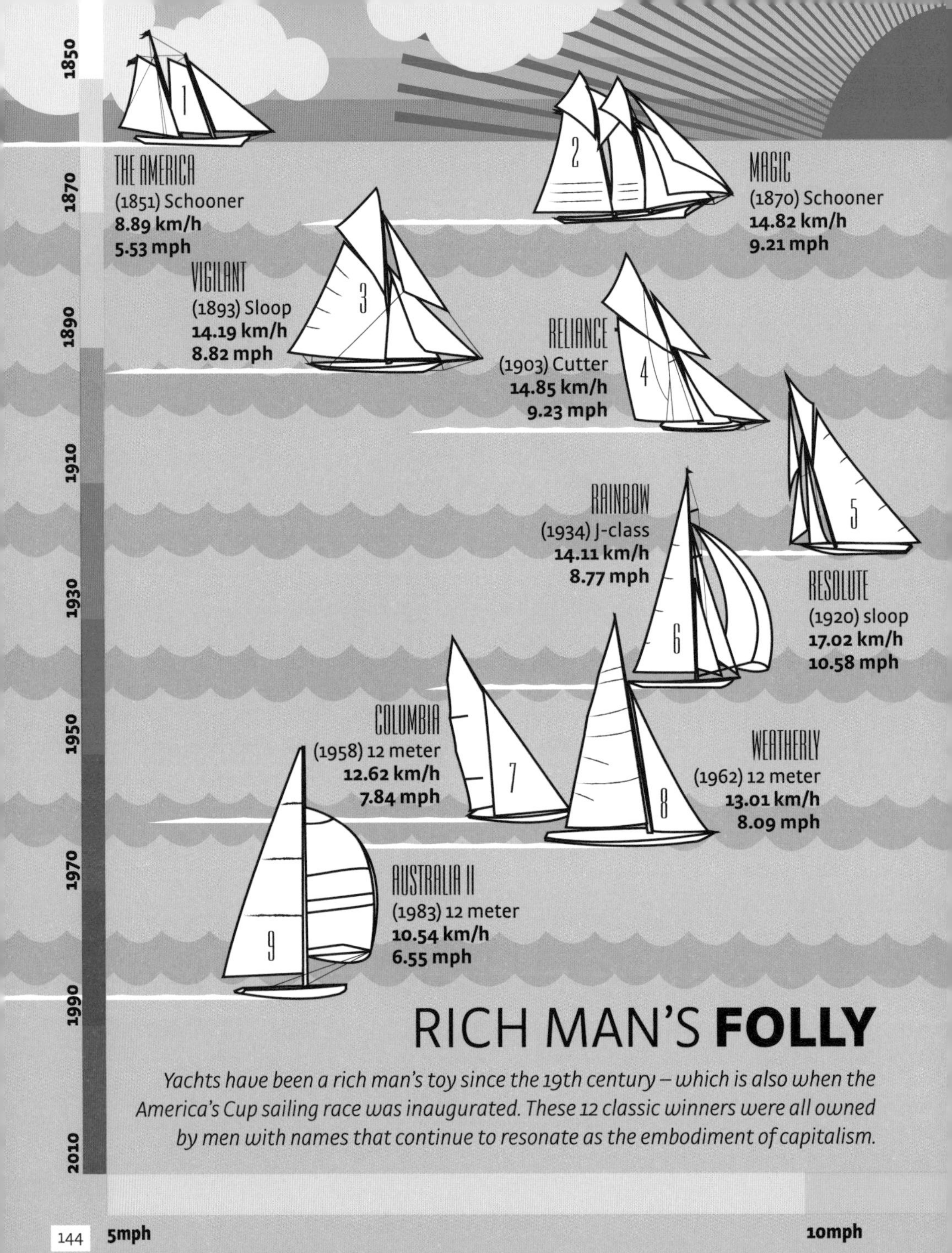

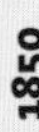

1850
1870
1890
1910
1930
1950
1970
1990
2010
1
THE AMERICA
(1851) Schooner
8.89 km/h
5.53 mph
2
MAGIC
(1870) Schooner
14.82 km/h
9.21 mph
3
VIGILANT
(1893) Sloop
14.19 km/h
8.82 mph
4
RELIANCE
(1903) Cutter
14.85 km/h
9.23 mph
5
RESOLUTE
(1920) sloop
17.02 km/h
10.58 mph
6
RAINBOW
(1934) J-class
14.11 km/h
8.77 mph
7
COLUMBIA
(1958) 12 meter
12.62 km/h
7.84 mph
8
WEATHERLY
(1962) 12 meter
13.01 km/h
8.09 mph
9
AUSTRALIA II
(1983) 12 meter
10.54 km/h
6.55 mph
5mph
10mph

RICH MAN'S **FOLLY**

Yachts have been a rich man's toy since the 19th century – which is also when the America's Cup sailing race was inaugurated. These 12 classic winners were all owned by men with names that continue to resonate as the embodiment of capitalism.

OWNER

1 Syndicate, led by **John Cox Stevens** (1785–1857), founder NY Yacht Club. Second place was 22 minutes behind.

2 **Franklin Osgood** (1826–1888), financier and mine owner. This winning boat was 13 years old.

3 Syndicate led by banker **Charles Oliver Iselin** (1854–1932). This was the first custom-built winner.

4 **William Rockefeller** (1841–1922), financier & oil magnate and **Cornelius Vanderbilt III** (1873– 1942), railway tycoon. This was the largest boat in the history of the race.

5 New York Yachting Club syndicate headed by **Henry Walters** (1848–1931), railway magnate and art collector. This boat broke the course record.

6 **Harold S. Vanderbilt** (1884–1970), shipping and railroad billionaire, plus 16 other millionaires. The first winner with aluminium hull.

7 Syndicate led by real estate owner and financier **Henry Sears** (1913–1982). This was the first race held since 1937.

8 Syndicate led by shipping millionaire **Henry D. Mercer** (1893–1974). The first Australian challenger.

9 **Alan Bond** (1938–), property, gold mining, brewing, TV, airship tycoon. The first non-American winner.

10 **Larry Ellison** (1944–), US software tycoon, fifth wealthiest man in world. The first winner to travel at twice speed of the wind.

11 **Larry Ellison** (1944–), US software tycoon, fifth wealthiest man in world. Reached a record top speed of 85 km/h (53mph).

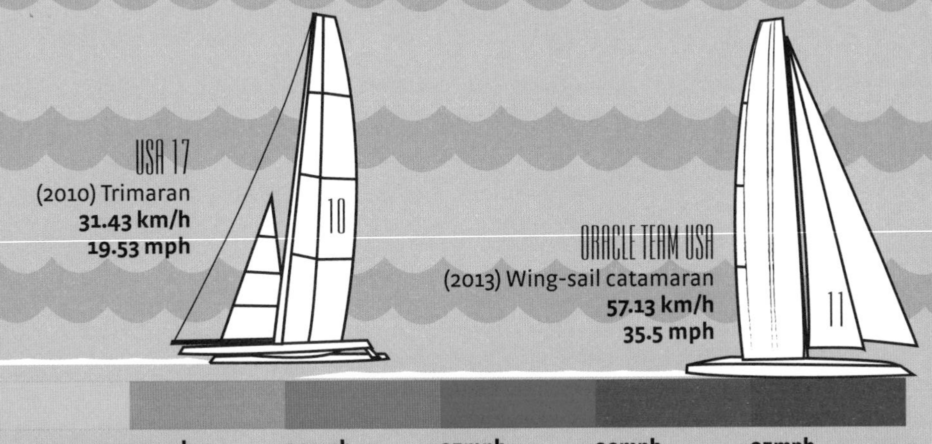
USA 17
(2010) Trimaran
31.43 km/h
19.53 mph
10
ORACLE TEAM USA
(2013) Wing-sail catamaran
57.13 km/h
35.5 mph
11
15mph
20mph
25mph
30mph
35mph

wikipedia.org

DAVID **BEATS** GOLIATH!

Sporting upsets are the stuff that dreams are made of. These examples of triumph of the unfancied underdog show why dreamers will always root for the small guy.

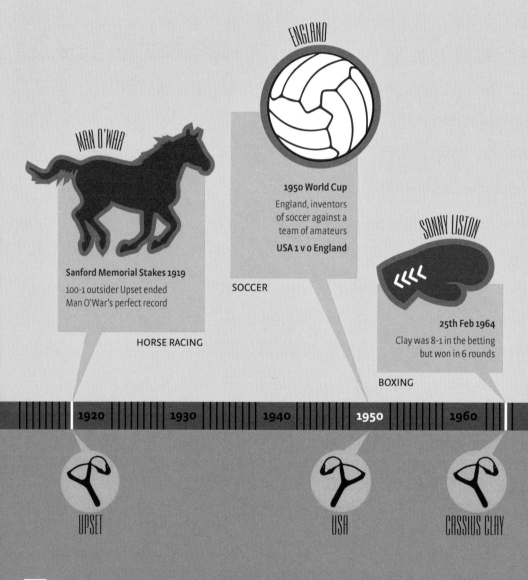

MAN O'WAR

Sanford Memorial Stakes 1919

100-1 outsider Upset ended Man O'War's perfect record

HORSE RACING

ENGLAND

1950 World Cup

England, inventors of soccer against a team of amateurs

USA 1 v 0 England

SOCCER

SONNY LISTON

25th Feb 1964

Clay was 8-1 in the betting but won in 6 rounds

BOXING

1920 1930 1940 1950 1960

UPSET

USA

CASSIUS CLAY

ARGENTINA

SOCCER

1990 World Cup

Argentina were the holders, Cameroon were in only their second finals and had not won a game the first time

Argentina 0 v 1 Cameroon

ALEKSANDR KARELIN

2000 Olympic Final

Gardner was the first man to beat the 3 x Olympic gold medalist in 13 years

WRESTLING

MIKE TYSON

1990 World Heavyweight Championship

Douglas was 40-1 against but KO'd Tyson in round 10; his first loss in 38 fights

BOXING

NEW ENGLAND PATRIOTS

2008 Super Bowl

New England were one of the shortest priced favourites ever

NY Giants 17 v 14 New England

FOOTBALL

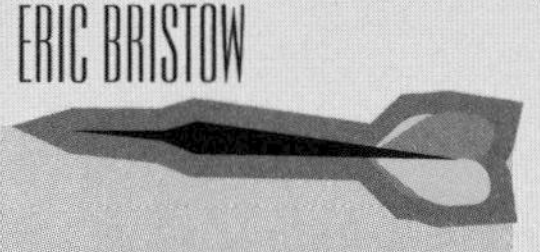
ERIC BRISTOW

1983 World Championship

Unranked, Deller beat the top 3 in the world to win

DARTS

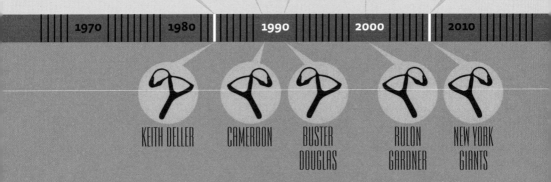

1970 1980 1990 2000 2010

KEITH DELLER

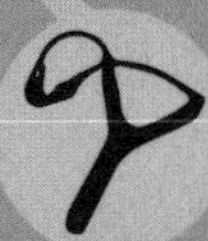
CAMEROON

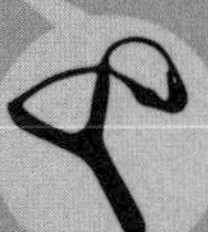
BUSTER DOUGLAS

RULON GARDNER

NEW YORK GIANTS

POT LUCK

On the face of it snooker and pool are very similar games, both employing a table with pockets, into which differently marked balls have to be propelled using a stick. Yet one is as British as tea and the other as American as cola, which could explain why each game is popular in different countries – although not why one is more lucrative to play than the other.

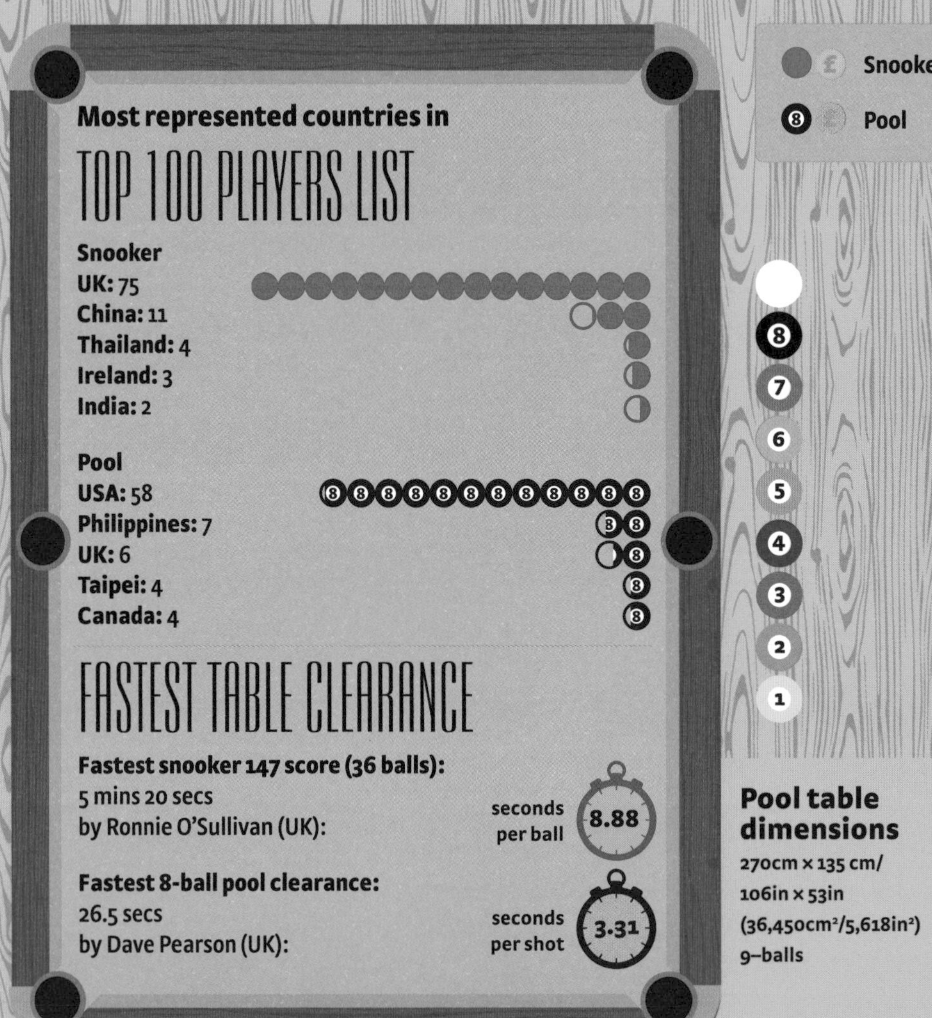

Snooker
Pool
Most represented countries in
TOP 100 PLAYERS LIST
Snooker
UK: 75
China: 11
Thailand: 4
Ireland: 3
India: 2
Pool
USA: 58
Philippines: 7
UK: 6
Taipei: 4
Canada: 4
FASTEST TABLE CLEARANCE
Fastest snooker 147 score (36 balls):
5 mins 20 secs
by Ronnie O'Sullivan (UK):
seconds per ball
8.88
Fastest 8-ball pool clearance:
26.5 secs
by Dave Pearson (UK):
seconds per shot
3.31

Pool table dimensions

270cm × 135 cm/
106in × 53in
(36,450cm²/5,618in²)
9–balls

 wikipedia.org

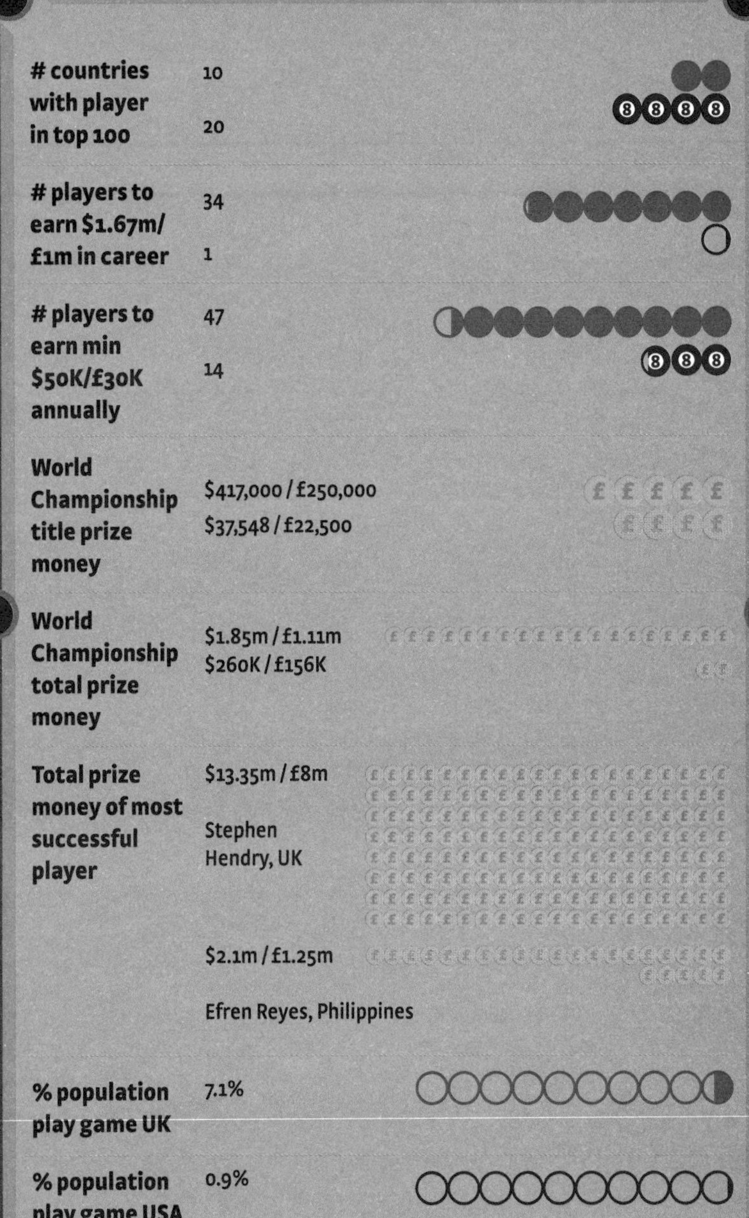

countries with player in top 100
10
20
players to earn $1.67m/ £1m in career
34
1
players to earn min $50K/£30K annually
47
14
World Championship title prize money
$417,000 / £250,000
$37,548 / £22,500
World Championship total prize money
$1.85m / £1.11m
$260K / £156K
Total prize money of most successful player
$13.35m / £8m
Stephen Hendry, UK
$2.1m / £1.25m
Efren Reyes, Philippines
% population play game UK
7.1%
% population play game USA
0.9%

Snooker table dimensions

357cm × 178 cm/ 140in × 70in (63,546cm²/ 9,800in²). 21 balls

SPORTING **CURSES**

Many people who play professional sport seem to have superstitions and good luck charms or routines, and there's no wonder when you consider these long-lasting curses. From baseball to golf, soccer to snooker, here are the most infamous curses in sport.

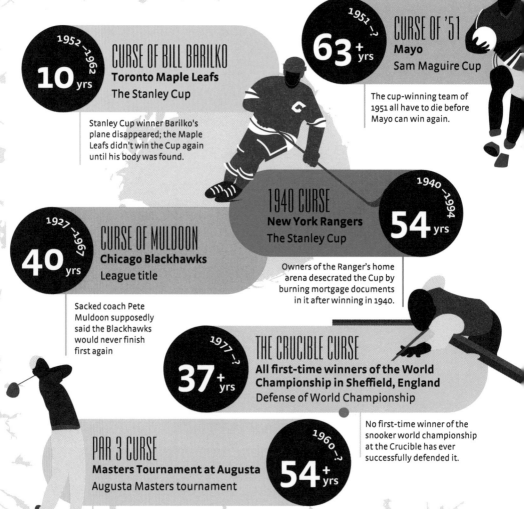

1952–1962
10 yrs

CURSE OF BILL BARILKO

Toronto Maple Leafs
The Stanley Cup

Stanley Cup winner Barilko's plane disappeared; the Maple Leafs didn't win the Cup again until his body was found.

1951–?
63+ yrs

CURSE OF '51

Mayo
Sam Maguire Cup

The cup-winning team of 1951 all have to die before Mayo can win again.

1940–1994
54 yrs

1940 CURSE

New York Rangers
The Stanley Cup

Owners of the Ranger's home arena desecrated the Cup by burning mortgage documents in it after winning in 1940.

1927–1967
40 yrs

CURSE OF MULDOON

Chicago Blackhawks
League title

Sacked coach Pete Muldoon supposedly said the Blackhawks would never finish first again

1977–?
37+ yrs

THE CRUCIBLE CURSE

All first-time winners of the World Championship in Sheffield, England
Defense of World Championship

No first-time winner of the snooker world championship at the Crucible has ever successfully defended it.

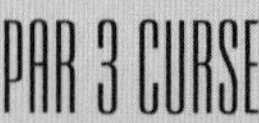

1960–?
54+ yrs

PAR 3 CURSE

Masters Tournament at Augusta
Augusta Masters tournament

No winner of the Par 3 competition played before the Augusta Masters has ever won the Masters itself.

CURSE OF THE COLONEL

29+ yrs (1985–?)

Hanshin Tigers (Japan)

Japanese Championship

Hanshin Tigers players threw a statue of Col. Sanders in the river after winning the championship in 1985, and have never won since.

CURSE OF THE BAMBINO

86 yrs (1918–2004)

Boston Red Sox

World Series

The Red Sox traded Babe Ruth to the Yankees after winning the World Series in 1918 and didn't win again until 2004.

CURSE OF BOBBY LAYNE

56+ yrs (1958–?)

Detroit Lions

Any trophy

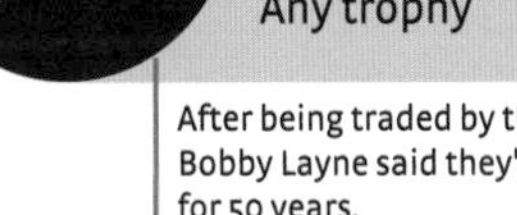

After being traded by the Lions, Bobby Layne said they'd not win for 50 years.

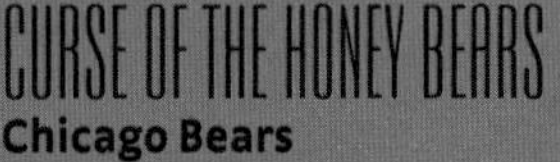

CURSE OF THE HONEY BEARS

28+ yrs (1986–?)

Chicago Bears

Super Bowl

The Chicago Bears won Super Bowl XX and then disbanded their cheerleaders, the Honey Bears; they haven't won since.

CURSE OF BIDDY EARLY

81 yrs (1914–1995)

Clare County

League title

A 19th-century 'witch' in County Clare cursed the team from beyond the grave.

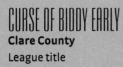

SOCCEROOS WITCH DOCTOR CURSE

34 yrs (1970–2004)

Australian National team

World Cup qualification

The Australian national soccer team hired a witch doctor to help them win a World Cup qualifying game, but didn't pay him...

CURSE OF BÉLA GUTTMANN

52+ yrs (1962–?)

Benfica

Any European trophy

Cup and league title-winning Hungarian-born soccer coach was sacked by Benfica, so he cursed them for 100 years.

wikipedia.org, reddit.com

IN AND **OUT** OF THE OLYMPICS

The Olympics have happened every four years (with a couple of breaks) since the beginning of the 20th century. They have become a definite date on the world's sporting calendar. Not that they've remained the same, though. Here is a guide to all of the sports that have been in and out of the Summer Games since 1896, including those that no longer appear.

TOTAL SUMMER EVENTS

0-59 | 60-120 | 121-180 | 181-240 | 240-302

Year	'96	'00	'04	'06	'08	'12	'20	'24	'28	'32	'36	'48	'52	'56	'60
Events	43	85	94	78	110	102	156	126	109	117	129	136	149	151	150

Year	'64	'68	'72	'76	'80	'84	'88	'92	'96	'00	'04	'08	'12	'16
Events	163	176	191	198	205	221	241	256	272	300	301	302	302	300

DISCONTINUED SUMMER SPORTS

Baseball 1912[D], 1936[D], 1952[D], 1956[D], 1964[D], 1984[D], 1988[D], 1992[1], 1996[1], 2000[1], 2004[1], 2008[1] | **Basque pelota** 1900[1], 1924[D], 1968[D], 1992[D] | **Cricket** 1900[1] | **Croquet** 1900[3] | **Equestrian / Vaulting** 1920[2] | **Figure skating** 1908[4], 1920[4], 1924–2016 | **Ice hockey** 1920[1], 1924–2016 | **Jeu de paume** 1900[D], 1908[1], 1924[D] | **Lacrosse** 1904[1], 1908[1], 1928[D], 1932[D], 1948[D] | **Polo** 1900[1], 1908[1], 1920[1], 1924[1], 1936[1] | **Rackets** 1908[2] | **Roque** 1904[1], |**Softball** 1996–2008[1] | **Tug of war** 1900–1920[1] | **Water motorsports** 1900[D], 1908[3]

1) *Number of current* D) *Demo*

KEY

Aquatics
- Diving
- Swimming
- Synchronized swimming
- Water polo

- Archery
- Athletics
- Badminton
- Basketball
- Boxing

Canoeing / Kayak
- Slalom
- Sprint

Cycling
- BMX
- Mountain biking
- Road cycling
- Track cycling

Equestrian
- Dressage
- Eventing
- Jumping

- Fencing
- Field hockey
- Football
- Golf

Gymnastics
- Artistic
- Rhythmic
- Trampoline

- Handball
- Judo
- Modern pentathlon
- Rowing
- Rugby union
- Sailing
- Shooting
- Table tennis
- Taekwondo
- Tennis
- Triathlon
- Volleyball (beach)
- Volleyball (indoor)
- Weightlifting

Wrestling
- Freestyle
- Greco-Roman

D* *Demo*

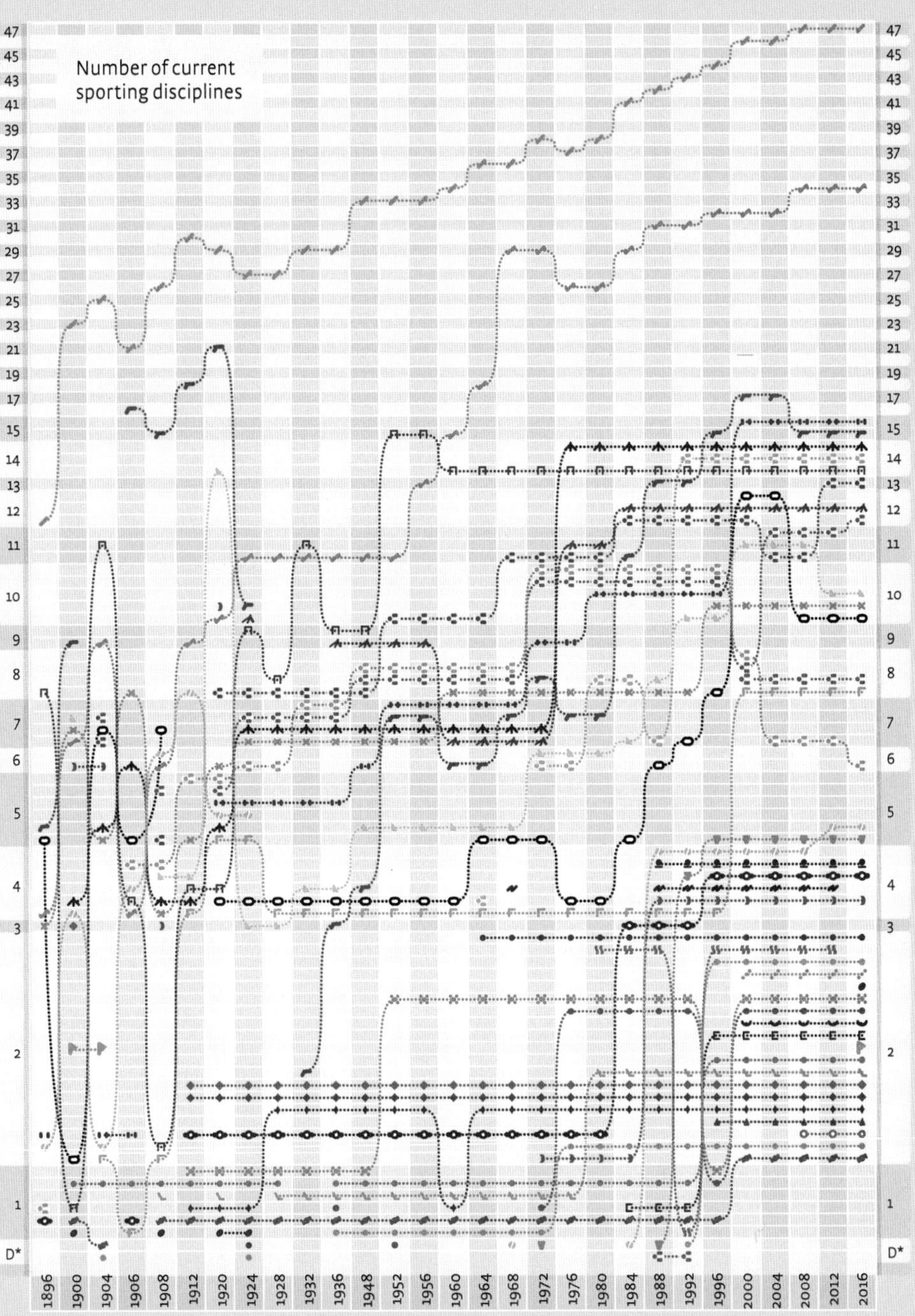
Number of current sporting disciplines
47
45
43
41
39
37
35
33
31
29
27
25
23
21
19
17
15
14
13
12
11
10
9
8
7
6
5
4
3
2
1
D*
1896
1900
1904
1906
1908
1912
1920
1924
1928
1932
1936
1948
1952
1956
1960
1964
1968
1972
1976
1980
1984
1988
1992
1996
2000
2004
2008
2012
2016

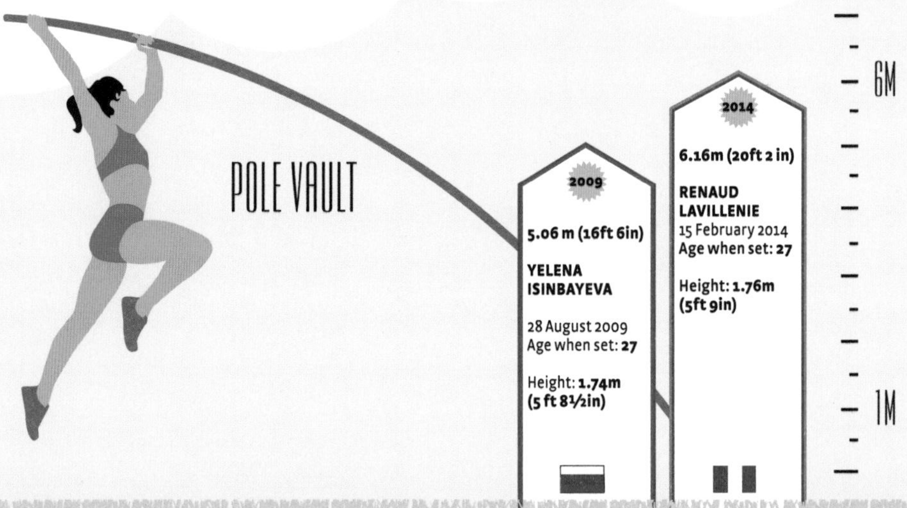
POLE VAULT
2009
5.06 m (16ft 6in)
YELENA ISINBAYEVA
28 August 2009
Age when set: 27
Height: 1.74m (5 ft 8½in)
2014
6.16m (20ft 2 in)
RENAUD LAVILLENIE
15 February 2014
Age when set: 27
Height: 1.76m (5ft 9in)
6M
1M

WHO'S FOR THE **HIGH JUMP**?

World records in athletics get broken all the time, at international track meets, Olympics and major events. Or, at least they do in most events except those that involve jumping, it appears. The Olympic records have changed more recently than World, but still many persist for decades.

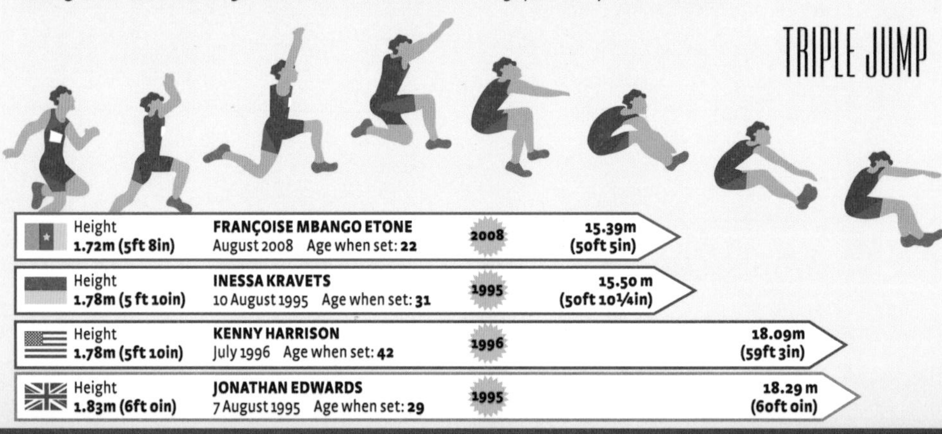
TRIPLE JUMP
Height 1.72m (5ft 8in)
FRANÇOISE MBANGO ETONE
August 2008 Age when set: 22
2008
15.39m (50ft 5in)
Height 1.78m (5 ft 10in)
INESSA KRAVETS
10 August 1995 Age when set: 31
1995
15.50 m (50ft 10¼in)
Height 1.78m (5ft 10in)
KENNY HARRISON
July 1996 Age when set: 42
1996
18.09m (59ft 3in)
Height 1.83m (6ft 0in)
JONATHAN EDWARDS
7 August 1995 Age when set: 29
1995
18.29 m (60ft 0in)
6M
10M
18M

sports-reference.com, wikipedia.org

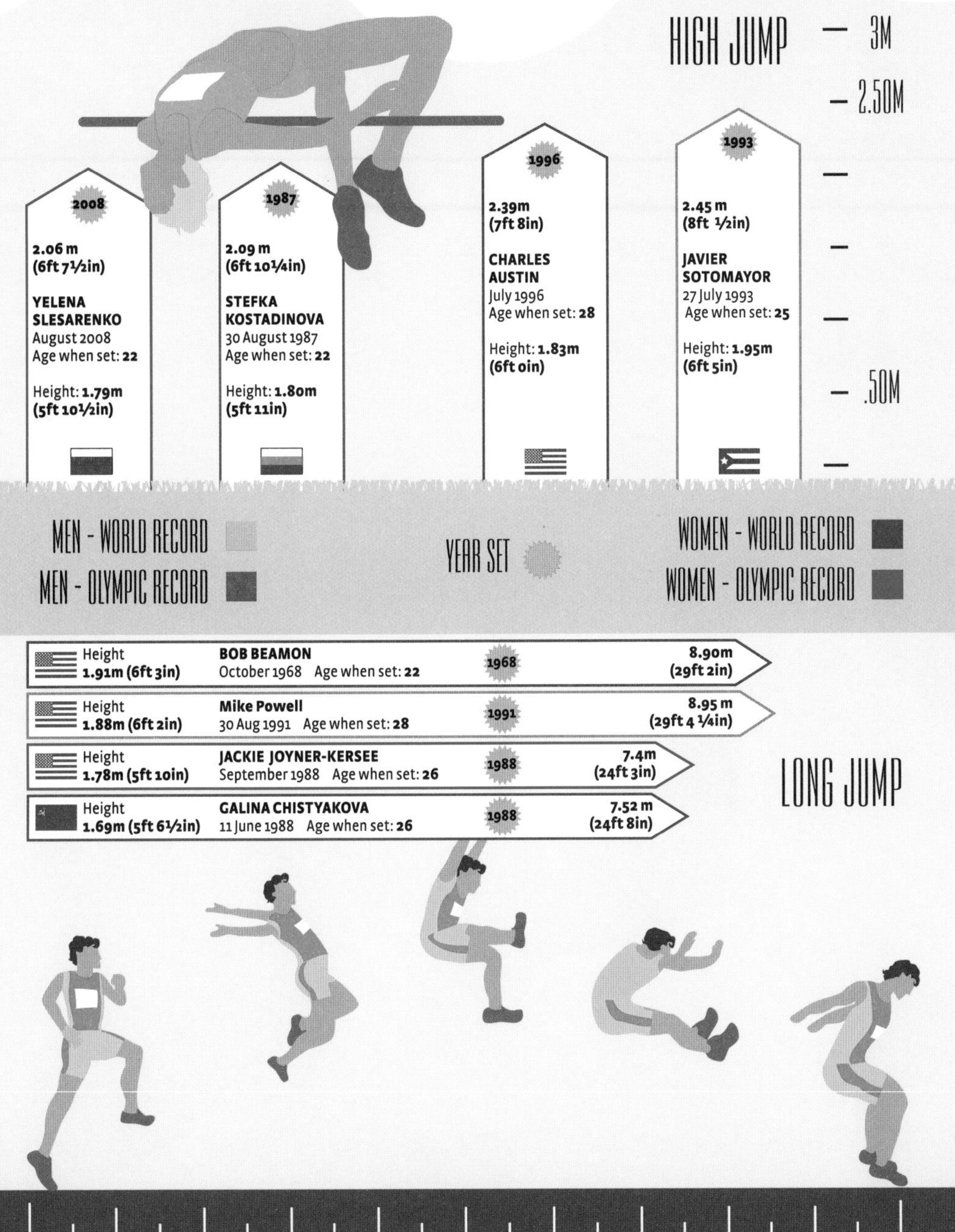

HIGH JUMP
3M
2.50M
.50M
2008
2.06 m (6ft 7½in)
YELENA SLESARENKO
August 2008
Age when set: 22
Height: 1.79m (5ft 10½in)
1987
2.09 m (6ft 10¼in)
STEFKA KOSTADINOVA
30 August 1987
Age when set: 22
Height: 1.80m (5ft 11in)
1996
2.39m (7ft 8in)
CHARLES AUSTIN
July 1996
Age when set: 28
Height: 1.83m (6ft 0in)
1993
2.45 m (8ft ½in)
JAVIER SOTOMAYOR
27 July 1993
Age when set: 25
Height: 1.95m (6ft 5in)
MEN - WORLD RECORD
MEN - OLYMPIC RECORD
YEAR SET
WOMEN - WORLD RECORD
WOMEN - OLYMPIC RECORD
Height 1.91m (6ft 3in)
BOB BEAMON
October 1968 Age when set: 22
1968
8.90m (29ft 2in)
Height 1.88m (6ft 2in)
Mike Powell
30 Aug 1991 Age when set: 28
1991
8.95 m (29ft 4 ¼in)
Height 1.78m (5ft 10in)
JACKIE JOYNER-KERSEE
September 1988 Age when set: 26
1988
7.4m (24ft 3in)
Height 1.69m (5ft 6½in)
GALINA CHISTYAKOVA
11 June 1988 Age when set: 26
1988
7.52 m (24ft 8in)
LONG JUMP
1M
3M
5M
7M
9M

BULLS**EYE!**

Exactly how difficult is it to pot a ball on a pool table, dunk a basketball or sink a putt? Here's how much bigger targets are than the things being aimed at them, what degree of difficulty is involved in getting a direct score, and whether anyone is trying to stop the object hitting the target.

SPORT	TARGET	AREA (FEET2/METERS2)	OBJECT
Pool (Corner – max width)	Pocket	0.385 / 0.117	Ball (Diameter)
Basketball	Hoop	1.77 / 0.164	Ball
Golf	Hole	0.098 / 0.108	Ball
Clay Pigeon Shooting	Clay Pigeon	0.102 / 0.0095	Shot (c.250 per shell)
Soccer	Goal	192 / 17.84	Soccer ball
Ice Hockey	Net	24 / 2.23	Puck
Table Tennis (Serve)	Service Side	11.225 / 1.037	Ball
Tennis (Serve)	Service Box	141.75 / 13.17	Ball
American Football	End Zone	4800 / 446	Football
Archery	Target	12.566 / 1.169	Arrow
Darts	Board	1.77 / 0.164	Dart

AREA (FEET2/METRES2)
0.187 / 0.057
0.49 / 0.0458
0.0153/ 0.00143
0.000063 / 0.00005 x 250
0.417 / 0.0378
0.049 / 0.00456
0.0135 / 0.00126
0.037 / 0.0034
0.266 / 0.0248
0.00064 / 0.000059
0.000008 / 0.00000079
SIZE OF OBJECT IN RELATION TO TARGET
0.48
0.28
0.16
0.1375
0.002
0.002
0.0012
0.00026
0.000055
0.00005
0.000005
TARGET DEFENDED?
No
Yes
No
No
Yes
Yes
No
No
Yes
No
No

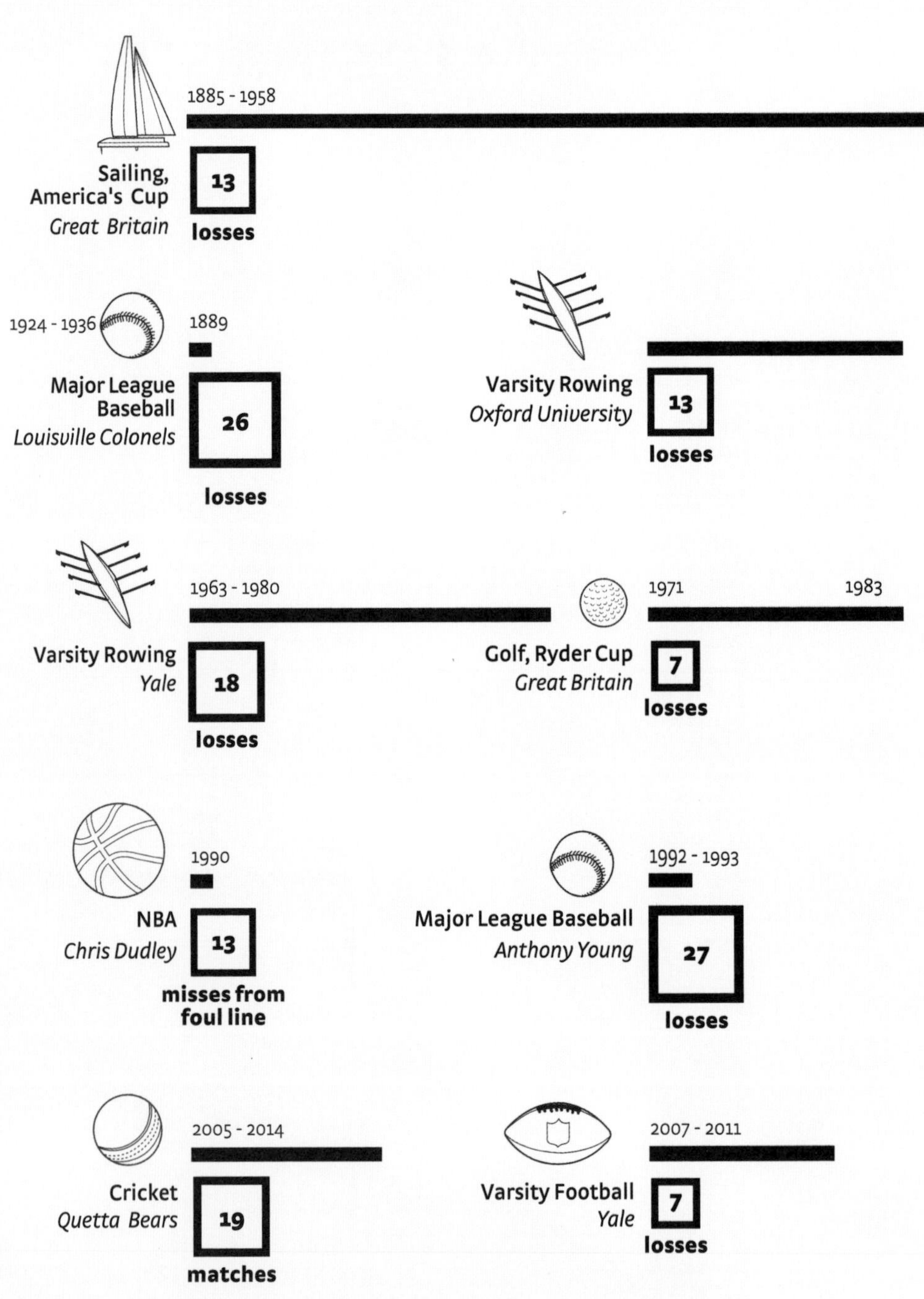
1885 - 1958
Sailing,
America's Cup
Great Britain
13
losses
1924 - 1936
1889
Major League
Baseball
Louisville Colonels
26
losses
Varsity Rowing
Oxford University
13
losses
1963 - 1980
Varsity Rowing
Yale
18
losses
1971
1983
Golf, Ryder Cup
Great Britain
7
losses
1990
NBA
Chris Dudley
13
misses from
foul line
1992 - 1993
Major League Baseball
Anthony Young
27
losses
2005 - 2014
Cricket
Quetta Bears
19
matches
2007 - 2011
Varsity Football
Yale
7
losses

ON A **LOSING** STREAK

By its very nature, sport has to have a loser, but these teams and individuals have taken losing to a new level of achievement. Here are the longest losing streaks – consecutive losses without a win – in eight major sports.

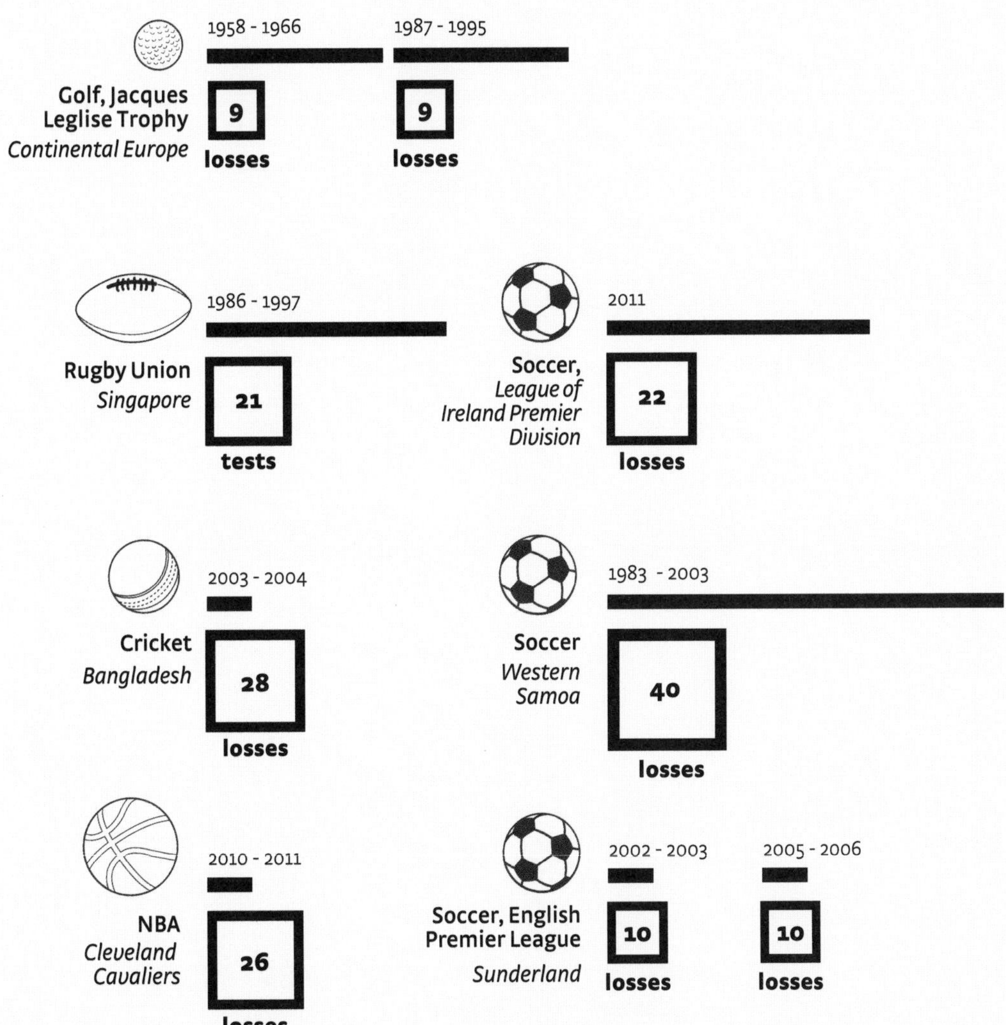

Golf, Jacques Leglise Trophy
Continental Europe
1958 - 1966
9
losses
1987 - 1995
9
losses
Rugby Union
Singapore
1986 - 1997
21
tests
Soccer, League of Ireland Premier Division
2011
22
losses
Cricket
Bangladesh
2003 - 2004
28
losses
Soccer
Western Samoa
1983 - 2003
40
losses
NBA
Cleveland Cavaliers
2010 - 2011
26
losses
Soccer, English Premier League
Sunderland
2002 - 2003
10
losses
2005 - 2006
10
losses

Credits

Produced by Essential Works Ltd
essentialworks.co.uk

Essential Works

Art Director: Gemma Wilson
Supervising Editor:
Mal Peachey
Editor: Fiona Screen
Researchers: Brianna Lester, Kiril Petrov, Duncan Steer, Giulia Vallone, Barney White
Layout: Ben Cracknell

Octopus Books

Editorial Director:
Trevor Davies

Senior Production Manager:
Peter Hunt

Designers/Illustrators

Marc Morera Agustí (18–19, 24–25, 54–55)
Meegan Barnes (42)
Federica Bonfanti (14–15, 66–67)
Kuo Kang Chen (48–49, 62–63)
Ian Cowles (43)
Ben Cracknell (70–71, 82–83)
Giulia De Amicis (158–159)
Barbara Doherty (10–11, 22–23, 28, 36–37, 50–51, 72–73, 78–79, 92–93, 96–97, 106–107, 117, 132, 146–147)
Cristian Enache (40–41, 44–45, 46–47, 56–57, 102–103, 124–125, 128–129, 136–137)
Marco Giannini (76–77)
Nick Graves (74–75, 80–81, 84–85)
Lorena Guerra (12)
Natasha Hellegouarch (60–61, 140–141)
Diana Coral Hernandez (86–87, 154–155)
Erwin Hilao (16–17, 34–35)
Tomasz Kłosinski (152–153)
Stephen Lillie (118–119, 130–131)
Mish Maudsley (68–69, 126–127, 144–145, 148–149)
Priscila Mendoza, Yazmin Alanis (20–21, 29, 32–33, 52–53, 94–95)
Milkwhale.com (114–115, 122–123, 134–135, 150–151)
Aleksandar Savic (108–109, 112–113, 133)
Yael Shinkar (13, 26–27, 100–101, 142–143)
Arnold Skawinski (64–65, 88–89, 90–91, 98–99, 138–139)
Ryan Welch (30–31, 110–111, 116)
Gemma Wilson (38–39, 104–105, 156–157)
Anil Yanik (58–59)